# THE PEOPLE'S LIBRARY

# THE CROWN OF WILD OLIVE
### AND THE
# ETHICS OF THE DUST

## JOHN RUSKIN

## EDITOR'S NOTE

The book of Ruskin's that one likes best
is the book of Ruskin's that one reads best.
There seems no other way, at the moment, of
expressing the magical charm of his prose, to
tell of his qualities, so many-sided in its
effect upon an ear attuned to the melody of
diction.

Ruskin himself believed, we are told, that
"Unto this Last" that thing would be the most
permanent of all his works. "If it should fail
to become so—and the present century will
decide the good and ill—It will probably be
because it lacks a certain meaning of those
to whom ...                  "Everything may made of
himself ....  Yet, whatever is complete, for the
adorned thought, it contains, it is well labored
of those who like the high in literature.

We have nothing to do here with the
economic theories propounded in either The
Crown of Wild Olive, or Fors Clavigera, the
...a... Each reader may accept or reject
them as they were accepted or rejected by
the students, men and women, before whom,
at Manchester in 1864, they were delivered.
The day has passed, in any case, for any
violent controversies over Ruskin's opinions
upon economics. One reads his books to-day
simply for ... after the real matter is
over, for the mental and moral uplift in
them. And one does not come from them
with disappointment.

John Ruskin was born in London in 1819,
and died at Coniston, in the Lake District,
in 1900.

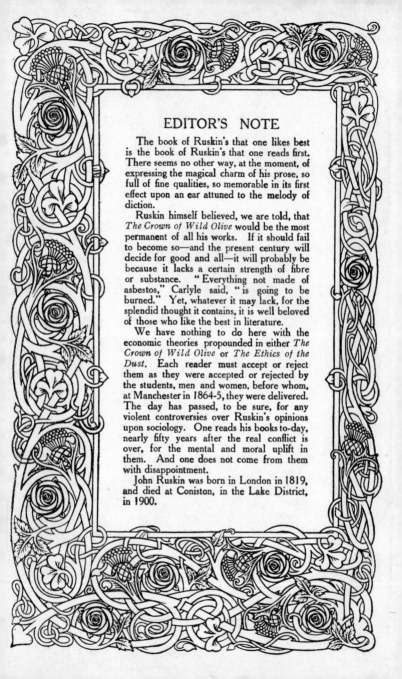

## EDITOR'S NOTE

The book of Ruskin's that one likes best is the book of Ruskin's that one reads first. There seems no other way, at the moment, of expressing the magical charm of his prose, so full of fine qualities, so memorable in its first effect upon an ear attuned to the melody of diction.

Ruskin himself believed, we are told, that *The Crown of Wild Olive* would be the most permanent of all his works. If it should fail to become so—and the present century will decide for good and all—it will probably be because it lacks a certain strength of fibre or substance. "Everything not made of asbestos," Carlyle said, "is going to be burned." Yet, whatever it may lack, for the splendid thought it contains, it is well beloved of those who like the best in literature.

We have nothing to do here with the economic theories propounded in either *The Crown of Wild Olive* or *The Ethics of the Dust*. Each reader must accept or reject them as they were accepted or rejected by the students, men and women, before whom, at Manchester in 1864-5, they were delivered. The day has passed, to be sure, for any violent controversies over Ruskin's opinions upon sociology. One reads his books to-day, nearly fifty years after the real conflict is over, for the mental and moral uplift in them. And one does not come from them with disappointment.

John Ruskin was born in London in 1819, and died at Coniston, in the Lake District, in 1900.

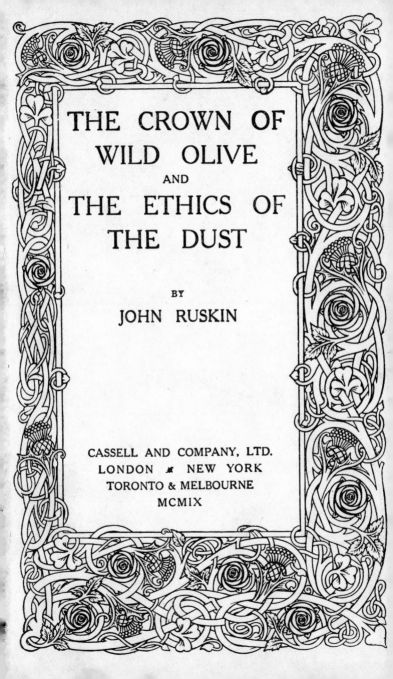

# THE CROWN OF WILD OLIVE

## AND

# THE ETHICS OF THE DUST

BY

JOHN RUSKIN

CASSELL AND COMPANY, LTD.
LONDON   NEW YORK
TORONTO & MELBOURNE
MCMIX

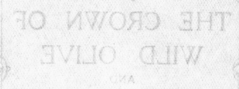

# CONTENTS

## THE CROWN OF WILD OLIVE

## THE ETHICS OF THE DUST

# THE CROWN OF WILD OLIVE

## THREE LECTURES

### ON

## WORK, TRAFFIC, AND WAR

'And indeed it should have been of gold, had not Jupiter been so poor.'—ARISTOPHANES (*Plutus*)

# PREFACE

Twenty years ago there was no lovelier piece of lowland scenery in South England, nor any more pathetic, in the world, by its expression of sweet human character and life, than that immediately bordering on the sources of the Wandle, and including the lower moors of Addington, and the villages of Beddington and Carshalton, with all their pools and streams. No clearer or diviner waters ever sang with constant lips of the hand which 'giveth rain from heaven '; no pastures ever lightened in spring time with more passionate blossoming; no sweeter homes ever hallowed the heart of the passer-by with their pride of peaceful gladness—fain-hidden—yet full-confessed. The place remains, or, until a few months ago, remained, nearly unchanged in its larger features ; but, with deliberate mind I say, that I have never seen anything so ghastly in its inner tragic meaning—not in Pisan Maremma, —not by Campagna tomb,—not by the sand-isles of the Torcellan shore,—as the slow stealing of aspects of reckless, indolent, animal neglect, over the delicate sweetness of that English scene : nor is any blasphemy or impiety— any frantic saying or godless thought—more appalling to me, using the best power of judgment I have to discern its sense and scope, than the insolent defiling of those springs by the human herds that drink of them. Just where the welling of stainless water, trembling and pure, like a body of light, enters the pool of Carshalton, cutting itself a radiant channel down to the gravel, through warp of feathery weeds, all waving, which it traverses with its deep threads of clearness, like the chalcedony in moss-agate, starred here and there with the white grenouillette ;

just in the very rush and murmur of the first spreading currents, the human wretches of the place cast their street and house foulness ; heaps of dust and slime, and broken shreds of old metal, and rags of putrid clothes ; they having neither energy to cart it away, nor decency enough to dig it into the ground, thus shed into the stream, to diffuse what venom of it will float and melt, far away, in all places where God meant those waters to bring joy and health. And, in a little pool, behind some houses farther in the village, where another spring rises, the shattered stones of the well, and of the little fretted channel which was long ago built and traced for it by gentler hands, lie scattered, each from each, under a ragged bank of mortar, and scoria ; and bricklayers' refuse, on one side, which the clean water nevertheless chastises to purity ; but it cannot conquer the dead earth beyond ; and there, circled and coiled under festering scum, the stagnant edge of the pool effaces itself into a slope of black slime, the accumulation of indolent years. Half a dozen men, with one day's work, could cleanse those pools, and trim the flowers about their banks, and make every breath of summer air above them rich with cool balm ; and every glittering wave medicinal, as if it ran, troubled of angels, from the porch of Bethesda. But that day's work is never given, nor will be ; nor will any joy be possible to heart of man for evermore, about those wells of English waters.

When I last left them, I walked up slowly through the back streets of Croydon, from the old church to the hospital ; and, just on the left, before coming up to the crossing of the High Street, there was a new public-house built. And the front of it was built in so wise manner, that a recess of two feet was left below its front windows, between them and the street-pavement—a recess too narrow for any possible use (for even if it had been occupied by a seat, as in old time it might have been, everybody walking along the street would have fallen over the

legs of the reposing wayfarers). But, by way of making
this two feet depth of freehold land more expressive of the
dignity of an establishment for the sale of spirituous
liquors, it was fenced from the pavement by an imposing
iron railing, having four or five spearheads to the yard of
it, and six feet high ; containing as much iron and iron-
work, indeed, as could well be put into the space ; and by
this stately arrangement, the little piece of dead ground
within, between wall and street, became a protective
receptacle of refuse ; cigar ends, and oyster shells, and the
like, such as an open-handed English street-populace
habitually scatters from its presence, and was thus left,
unsweepable by any ordinary methods. Now the iron
bars which, uselessly (or in great degree worse than uselessly), enclosed this bit of ground and made it pestilent,
represented a quantity of work which would have cleansed
the Carshalton pools three times over ;—of work, partly
cramped and deadly, in the mine ; partly fierce * and
exhaustive, at the furnace ; partly foolish and sedentary,
of ill-taught students making bad designs : work from
the beginning to the last fruits of it, and in all the branches
of it, venomous, deathful, and miserable. Now, how did
it come to pass that this work was done instead of the
other ; that the strength and life of the English operative

---

* ' A fearful occurrence took place a few days since, near Wolver-
hampton. Thomas Snape, aged nineteen, was on duty as the
" keeper " of a blast furnace at Deepfield, assisted by John
Gardner, aged eighteen, and Joseph Swift, aged thirty-seven. The
furnace contained four tons of molten iron, and an equal amount
of cinders, and ought to have been run out at 7.30 p.m. But Snape
and his mates, engaged in talking and drinking, neglected their
duty, and, in the meantime, the iron rose in the furnace until it
reached a pipe wherein water was contained. Just as the men had
stripped, and were proceeding to tap the furnace, the water in the
pipe, converted into steam, burst down its front and let loose on
them the molten metal, which instantaneously consumed Gardner ;
Snape, terribly burnt, and mad with pain, leaped into the canal and
then ran home and fell dead on the threshold ; Swift survived to
reach the hospital, where he died too.'

were spent in defiling ground, instead of redeeming it ;
and in producing an entirely (in that place) valueless piece
of metal, which can neither be eaten nor breathed, instead
of medicinal fresh air and pure water ?

There is but one reason for it, and at present a conclusive one—that the capitalist can charge percentage on
the work in the one case, and cannot in the other.    If,
having certain funds for supporting labour at my disposal,
I pay men merely to keep my ground in order, my money
is, in that function, spent once for all ; but if I pay them
to dig iron out of my ground, and work it, and sell it, I
can charge rent for the ground, and percentage both on
the manufacture and the sale, and make my capital profitable in these three bye-ways.    The greater part of the
profitable investment of capital, in the present day, is in
operations of this kind, in which the public is persuaded
to buy something of no use to it, on production, or sale,
of which, the capitalist may charge percentage ; the said
public remaining all the while under the persuasion that
the percentages thus obtained are real national gains,
whereas, they are merely filchings out of partially light
pockets to swell heavy ones.

Thus, the Croydon publican buys the iron railing to
make himself more conspicuous to drunkards.    The
public-house-keeper on the other side of the way presently
buys another railing, to out-rail him with.    Both are, as
to their *relative* attractiveness to customers of taste, just
where they were before ; but they have lost the price of
the railings ; which they must either themselves finally
lose, or make their aforesaid customers of taste pay, by
raising the price of the beer, or adulterating it.    Either the
publicans, or their customers, are thus poorer by precisely
what the capitalist has gained ; and the value of the
work itself, meantime, has been lost to the nation ; the
iron bars in that form and place being wholly useless.
It is this mode of taxation of the poor by the rich which

is referred to in the text (page 42), in comparing the
modern acquisitive power of capital with that of the
lance and sword ; the only difference being that the levy
of blackmail in old times was by force, and is now by
cozening. The old rider and riever frankly quartered himself on the publican for the night ; the modern one merely
makes his lance into an iron spike, and persuades his host
to buy it. One comes as an open robber, the other as a
cheating pedlar ; but the result, to the injured person's
pocket, is absolutely the same. Of course many useful
industries mingle with, and disguise the useless ones ; and,
in the habits of energy aroused by the struggle, there is
a certain direct good. It is far better to spend four
thousand pounds in making a good gun, and then to blow
it to pieces, than to pass life in idleness. Only do not let
it be called ' political economy.' There is also a confused
notion in the minds of many persons, that the gathering
of the property of the poor into the hands of the rich does
no ultimate harm ; since, in whosesoever hands it may
be, it must be spent at last, and thus, they think, return to
the poor again. This fallacy has been again and again
exposed ; but grant the plea true, and the same apology
may, of course, be made for blackmail, or any other form
of robbery. It might be (though practically it never is) as
advantageous for the nation that the robber should have
the spending of the money he extorts, as that the person
robbed should have spent it. But this is no excuse for
the theft. If I were to put a turnpike on the road where
it passes my own gate, and endeavour to exact a shilling
from every passenger, the public would soon do away with
my gate, without listening to any plea on my part that
' it was as advantageous to them, in the end, that I should
spent their shillings, as that they themselves should.'
But if, instead of out-facing them with a turnpike, I can
only persuade them to come in and buy stones, or old iron,
or any other useless thing, out of my ground, I may rob

them to the same extent, and be, moreover, thanked as a
public benefactor, and promoter of commercial prosperity.
And this main question for the poor of England—for the
poor of all countries—is wholly omitted in every common
treatise on the subject of wealth.   Even by the labourers
themselves, the operation of capital is regarded only in its
effect on their immediate interests ; never in the far more
terrific power of its appointment of the kind and the object
of labour.   It matters little, ultimately, how much a
labourer is paid for making anything ; but it matters
fearfully what the thing is which he is compelled to make.
If his labour is so ordered as to produce food and fresh air,
and fresh water—no matter that his wages are low—the
food and fresh air and water will be at last there ;  and he
will at last get them.   But if he is paid to destroy food
and fresh air, or to produce iron bars instead of them, the
food and air will finally *not* be there, and he will *not* get
them, to his great and final inconvenience.   So that,
conclusively, in political as in household economy, the
great question is, not so much what money you have in
your pocket, as what you will buy with it, and do with it.

I have been long accustomed, as all men engaged in
work of investigation must be, to hear my statements
laughed at for years, before they are examined or believed ;
and I am generally content to wait the public's time.
But it has not been without displeased surprise that I
have found myself totally unable, as yet, by any repetition,
or illustration, to force this plain thought into my readers'
heads—that the wealth of nations, as of men, consists in
substance, not in ciphers ;  and that the real good of all
work and of all commerce depends on the final worth of
the thing you make, or get by it.   This is a practical
enough statement, one would think : but the English
public has been so possessed by its modern school of
economists with the notion that Business is always good,
whether it be busy in mischief or in benefit ; and that

buying and selling are always salutary, whatever the
intrinsic worth of what you buy or sell,—that it seems
impossible to gain so much as a patient hearing for any
inquiry respecting the substantial result of our eager
modern labours.   I have never felt more checked by the
sense of this impossibility than in arranging the heads of
the following three lectures, which, though delivered at
considerable intervals of time, and in different places,
were not prepared without reference to each other.   Their
connection would, however, have been made far more
distinct, if I had not been prevented, by what I feel to be
another great difficulty in addressing English audiences,
from enforcing, with any decision, the common, and to me
the most important, part of their subjects.   I chiefly
desired (as I have just said) to question my hearers—
operatives, merchants, and soldiers—as to the ultimate
meaning of the *business* they had in hand ; and to know
from them what they expected or intended their manufacture to come to, their selling to come to, and their killing
to come to.   That appeared the first point needing deter-
mination before I could speak to them with any real
utility or effect.   ' You craftsmen—salesmen—swordsmen
—do but tell me clearly what you want ; then, if I can
say anything to help you, I will ; and if not, I will account
to you as I best may for my inability.'   But in order to
put this question into any terms, one had first of all to
face the difficulty just spoken of—to me for the present
insuperable—the difficulty of knowing whether to address
one's audience as believing, or not believing, in any other
world than this.   For if you address any average modern
English company as believing in an Eternal life, and
endeavour to draw any conclusions, from this assumed
belief, as to their present business, they will forthwith
tell you that ' what you say is very beautiful, but it is not
practical.'   If, on the contrary, you frankly address them
as unbelievers in Eternal life, and try to draw any conse-

quences from that unbelief,—they immediately hold you
for an accursed person, and shake off the dust from their
feet at you. And the more I thought over what I had
got to say, the less I found I could say it, without some
reference to this intangible or intractable part of the
subject. It made all the difference, in asserting any
principle of war, whether one assumed that a discharge of
artillery would merely knead down a certain quantity of
red clay into a level line, as in a brick-field ; or whether,
out of every separately Christian-named portion of the
ruinous heap, there went out, into the smoke and dead-
fallen air of battle, some astonished condition of soul,
unwillingly released. It made all the difference, in speaking
of the possible range of commerce, whether one assumed
that all bargains related only to visible property—or
whether property, for the present invisible, but nevertheless real, was elsewhere purchasable on other terms. It
made all the difference, in addressing a body of men
subject to considerable hardship, and having to find some
way out of it, whether one could confidently say to them,
' My friends, you have only to die, and all will be right ' ;
or whether one had any secret misgiving that such advice
was more blessed to him that gave than to him that took
it. And therefore the deliberate reader will find, throughout these lectures, a hesitation in driving points home,
and a pausing short of conclusions which he will feel I
would fain have come to ; hesitation which arises wholly
from this uncertainty of my hearers' temper. For I do
not now speak, nor have I ever spoken, since the time
of first forward youth, in any proselyting temper, as desiring to persuade any one of what, in such matters, I
thought myself ; but, whomsoever I venture to address,
I take for the time his creed as I find it ; and endeavour
to push it into such vital fruit as it seems capable of.
Thus, it is a creed with a great part of the existing English
people that they are in possession of a book which tells

them, straight from the lips of God, all they ought to do, and need to know. I have read that book, with as much care as most of them, for some forty years ; and am thankful that, on those who trust it, I can press its pleadings. My endeavour has been uniformly to make them trust it more deeply than they do ; trust it, not in their own favourite verses only, but in the sum of all ; trust it, not as a fetish or talisman, which they are to be saved by daily repetitions of ; but as a Captain's order, to be heard and obeyed at their peril. I was always encouraged by supposing my hearers to hold such belief. To these, if to any, I once had hope of addressing, with acceptance, words which insisted on the guilt of pride, and the futility of avarice ; from these, if from any, I once expected ratification of a political economy, which asserted that the life was more than the meat, and the body than raiment ; and these, it once seemed to me, I might ask, without accusation of fanaticism, not merely in doctrine of the lips, but in the bestowal of their heart's treasure, to separate themselves from the crowd of whom it is written ' After all these things do the Gentiles seek.'

It cannot, however, be assumed, with any semblance of reason, that a general audience is now wholly, or even in majority, composed of these religious persons. A large portion must always consist of men who admit no such creed ; or who, at least, are inaccessible to appeals founded on it. And as, with the so-called Christian, I desired to plead for honest declaration and fulfilment of his belief in life, with the so-called Infidel, I desired to plead for an honest declaration and fulfilment of his belief in death. The dilemma is inevitable. Men must either hereafter live, or hereafter die ; fate may be bravely met, and conduct wisely ordered, on either expectation ; but never in hesitation between ungrasped hope, and unconfronted fear. We usually believe in immortality, so far as to avoid preparation for death ; and in mortality, so far as to avoid preparation for anything after death. Whereas, a wise man will at least hold himself prepared for one or other of two events, of which one or other is inevitable ; and will have all things in order, for his sleep, or in readiness, for his awakening.

Nor have we any right to call it an ignoble judgment, if he determine to put them in order, as for sleep. A brave belief in life is indeed an enviable state of mind, but, as far as I can discern, an unusual one. I know few Christians so convinced of the splendour of the rooms in their Father's house, as to be happier when their friends are called to those mansions, than they would have been if the Queen had sent for them to live at court : nor has the Church's most ardent ' desire to part, and be with Christ,' ever cured it of the singular habit of putting on mourning for every person summoned to such departure. On the contrary, a brave belief in death has been assuredly held by many not ignoble persons, and it is a sign of the last depravity in the Church itself, when it assumes that such a belief is inconsistent with either purity of character, or energy of hand. The shortness of life is not, to any rational person, a conclusive reason for wasting the space of it which may be granted him ; nor does the anticipation of death to-morrow suggest, to any one but a drunkard, the expediency of drunkenness to-day. To teach that there is no device in the grave may indeed make the deviceless person more contented in his dullness ; but it will make the deviser only more earnest in devising : nor is human conduct likely, in every case, to be purer, under the conviction that all its evil may in a moment be pardoned, and all its wrong-doing in a moment redeemed ; and that the sigh of repentance, which purges the guilt of the past, will waft the soul into a felicity which forgets its pain,—than it may be under the sterner, and to many not unwise minds, more probable, apprehension, that ' what a man soweth that shall he also reap '—or others reap,—when he, the living seed of pestilence, walked no more in darkness, but lies down therein.

But to men whose feebleness of sight, or bitterness of soul, or the offence given by the conduct of those who claim higher hope, may have rendered this painful creed the only possible one, there is an appeal to be made, more secure in its ground than any which can be addressed to happier persons. I would fain, if I might offencelessly, have spoken to them as if none others heard ; and have said thus : Hear me, you dying men, who will soon be deaf for ever. For these others, at your right hand and your left, who look forward to a state of infinite existence, in which all their errors will be overruled, and all their faults forgiven ; for these, who, stained and blackened in the battle smoke of mortality, have but to dip themselves for an instant in the font of death, and to rise renewed of plumage, as a dove that is covered with silver, and her feathers like gold ; for these, indeed, it may be permissible to waste their numbered moments, through faith in a future of innumerable hours ; to these, in their weakness, it may be conceded that they should tamper with sin which can only bring forth fruit of righteousness, and profit by the iniquity which, one day, will be remembered no more. In them, it may be no sign of hardness of heart to neglect the poor, over whom they know their Master is watching ; and to leave those to perish temporarily, who cannot perish eternally. But, for you, there is no such hope, and therefore no such excuse. This fate, which you ordain for the wretched, you believe to be all their inheritance ; you may crush them, before the moth, and they will never rise to rebuke you ;—their breath, which fails for lack of food, once expiring, will never be recalled to whisper against you a word of accusing ;—they and you, as you think, shall lie down together in the dust, and the worms cover you ;—and for them there shall be no consolation, and on you no vengeance—only the question murmured above your grave : ' Who shall repay him what he hath done ? ' Is it therefore easier for you in your heart to inflict the sorrow for which there is no remedy ? Will you take, wantonly, this little all of his life from your poor brother, and make his brief hours long to him with pain ? Will you be readier to the injustice which can never be redressed ; and niggardly of mercy which you *can* bestow but once, and which, refusing, you refuse for ever ? I think better of you, even of the most selfish, than that you would do this, well understood. And for yourselves, it seems to me, the question becomes not less grave, in these curt limits. If your life were but a fever fit—the madness of a night, whose follies were all to be forgotten in the dawn, it might matter little how you fretted away the sickly hours,—what toys you snatched at, or let fall,— what visions you followed wistfully with the deceived eyes of sleepless phrenzy. Is the earth only an hospital ? Play, if you care to play, on the floor of the hospital dens. Knit its straw into what crowns please you ; gather the dust of it for treasure, and die rich in that clutching at the black motes in the air with your dying hands ;—and yet, it may be well with you. But if this life be no dream, and the world no hospital ; if all the peace and power and joy you can ever win, must be won now ; and all fruit of victory gathered here, or never ;—will you still, through- out the puny totality of your life, weary yourselves in the fire for vanity ? If there is no rest which remaineth for you, is there none you might presently take ? was this grass of the earth made green for your shroud only, not for your bed ? and can you never lie down *upon* it, but only *under* it ? The heathen, to whose creed you have returned, thought not so. They knew that life brought its contest, but they expected from it also the crown of all contest : No proud one ! no jewelled circlet flaming through Heaven above the height of the unmerited throne ; only some few leaves of wild olive, cool to the tired brow, through a few years of peace.   It should have been of gold they thought ;  but Jupiter was poor ;  this was the best the god could give them.   Seeking a greater than this, they had known it a mockery.   Not in war, not in wealth, not in tyranny, was there any happiness to be found for them—only in kindly peace, fruitful and free.   The wreath was to be of *wild* olive, mark you :—the tree that grows carelessly, tufting the rocks with no vivid bloom, no verdure of branch ;  only with soft snow of blossom, and scarcely fulfilled fruit, mixed with grey leaf and thornset stem ;  no fastening of diadem for you but with such sharp embroidery !   But this, such as it is, you may win while yet you live ;  type of grey honour and sweet rest.*   Free-heartedness, and graciousness, and undisturbed trust, and requited love, and the sight of the peace of others, and the ministry to their pain ;—these, and the blue sky above you, and the sweet waters and flowers of the earth beneath ; and mysteries and presences innumerable, of living things,—these may yet be here your riches ;  untormenting and divine :  serviceable for the life that now is ;  nor, it may be, without promise of that which is to come.

* μελιτόεσσα ἀέθλων γ᾽ ἕνεκεν.

# LECTURE I *

## WORK

My Friends,—I have not come among you to-night to endeavour to give you an entertaining lecture ; but to tell you a few plain facts, and ask you some plain, but necessary, questions.  I have seen and known too much of the struggle for life among our labouring population, to feel at ease, even under any circumstances, in inviting them to dwell on the trivialities of my own studies ; but, much more, as I meet to-night, for the first time, the members of a working Institute established in the district in which I have passed the greater part of my life, I am desirous that we should at once understand each other, on graver matters.  I would fain tell you, with what feelings, and with what hope, I regard this Institution, as one of many such, now happily established throughout England, as well as in other countries ;—Institutions which are preparing the way for a great change in all the circumstances of industrial life ; but of which the success must wholly depend upon our clearly understanding the circumstances and necessary *limits* of this change.  No teacher can truly promote the cause of education, until he knows the conditions of the life for which that education is to prepare his pupil.  And the fact that he is called upon to address you, nominally, as a ' Working Class,' must compel him, if he is in any wise earnest or thoughtful, to inquire, in the outset, on what you yourselves suppose this class distinction has been founded in the past, and must be founded in the future.  The manner of the amuse-

* Delivered before the Working Men's Institute, at Camberwell.

ment, and the matter of the teaching, which any of us can offer you, must depend wholly on our first understanding from you, whether you think the distinction heretofore drawn between working men and others, is truly or falsely founded. Do you accept it as it stands ? do you wish it to be modified ? or do you think the object of education is to efface it, and make us forget it for ever ?

Let me make myself more distinctly understood. We call this—you and I—a 'Working Men's' Institute, and our college in London, a 'Working Men's' College. Now, how do you consider that these several institutes differ, or ought to differ, from 'idle men's' institutes and 'idle men's' colleges ? Or by what other word than 'idle' shall I distinguish those whom the happiest and wisest of working men do not object to call the 'Upper Classes' ? Are there really upper classes—are there lower ? How much should they always be elevated, how much always depressed ? And, gentlemen and ladies—I pray those of you who are here to forgive me the offence there may be in what I am going to say. It is not *I* who wish to say it. Bitter voices say it ; voices of battle and of famine through all the world, which must be heard some day, whoever keeps silence. Neither is it to *you* specially that I say it. I am sure that most now present know their duties of kindness, and fulfil them, better perhaps than I do mine. But I speak to you as representing your whole class, which errs, I know, chiefly by thoughtlessness, but not therefore the less terribly. Wilful error is limited by the will, but what limit is there to that of which we are unconscious ?

Bear with me, therefore, while I turn to these workmen, and ask them, also as representing a great multitude, what they think the 'upper classes' are, and ought to be, in relation to them. Answer, you workmen who are here, as you would among yourselves, frankly ; and tell me how you would have me call those classes. Am I to call them—

would *you* think me right in calling them—the idle classes ?
I think you would feel somewhat uneasy, and as if I were
not treating my subject honestly, or speaking from my
heart, if I went on under the supposition that all rich
people were idle. You would be both unjust and unwise
if you allowed me to say that—not less unjust than the
rich people who say that all the poor are idle, and will
never work if they can help it, or more than they can
help.

For indeed the fact is, that there are idle poor and idle
rich ; and there are busy poor and busy rich. Many a
beggar is as lazy as if he had ten thousand a year ; and
many a man of large fortune is busier than his errand-boy,
and never would think of stopping in the street to play
marbles. So that, in a large view, the distinction between
workers and idlers, as between knaves and honest men,
runs through the very heart and innermost economies of
men of all ranks and in all positions. There is a working
class—strong and happy—among both rich and poor ;
there is an idle class—weak, wicked, and miserable—among
both rich and poor. And the worst of the misunder-
standings arising between the two orders come of the
unlucky fact that the wise of one class habitually con-
template the foolish of the other. If the busy rich people
watched and rebuked the idle rich people, all would be
right ; and if the busy poor people watched and rebuked
the idle poor people, all would be right. But each class
has a tendency to look for the faults of the other. A hard-
working man of property is particularly offended by an
idle beggar ; and an orderly, but poor, workman is naturally
intolerant of the licentious luxury of the rich. And what
is severe judgment in the minds of the just men of either
class, becomes fierce enmity in the unjust—but among the
unjust *only*. None but the dissolute among the poor look
upon the rich as their natural enemies, or desire to pillage
their houses and divide their property. None but the

dissolute among the rich speak in opprobrious terms of
the vices and follies of the poor.

There is, then, no class distinction between idle and
industrious people ; and I am going to-night to speak only
of the industrious.   The idle people we will put out of our
thoughts at once—they are mere nuisances : what ought
to be done with *them*, we'll talk of at another time.   But
there are class distinctions among the industrious themselves ; tremendous distinctions, which rise and fall to
every degree in the infinite thermometer of human pain
and of human power, distinctions of high and low, of lost
and won, to the whole reach of man's soul and body.

These separations we will study, and the laws of them,
among energetic men only, who, whether they work or
whether they play, put their strength into the work, and
their strength into the game ; being in the full sense of
the word ' industrious,' one way or another—with a
purpose, or without.   And these distinctions are mainly
four :

I. Between those who work, and those who play.

II. Between those who produce the means of life, and
those who consume them.

III. Between those who work with the head, and those
who work with the hand.

IV. Between those who work wisely, and who work
foolishly.

For easier memory, let us say we are going to oppose,
in our examination—

    I. Work to play ;
    II. Production to consumption ;
    III. Head to hand ; and,
    IV. Sense to nonsense.

I. First, then, of the distinction between the classes
who work and the classes who play.   Of course we must

agree upon a definition of these terms—work and play—
before going farther. Now, roughly, not with vain subtlety
of definition, but for plain use of the words, ' play ' is an
exertion of body or mind, made to please ourselves, and
with no determined end ; and work is a thing done because
it ought to be done, and with a determined end. You
play, as you call it, at cricket, for instance. That is as
hard work as anything else ; but it amuses you, and it
has no result but the amusement. If it were done as an
ordered form of exercise, for health's sake, it would become
work directly. So, in like manner, whatever we do to
please ourselves, and only for the sake of the pleasure,
not for an ultimate object, is ' play,' the ' pleasing thing,'
not the useful thing. Play may be useful, in a secondary
sense (nothing is indeed more useful or necessary) ; but
the use of it depends on its being spontaneous.

Let us, then, inquire together what sort of games the
playing class in England spend their lives in playing at.

The first of all English games is making money. That
is an all-absorbing game ; and we knock each other down
oftener in playing at that, than at football, or any other
roughest sport ; and it is absolutely without purpose ;
no one who engages heartily in that game ever knows why.
Ask a great money-maker what he wants to do with his
money—he never knows. He doesn't make it to do
anything with it. He gets it only that he *may* get it.
' What will you make of what you have got ? ' you ask.
' Well, I'll get more ' he says. Just as, at cricket, you get
more runs. There's no use in the runs, but to get more
of them than other people is the game. And there's no
use in the money, but to have more of it than other people
is the game. So all that great foul city of London there—
rattling, growling, smoking, stinking—a ghastly heap of
fermenting brickwork, pouring out poison at every pore—
you fancy it is a city of work ? Not a street of it ! It is
a great city of play ; very nasty play, and very hard

play; but still play. It is only Lord's cricket ground without the turf: a huge billiard table without the cloth, and with pockets as deep as the bottomless pit; but mainly a billiard table, after all.

Well, the first great English game is this playing at counters. It differs from the rest in that it appears always to be producing money, while every other game is expensive. But it does not always produce money. There's a great difference between ' winning ' money and ' making ' it : a great difference between getting it out of another man's pocket into ours, or filling both. Collecting money is by no means the same thing as making it ; the tax-gatherer's house is not the Mint ; and much of the apparent gain (so called), in commerce, is only a form of taxation on carriage or exchange.

Our next great English game, however, hunting and shooting, is costly altogether ; and how much we are fined for it annually in land, horses, gamekeepers, and game laws, and all else that accompanies that beautiful and special English game, I will not endeavour to count now ; but note only that, except for exercise, this is not merely a useless game, but a deadly one, to all connected with it. For through horse-racing, you get every form of what the higher classes everywhere call ' Play,' in distinction from all other plays ; that is, gambling ; by no means a beneficial or recreative game ; and, through game-preserving, you get also some curious laying out of ground ; that beautiful arrangement of dwelling-house for man and beast, by which we have grouse and blackcock— so many brace to the acre, and men and women—so many brace to the garret. I often wonder that the angelic builders and surveyors—the angelic builders who build the ' many mansions ' up above there ; and the angelic surveyors, who measured that four-square city with their measuring reeds—I wonder what they think, or are supposed to think, of the laying out of ground by this nation, which has set itself, as it seems, literally to accomplish, word for word, or rather fact for word, in the persons of those poor whom its Master left to represent Him, what that Master said of himself—that foxes and birds had homes, but He none.

Then, next to the gentlemen's game of hunting, we must put the ladies' game of dressing. It is not the cheapest of games. I saw a brooch at a jeweller's in Bond Street a fortnight ago, not an inch wide, and without any singular jewel in it, yet worth £3,000. And I wish I could tell you what this ' play ' costs, altogether, in England, France, and Russia annually. But it is a pretty game, and on certain terms, I like it ; nay, I don't see it played quite as much as I would fain have it. You ladies like to lead the fashion—by all means lead it—lead it thoroughly, lead it far enough. Dress yourselves nicely, and dress everybody else nicely. Lead the *fashions for the poor* first ; make *them* look well, and you yourselves will look, in ways of which you have now no conception, all the better. The fashions you have set for some time among your peasantry are not pretty ones ; their doublets are too irregularly slashed, and the wind blows too frankly through them.

Then there are other games, wild enough, as I could show you if I had time.

There's playing at literature, and playing at art—very different, both, from working at literature, or working at art, but I've no time to speak of these. I pass to the greatest of all—the play of plays, the great gentlemen's game, which ladies like them best to play at—the game of War. It is entrancingly pleasant to the imagination ; the facts of it, not always so pleasant. We dress for it, however, more finely than for any other sport ; and go out to it, not merely in scarlet, as to hunt, but in scarlet and gold, and all manner of fine colours : of course we could fight better in grey, and without feathers ; but all nations

have agreed that it is good to be well dressed at this play.
Then the bats and balls are very costly ; our English and
French bats, with the balls and wickets, even those which
we don't make any use of, costing, I suppose, now about
fifteen millions of money annually to each nation ; all
which you know is paid for by hard labourer's work in the
furrow and furnace. A costly game !—not to speak of
its consequences ; I will say at present nothing of these.
The mere immediate cost of all these plays is what I want
you to consider ; they all cost deadly work somewhere,
as many of us know too well. The jewel-cutter, whose
sight fails over the diamonds ; the weaver, whose arm
fails over the web ; the iron-forger, whose breath fails
before the furnace—*they* know what work is—they, who
have all the work, and none of the play, except a kind
they have named for themselves down in the black north
country where ' play ' means being laid up by sickness.
It is a pretty example for philologists, of varying dialect,
this change in the sense of the word ' play,' as used in the
black country of Birmingham, and the red and black
country of Baden Baden. Yes, gentlemen, and gentle-
women, of England, who think ' one moment unamused a
misery, not made for feeble man,' this is what you have
brought the word ' play ' to mean, in the heart of merry
England ! You may have your fluting and piping ; but
there are sad children sitting in the market-place, who
indeed cannot say to you ' We have piped unto you, and
ye have not danced ' : but eternally shall say to you ' We
have mourned unto you, and ye have not lamented.'

This, then, is the first distinction between the ' upper
and lower ' classes. And this is one which is by no means
necessary ; which indeed must, in process of good time,
be by all honest men's consent abolished. Men will be
taught that an existence of play, sustained by the blood
of other creatures, is a good existence for gnats and sucking
fish ; but not for men : that neither days, nor lives, can

be made holy by doing nothing in them : that the best prayer at the beginning of a day is that we may not lose its moments ; and the best grace before meat, the consciousness that we have justly earned our dinner. And when we have this much of plain Christianity preached to us again, and enough respect what we regard as inspiration, as not to think that ' Son, go work to-day in my vineyard ' means ' Fool, go play to-day in my vineyard,' we shall all be workers, in one way or another ; and this much at least of the distinction between ' upper ' and ' lower ' forgotten.

II. I pass then to our second distinction ; between the rich and poor, between Dives and Lazarus—distinction which exists more sternly, I suppose, in this day, than ever in the world, Pagan or Christian, till now. I will put it sharply before you, to begin with, merely by reading two paragraphs which I cut from two papers that lay on my breakfast table on the same morning, the 25th of November, 1864. The piece about the rich Russian at Paris is commonplace enough, and stupid besides ; (for fifteen francs, 12s. 6d., is nothing for a rich man to give for a couple of peaches, out of season). Still, the two paragraphs printed on the same day are worth putting side by side.

' Such a man is now here. He is a Russian, and, with your permission, we will call him Count Teufelskine. In dress he is sublime ; art is considered in that toilet, the harmony of colour respected, the *chiar' oscuro* evident in well-selected contrast. In manners he is dignified—nay, perhaps apathetic ; nothing disturbs the placid serenity of that calm exterior. One day our friend breakfasted *chez* Bignon. When the bill came he read " Two peaches, 15f." He paid. " Peaches scarce, I presume ? " was his sole remark. " No, sir," replied the waiter, " but Teufelskines are." ' *Telegraph*, November 25, 1864.

' Yesterday morning, at eight o'clock, a woman, passing

a dung heap in the stone yard near the recently-erected almshouses in Shadwell Gap, High Street, Shadwell, called the attention of a Thames police-constable to a man in a sitting position on the dung heap, and said she was afraid he was dead. Her fears proved to be true. The wretched creature appeared to have been dead several hours. He had perished of cold and wet, and the rain had been beating down on him all night. The deceased was a bone-picker. He was in the lowest stage of poverty, poorly clad, and half-starved. The police had frequently driven him away from the stone yard, between sunset and sunrise, and told him to go home. He selected a most desolate spot for his wretched death. A penny and some bones were found in his pockets. The deceased was between fifty and sixty years of age. Inspector Roberts, of the K division, has given directions for inquiries to be made at the lodging-houses respecting the deceased, to ascertain his identity if possible.'—*Morning Post*, November 25, 1864.

You have the separation thus in brief compass ; and I want you to take notice of the ' a penny and some bones were found in his pockets,' and to compare it with this third statement, from the *Telegraph* of January 16th of this year :

' Again, the dietary scale for adult and juvenile paupers were drawn up by the most conspicuous political economists in England. It is low in quantity, but it is sufficient to support nature ; yet within ten years of the passing of the Poor Law Act, we heard of the paupers in the Andover Union gnawing the scraps of putrid flesh and sucking the marrow from the bones of horses which they were employed to crush.'

You see my reason for thinking that our Lazarus of Christianity has some advantage over the Jewish one. Jewish Lazarus expected, or at least prayed, to be fed with crumbs from the rich man's table ; but *our* Lazarus is fed with crumbs from the dog's table.

Now this distinction between rich and poor rests on two bases. Within its proper limits, on a basis which is lawful and everlastingly necessary; beyond them, on a basis unlawful, and everlastingly corrupting the framework of society. The lawful basis of wealth is, that a man who works should be paid the fair value of his work; and that if he does not choose to spend it to-day, he should have free leave to keep it, and spent it to-morrow. Thus, an industrious man working daily, and laying by daily, attains at last the possession of an accumulated sum of wealth, to which he has absolute right. The idle person who will not work, and the wasteful person who lays nothing by, at the end of the same time will be doubly poor—poor in possession, and dissolute in moral habit; and he will then naturally covet the money which the other has saved. And if he is then allowed to attack the other, and rob him of his well-earned wealth, there is no more any motive for saving, or any reward for good conduct; and all society is thereupon dissolved, or exists only in systems of rapine. Therefore the first necessity of social life is the clearness of national conscience in enforcing the law—that he should keep who has JUSTLY EARNED.

That law, I say, is the proper basis of distinction between rich and poor. But there is also a false basis of distinction; namely, the power held over those who earn wealth by those who levy or exact it. There will be always a number of men who would fain set themselves to the accumulation of wealth as the sole object of their lives. Necessarily, that class of men is an uneducated class, inferior in intellect, and more or less cowardly. It is physically impossible for a well-educated, intellectual, or brave man to make money the chief object of his thoughts; as physically impossible as it is for him to make his dinner the principal object of them. All healthy people like their dinners, but their dinner is not the main object of their lives. So all healthily

minded people like making money—ought to like it, and
to enjoy the sensation of winning it : but the main object
of their life is not money ; it is something better than
money.  A good soldier, for instance, mainly wishes to do
his fighting well.  He is glad of his pay—very properly so,
and justly grumbles when you keep him ten years without
it—still, his main notion of life is to win battles, not to
be paid for winning them.  So of clergymen.  They like
pew-rents, and baptismal fees, of course ; but yet, if they
are brave and well educated, the pew-rent is not the sole
object of their lives, and the baptismal fee is not the sole
purpose of the baptism ; the clergyman's object is essentially to baptize and preach, not to be paid for preaching.
So of doctors.  They like fees no doubt—ought to like
them ; yet if they are brave and well educated, the entire
object of their lives is not fees.  They, on the whole,
desire to cure the sick ; and—if they are good doctors,
and the choice were fairly put to them—would rather cure
their patient, and lose their fee, than kill him, and get it.
And so with all other brave and rightly trained men ;
their work is first, their fee second—very important always,
but still *second*.  But in every nation, as I said, there are
a vast class who are ill-educated, cowardly, and more or
less stupid.  And with these people, just as certainly the
fee is first, and the work second, as with brave people the
work is first and the fee second.  And this is no small
distinction.  It is the whole distinction in a man ; distinction between life and death *in* him, between heaven
and hell *for* him.  You cannot serve two masters—you
*must* serve one or other.  If your work is first with you,
and your fee second, work is your master, and the lord of
work, who is God.  But if your fee is first with you, and
your work second, fee is your master, and the lord of fee,
who is the Devil ; and not only the Devil, but the lowest
of devils—' the least erected fiend that fell.'  So there
you have it in brief terms ; Work first—you are God's

servants ; Fee first—you are the Fiend's.  And it makes a difference, now and ever, believe me, whether you serve Him who has on His vesture and thigh written, ' King of Kings,' and whose service is perfect freedom ; or him on whose vesture and thigh the name is written, ' Slave of Slaves,' and whose service is perfect slavery.

However, in every nation there are, and must always be, a certain number of these Fiend's servants, who have it principally for the object of their lives to make money. They are always, as I said, more or less stupid, and cannot conceive of anything else so nice as money.  Stupidity is always the basis of the Judas bargain.  We do great injustice to Iscariot, in thinking him wicked above all common wickedness.  He was only a common money-lover, and, like all money-lovers, didn't understand Christ —couldn't make out the worth of Him, or meaning of Him. He didn't want Him to be killed.  He was horror-struck when he found that Christ would be killed ;  threw his money away instantly, and hanged himself.  How many of our present money-seekers, think you, would have the grace to hang themselves, whoever was killed ?  But Judas was a common, selfish, muddle-headed, pilfering fellow ;  his hand always in the bag of the poor, not caring for them.  He didn't understand Christ ;  yet believed in Him, much more than most of us do ;  had seen Him do miracles, thought He was quite strong enough to shift for Himself, and he, Judas, might as well make his own little bye-perquisites out of the affair.  Christ would come out of it well enough, and he have his thirty pieces.  Now, that is the money-seeker's idea, all over the world.  He doesn't hate Christ, but can't understand Him—doesn't care for Him—sees no good in that benevolent business ; makes his own little job out of it at all events, come what will.  And thus, out of every mass of men, you have a certain number of bagmen—your ' fee-first ' men, whose main object is to make money.  And they do make it—

make it in all sorts of unfair ways, chiefly by the weight and force of money itself, or what is called the power of capital ; that is to say, the power which money, once obtained, has over the labour of the poor, so that the capitalist can take all its produce to himself, except the labourer's food. That is the modern Judas's way of ' carrying the bag,' and ' bearing what is put therein.'

Nay, but (it is asked) how is that an unfair advantage ? Has not the man who has worked for the money a right to use it as he best can ? No ; in this respect, money is now exactly what mountain promontories over public roads were in old times. The barons fought for them fairly : the strongest and cunningest got them ; then fortified them, and made every one who passed below pay toll. Well, capital now is exactly what crags were then. Men fight fairly (we will, at least, grant so much, though it is more than we ought) for their money : but, once having got it, the fortified millionaire can make everybody who passes below pay toll to his million, and build another tower of his money castle. And I can tell you, the poor vagrants by the roadside suffer now quite as much from the bag-baron, as ever they did from the crag-baron. Bags and crags have just the same result on rags. I have not time, however, to-night to show you in how many ways the power of capital is unjust : but this one great principle I have to assert—you will find it quite indis- putably true—that whenever money is the principal object of life with either man or nation, it is both got ill, and spent ill ; and does harm both in the getting and spending ; but when it is not the principal object, it and all other things will be well got, and well spent. And here is the test, with every man, of whether money is the principal object with him, or not. If in mid-life he could pause and say, ' Now I have enough to live upon, I'll live upon it ; and having well earned it, I will also well spend it, and go out of the world poor, as I came into it,' then money is

not principal with him ; but, if, having enough to live
upon in the manner befitting his character and rank, he
still wants to make more, and to *die* rich, then money is
the principal object with him, and it becomes a curse to
himself, and generally to those who spend it after him.
For you know it *must* be spent some day ; the only question
is whether the man who makes it shall spend it, or some one
else. And generally it is better for the maker to spend it,
for he will know best its value and use. This is the true
law of life. And if a man does not choose thus to spend
his money, he must either hoard it or lend it, and the
worst thing he can generally do is to lend it ; for borrowers
are nearly always ill-spenders, and it is with lent money
that all evil is mainly done, and all unjust war protracted.

For observe what the real fact is, respecting loans to
foreign military governments, and how strange it is. If
your little boy came to you to ask for money to spend in
squibs and crackers, you would think twice before you
gave it him ; and you would have some idea that it was
wasted, when you saw it fly off in fireworks, even though
he did no mischief with it. But the Russian children, and
Austrian children, come to you, borrowing money, not to
spend in innocent squibs, but in cartridges and bayonets
to attack you in India with, and to keep down all noble
life in Italy with, and to murder Polish women and children
with ; and *that* you will give at once, because they pay
you interest for it. Now, in order to pay you that interest,
they must tax every working peasant in their dominions ;
and on that work you live. You therefore at once rob
the Austrian peasant, assassinate or banish the Polish
peasant, and you live on the produce of the theft, and the
bribe for the assassination ! That is the broad fact—
that is the practical meaning of your foreign loans, and
of most large interest of money ; and then you quarrel
with Bishop Colenso, forsooth, as if *he* denied the Bible,
and you believed it ! though, wretches as you are, every

deliberate act of your lives is a new defiance of its primary orders ; and as if, for most of the rich men of England at this moment, it were not indeed to be desired, as the best thing at least for *them*, that the Bible should *not* be true, since against them these words are written in it : ' The rust of your gold and silver shall be a witness against you, and shall eat your flesh, as it were fire.'

III. I pass now to our third condition of separation, between the men who work with the hand, and those who work with the head.

And here we have at last an inevitable distinction. There *must* be work done by the arms, or none of us could live. There *must* be work done by the brains, or the life we get would not be worth having. And the same men cannot do both. There is rough work to be done, and rough men must do it ; there is gentle work to be done, and gentlemen must do it ; and it is physically impossible that one class should do, or divide, the work of the other. And it is of no use to try to conceal this sorrowful fact by fine words, and to talk to the workman about the honour-ableness of manual labour, and the dignity of humanity. That is a grand old proverb of Sancho Panza's, ' Fine words butter no parsnips' ; and I can tell you that, all over England just now, you workmen are buying a great deal too much butter at that dairy. Rough work, honourable or not, takes the life out of us ; and the man who has been heaving clay out of a ditch all day, or driving an express train against the north wind all night, or holding a collier's helm in a gale on a lee shore, or whirling white-hot iron at a furnace mouth, that man is not the same at the end of his day, or night, as one who has been sitting in a quiet room, with everything comfortable about him, reading books, or classing butterflies, or painting pictures. If it is any comfort to you to be told that the rough work is the more honourable of the two, I should be sorry to take that much of consolation from you ; and in some sense I need not. The rough work is at all events real, honest, and, generally, though not always, useful ; while the fine work is, a great deal of it, foolish and false as well as fine, and therefore dishonourable : but when both kinds are equally well and worthily done, the head's is the noble work, and the hand's the ignoble ; and of all hand work whatsoever, necessary for the maintenance of life, · those old words ' In the sweat of thy face thou shalt eat bread ' indicate that the inherent nature of it is one of calamity ; and that the ground, cursed for our sake, casts also some shadow of degradation into our contest with its thorn and its thistle ; so that all nations have held their days honourable, or ' holy,' and constituted them ' holydays ' or ' holidays,' by making them days of rest ; and the promise, which, among all our distant hopes, seems to cast the chief brightness over death, is that blessing of the dead who die in the Lord, that ' they rest from their labours, and their works do follow them.'

And thus the perpetual question and contest must arise, who is to do this rough work ? and how is the worker of it to be comforted, redeemed, and rewarded ? and what kind of play should he have, and what rest, in this world, sometimes, as well as in the next ? Well, my good working friends, these questions will take a little time to answer yet. They must be answered : all good men are occupied with them, and all honest thinkers. There's grand head work doing about them ; but much must be discovered, and much attempted in vain, before anything decisive can be told you. Only note these few particulars, which are already sure.

As to the distribution of the hard work. None of us, or very few of us, do either hard or soft work because we think we ought ; but because we have chanced to fall into the way of it, and cannot help ourselves. Now, nobody does anything well that they cannot help doing : work is only done well when it is done with a will ; and no man has a thoroughly sound will unless he knows he is doing what he should, and is in his place. And, depend upon it, all work must be done at last, not in a disorderly, scrambling, doggish way, but in an ordered, soldierly, human way—a lawful way. Men are enlisted for the labour that kills—the labour of war : they are counted, trained, fed, dressed, and praised for that. Let them be enlisted also for the labour that feeds : let them be counted, trained, fed, dressed, praised for that. Teach the plough exercise as carefully as you do the sword exercise, and let the officers of troops of life be held as much gentlemen as the officers of troops of death ; and all is done : but neither this, nor any other right thing, can be accomplished— you can't even see your way to it—unless, first of all, both servant and master are resolved that, come what will of it, they will do each other justice. People are perpetually squabbling about what will be best to do, or easiest to do, or adviseablest to do, or profitablest to do ; but they never, so far as I hear them talk, ever ask what it is *just* to do. And it is the law of heaven that you shall not be able to judge what is wise or easy, unless you are first resolved to judge what is just, and to do it. That is the one thing constantly reiterated by our Master—the order of all others that is given oftenest—'Do justice and judgment.' That's your Bible order ; that's the ' Service of God,' not praying nor psalm-singing. You are told, indeed, to sing psalms when you are merry, and to pray when you need anything ; and, by the perversion of the Evil Spirit, we get to think that praying and psalm-singing are ' service.' If a child finds itself in want of anything, it runs in and asks its father for it—does it call that, doing its father a service ? If it begs for a toy or a piece of cake—does it call that serving its father ? That, with God, is prayer, and He likes to hear it : He likes you to ask Him for cake when you want it ; but He doesn't call that ' serving Him.' Begging is not serving : God likes mere beggars as little as you do—He likes honest servants, not beggars. So when a child loves its father very much, and is very happy, it may sing little songs about him ; but it doesn't call that, serving its father ; neither is singing songs about God, serving God. It is enjoying ourselves if it's anything ; most probably it is nothing : but if it's anything, it is serving ourselves, not God. And yet we are impudent enough to call our beggings and chauntings ' Divine Service ' ; we say ' Divine service will be " performed " ' (that's our word—the form of it gone through) ' at eleven o'clock.' Alas !—unless we perform Divine service in every willing act of life, we never perform it at all. The one Divine work—the one ordered sacrifice—is to do justice ; and it is the last we are ever inclined to do. Anything rather than that ! As much charity as you choose, but no justice. ' Nay,' you will say, ' charity is greater than justice.' Yes, it is greater ; it is the summit of justice—it is the temple of which justice is the foundation. But you can't have the top without the bottom ; you cannot build upon charity. You must build upon justice, for this main reason, that you have not, at first, charity to build with. It is the last reward of good work. Do justice to your brother (you can do that, whether you love him or not), and you will come to love him. But do injustice to him, because you don't love him ; and you will come to hate him. It is all very fine to think you can build upon charity to begin with ; but you will find all you have got to begin with begins at home, and is essentially love of yourself. You well-to-do people, for instance, who are here to-night, will go to ' Divine service ' next Sunday, all nice and tidy, and your little children will have their tight little Sunday boots on, and lovely little Sunday feathers in their hats ; and you'll think, complacently and piously, how lovely they look ! So they do : and you love them heartily, and you like sticking feathers in their hats.

That's all right : that *is* charity ; but it is charity beginning at home. Then you will come to the poor little crossing-sweeper, got up also—it, in its Sunday dress—the dirtiest rags it has—that it may beg the better : we shall give it a penny, and think how good we are. That's charity going abroad. But what does Justice say, walking and watching near us ? Christian Justice has been strangely mute, and seemingly blind ; and, if not blind, decrepit, this many a day : she keeps her accounts still, however—quite steadily—doing them at nights, carefully, with her bandage off, and through acutest spectacles (the only modern scientific invention she cares about). You must put your ear down ever so close to her lips to hear her speak ; and then you will start at what she first whispers, for it will certainly be ' Why shouldn't that little crossing-sweeper have a feather on its head, as well as your own child ? ' Then you may ask Justice, in an amazed manner, ' How she can possibly be so foolish as to think children could sweep crossings with feathers on their heads ? ' Then you stoop again, and Justice says—still in her dull, stupid way—' Then, why don't you, every other Sunday, leave your child to sweep the crossing, and take the little sweeper to church in a hat and feather ? ' Mercy on us (you think), what will she say next ? And you answer, of course, that ' you don't, because everybody ought to remain content in the position in which Providence has placed them.' Ah, my friends, that's the gist of the whole question. *Did* Providence put them in that position, or did *you* ? You knock a man into a ditch, and then you tell him to remain content in the ' position in which Providence has placed him.' That's modern Christianity. You say—' *We* did not knock him into the ditch.' How do you know what you have done, or are doing ? That's just what we have all got to know, and what we shall never know, until the question with us, every morning, is, not how to do the gainful thing, but how to do the just thing ;

nor until we are at least so far on the way to being Christian,
as to have understood that maxim of the poor half-way
Mahometan, ' One hour in the execution of justice is worth
seventy years of prayer.'

Supposing, then, we have it determined with appropriate
justice, *who* is to do the hand work, the next questions
must be how the hand-workers are to be paid, and how
they are to be refreshed, and what play they are to have.
Now, the possible quantity of play depends on the possible
quantity of pay ; and the quantity of pay is not a matter
for consideration to hand-workers only, but to all workers.
Generally, good, useful work, whether of the hand or head,
is either ill-paid, or not paid at all.  I don't say it should
be so, but it always is so.  People, as a rule, only pay for
being amused or being cheated, not for being served.
Five thousand a year to your talker, and a shilling a day
to your fighter, digger, and thinker, is the rule.  None of
the best head work in art, literature, or science, is ever
paid for.  How much do you think Homer got for his
*Iliad* ? or Dante for his *Paradise* ? only bitter bread and
salt, and going up and down other people's stairs.  In
science, the man who discovered the telescope, and first
saw heaven, was paid with a dungeon ; the man who
invented the microscope, and first saw earth, died of
starvation, driven from his home : it is indeed very clear
that God means all thoroughly good work and talk to be
done for nothing.  Baruch, the scribe, did not get a penny
a line for writing Jeremiah's second roll for him, I fancy ;
and St. Stephen did not get bishop's pay for that long
sermon of his to the Pharisees ; nothing but stones.  For
indeed that is the world-father's proper payment.  So
surely as any of the world's children work for the world's
good, honestly, with head and heart ; and come to it,
saying ' Give us a little bread, just to keep the life in us,'
the world-father answers them, ' No, my children, not
bread ; a stone, if you like, or as many as you need, to
105—c *

keep you quiet.' But the hand-workers are not so ill off as all this comes to. The worst that can happen to *you* is to break stones ; not be broken by them. And for you there will come a time for better payment ; some day, assuredly, more pence will be paid to Peter the Fisherman, and fewer to Peter the Pope ; we shall pay people not quite so much for talking in Parliament and doing nothing, as for holding their tongues out of it and doing something ; we shall pay our ploughman a little more, and our lawyer a little less, and so on : but, at least, we may even now take care that whatever work is done shall be fully paid for ; and the man who does it paid for it, not somebody else ; and that it shall be done in an orderly, soldierly, well-guided, wholesome way, under good captains and lieutenants of labour ; and that it shall have its appointed times of rest, and enough of them ; and that in those times the play shall be wholesome play, not in theatrical gardens, with tin flowers and gas sunshine, and girls dancing because of their misery ; but in true gardens, with real flowers and real sunshine, and children dancing because of their gladness ; so that truly the streets shall be full (the ' streets,' mind you, not the gutters) of children, playing in the midst thereof. We may take care that working men shall have at least as good books to read as anybody else, when they've time to read them ; and as comfortable firesides to sit at as anybody else, when they've time to sit at them. This, I think, can be managed for you, my working friends, in the good time.

IV. I must go on, however, to our last head, concerning ourselves all, as workers. What is wise work, and what is foolish work ? What the difference between sense and nonsense, in daily occupation ?

Well, wise work is, briefly, work *with* God. Foolish work is work *against* God. And work done with God, which He will help, may be briefly described as ' Putting in Order '—that is, enforcing God's law of order, spiritual and material, over men and things. The first thing you have to do, essentially ; the real ' good work ' is, with respect to men, to enforce justice, and with respect to things, to enforce tidiness, and fruitfulness. And against these two great human deeds, justice and order, there are perpetually two great demons contending—the devil of iniquity, or inequity, and the devil of disorder, or of death ; for death is only consummation of disorder. You have to fight these two fiends daily. So far as you don't fight against the fiend of iniquity, you work for him. You ' work iniquity,' and the judgment upon you, for all your ' Lord, Lord's,' will be ' Depart from me, ye that work iniquity.' And so far as you do not resist the fiend of disorder, you work disorder, and you yourself do the work of Death, which is sin, and has for its wages, Death himself.

Observe then, all wise work is mainly threefold in character. It is honest, useful, and cheerful.

I. It is HONEST. I hardly know anything more strange than that you recognise honesty in play, and you do not in work. In your lightest games, you always have some one to see what you call ' fair-play.' In boxing, you must hit fair ; in racing, start fair. Your English watchword is fair-play, your English hatred, foul-play. Did it ever strike you that you wanted another watchword also, fair-work, and another hatred also, foul-work ? Your prize-fighter has some honour in him yet ; and so have the men in the ring round him : they will judge him to lose the match, by foul hitting. But your prize-merchant gains his match by foul selling, and no one cries out against that. You drive a gambler out of the gambling-room who loads dice, but you leave a tradesman in flourishing business, who loads scales ! For observe, all dishonest dealing *is* loading scales. What does it matter whether I get short weight, adulterate substance, or dishonest fabric ? The fault in the fabric is incomparably the worst of the two.

Give me short measure of food, and I only lose by you ; but give me adulterate food, and I die by you. Here, then, is your chief duty, you workmen and tradesmen— to be true to yourselves, and to us who would help you. We can do nothing for you, nor you for yourselves, without honesty. Get that, you get all ; without that, your suffrages, your reforms, your free-trade measures, your institutions of science, are all in vain. It is useless to put your heads together, if you can't put your hearts together. Shoulder to shoulder, right hand to right hand, among yourselves, and no wrong hand to anybody else, and you'll win the world yet.

II. Then, secondly, wise work is USEFUL. No man minds, or ought to mind, its being hard, if only it comes to something ; but when it is hard, and comes to nothing ; when all our bees' business turns to spiders' ; and for honey-comb we have only resultant cobweb, blown away by the next breeze—that is the cruel thing for the worker. Yet do we ever ask ourselves, personally, or even nationally, whether our work is coming to anything or not ? We don't care to keep what has been nobly done ; still less do we care to do nobly what others would keep ; and, least of all, to make the work itself useful instead of deadly to the doer, so as to use his life indeed, but not to waste it. Of all wastes, the greatest waste that you can commit is the waste of labour. If you went down in the morning into your dairy, and you found that your youngest child had got down before you ; and that he and the cat were at play together, and that he had poured out all the cream on the floor for the cat to lap up, you would scold the child, and be sorry the milk was wasted. But if, instead of wooden bowls with milk in them, there are golden bowls with human life in them, and instead of the cat to play with—the devil to play with, and you yourself the player ; and instead of leaving that golden bowl to be broken by God at the fountain, you break it in the dust yourself,

and pour the human blood out on the ground for the fiend
to lick up—that is no waste ! What ! you perhaps think,
' to waste the labour of men is not to kill them.' Is it not ?
I should like to know how you could kill them more utterly
—kill them with second deaths, seventh deaths, hundred-
fold deaths ? It is the slightest way of killing to stop a
man's breath. Nay, the hunger, and the cold, and the
little whistling bullets—our love-messengers between
nation and nation—have brought pleasant messages
from us to many a man before now ; orders of sweet
release, and leave at last to go where he will be most
welcome and most happy. At the worst you do but
shorten his life, you do not corrupt his life. But if you
put him to base labour, if you bind his thoughts, if you
blind his eyes, if you blunt his hopes, if you steal his
joys, if you stunt his body, and blast his soul, and at last
leave him not so much as to reap the poor fruit of his
degradation, but gather that for yourself, and dismiss
him to the grave, when you have done with him, having,
so far as in you lay, made the walls of that grave everlasting
(though, indeed, I fancy the goodly bricks of some of our
family vaults will hold closer in the resurrection day than
the sod over the labourer's head), this you think is no
waste, and no sin !

III. Then, lastly, wise work is CHEERFUL as a child's
work is. And now I want you to take one thought home
with you, and let it stay with you.

Everybody in this room has been taught to pray daily
' Thy kingdom come.' Now, if we hear a man swear in
the streets, we think it very wrong, and say he ' takes
God's name in vain.' But there's a twenty times worse
way of taking His name in vain, than that. It is to *ask
God for what we don't want.* He doesn't like that sort of
prayer. If you don't want a thing, don't ask for it : such
asking is the worst mockery of your King you can mock
Him with ; the soldiers striking Him on the head with the

reed was nothing to that. If you do not wish for His kingdom, don't pray for it. But if you do, you must do more than pray for it; you must work for it. And, to work for it, you must know what it is : we have all prayed for it many a day without thinking. Observe, it is a kingdom that is to come to us ; we are not to go to it. Also, it is not to be a kingdom of the dead, but of the living. Also, it is not to come all at once, but quietly ; nobody knows how. ' The kingdom of God cometh not with observation.' Also, it is not to come outside of us, but in the hearts of us : ' the kingdom of God is within you.' And, being within us, it is not a thing to be seen, but to be felt ; and though it brings all substance of good with it, it does not consist in that : ' the kingdom of God is not meat and drink, but righteousness, peace, and joy in the Holy Ghost ' : joy, that is to say, in the holy, healthful, and helpful Spirit. Now if we want to work for this kingdom, and to bring it, and enter into it, there's just one condition to be first accepted. You must enter it as children, or not at all : ' Whosoever will not receive it as a little child shall not enter therein.' And, again, ' Suffer little children to come unto me, and forbid them not, for of such is the kingdom of heaven.'

*Of such*, observe. Not of children themselves, but of such as children. I believe most mothers who read that text think that all heaven is to be full of babies. But that's not so. There will be children there, but the hoary head is the crown. ' Length of days, and long life and peace,' that is the blessing, not to die in babyhood. Children die but for their parents' sins ; God means them to live, but He can't let them always ; then they have their earlier place in heaven : and the little child of David, vainly prayed for ; the little child of Jeroboam, killed by its mother's step on its own threshold—they will be there. But weary old David, and weary old Barzillai, having learned children's lessons at last, will be there too : and the one question for us all, young or old, is, have we learned our child's lesson ? It is the *character* of children we want, and must gain at our peril ; let us see, briefly, in what it consists.

The first character of right childhood is that it is Modest. A well-bred child does not think it can teach its parents, or that it knows everything. It may think its father and mother know everything—perhaps that all grown-up people know everything ; very certainly it is sure that *it* does not. And it is always asking questions, and wanting to know more. Well, that is the first character of a good and wise man at his work. To know that he knows very little ; to perceive that there are many above him wiser than he ; and to be always asking questions, wanting to learn, not to teach. No one ever teaches well who wants to teach, or governs well who wants to govern ; it is an old saying (Plato's, but I know not if his first), and as wise as old.

Then, the second character of right childhood is to be Faithful. Perceiving that its father knows best what is good for it, and having found always, when it has tried its own way against his, that he was right and it was wrong, a noble child trusts him at last wholly, gives him its hand, and will walk blindfold with him, if he bids it. And that is the true character of all good men also, as obedient workers, or soldiers under captains. They must trust their captains ; they are bound for their lives to choose none but those whom they *can* trust. Then, they are not always to be thinking that what seems strange to them, or wrong in what they are desired to do, *is* strange or wrong. They know their captain : where he leads they must follow, what he bids, they must do ; and without this trust and faith, without this captainship and soldiership, no great deed, no great salvation, is possible to man. Among all the nations it is only when this faith is attained by them that they become great : the Jew, the Greek, and the

Mahometan, agree at least in testifying to this. It was a deed of this absolute trust which made Abraham the father of the faithful ; it was the declaration of the power of God as captain over all men, and the acceptance of a leader appointed by Him as commander of the faithful, which laid the foundation of whatever national power yet exists in the East ; and the deed of the Greeks, which has become the type of unselfish and noble soldiership to all lands, and to all times, was commemorated, on the tomb of those who gave their lives to do it, in the most pathetic, so far as I know, or can feel, of all human utterances : ' Oh, stranger, go and tell our people that we are lying here, having *obeyed* their words.'

Then, the third character of right childhood is to be Loving and Generous. Give a little love to a child, and you get a great deal back. It loves everything near it, when it is a right kind of child—would hurt nothing, would give the best it has away, always, if you need it— does not lay plans for getting everything in the house for itself, and delights in helping people ; you cannot please it so much as by giving it a chance of being useful, in ever so little a way.

And because of all these characters, lastly, it is Cheerful. Putting its trust in its father, it is careful for nothing— being full of love to every creature, it is happy always, whether in its play or its duty. Well, that's the great worker's character also. Taking no thought for the morrow ; taking thought only for the duty of the day ; trusting somebody else to take care of to-morrow ; knowing indeed what labour is, but not what sorrow is ; and always ready for play—beautiful play—for lovely human play is like the play of the Sun. There's a worker for you. He, steady to his time, is set as a strong man to run his course, but also, he *rejoiceth* as a strong man to run his course. See how he plays in the morning, with the mists below, and the clouds above, with a ray here and a flash there, and a shower of jewels everywhere ; that's the Sun's play ; and great human play is like his—all various—all full of light and life, and tender, as the dew of the morning.

So then, you have the child's character in these four things—Humility, Faith, Charity, and Cheerfulness. That's what you have got to be converted to. ' Except ye be converted and become as little children '—You hear much of conversion now-a-days ; but people always seem to think they have got to be made wretched by conversion— to be converted to long faces. No, friend, you have got to be converted to short ones ; you have to repent into childhood, to repent into delight, and delightsomeness. You can't go into a conventicle but you'll hear plenty of talk of backsliding. Backsliding, indeed ! I can tell you, on the ways most of us go, the faster we slide back the better. Slide back into the cradle, if going on is into the grave—back, I tell you ; back—out of your long faces, and into your long clothes. It is among children only, and as children only, that you will find medicine for your healing and true wisdom for your teaching. There is poison in the counsels of the *men* of this world ; the words they speak are all bitterness, ' the poison of asps is under their lips,' but ' the sucking child shall play by the hole of the asp.' There is death in the looks of men. ' Their eyes are privily set against the poor ' ; they are as the uncharmable serpent, the cockatrice, which slew by seeing. But ' the weaned child shall lay his hand on the cockatrice den.' There is death in the steps of men : ' their feet are swift to shed blood ; they have compassed us in our steps like the lion that is greedy of his prey, and the young lion lurking in secret places,' but, in that kingdom, the wolf shall lie down with the lamb, and the fatling with the lion, and ' a little child shall lead them.' There is death in the thoughts of men : the world is one wide riddle to them, darker and darker as it draws to a close, but the secret of it is known to the child and the Lord of heaven and earth is most to be thanked in that 'He has hidden these things from the wise and prudent, and has revealed them unto babes.' Yes, and there is death—infinitude of death in the principalities and powers of men. As far as the east is from the west, so far our sins are—*not* set from us, but multiplied around us : the Sun himself, think you he *now* 'rejoices' to run his course, when he plunges westward to the horizon, so widely red, not with clouds, but blood ? And it will be red more widely yet. Whatever drought of the early and latter rain may be, there will be none of that red rain. You fortify yourselves, you arm yourselves against it in vain ; the enemy and avenger will be upon you also, unless you learn that it is not out of the mouths of the knitted gun, or the smoothed rifle, but 'out of the mouths of babes and sucklings' that the strength is ordained, which shall 'still the enemy and avenger.'

# TRAFFIC

# LECTURE II*

## TRAFFIC

My good Yorkshire friends, you asked me down here among your hills that I might talk to you about this Exchange you are going to build : but earnestly and seriously asking you to pardon me, I am going to do nothing of the kind. I cannot talk, or at least can say very little, about this same Exchange. I must talk of quite other things, though not willingly—I could not deserve your pardon, if, when you invited me to speak on one subject, I wilfully spoke on another. But I cannot speak, to purpose, of anything about which I do not care ; and most simply and sorrowfully I have to tell you, in the outset, that I do *not* care about this Exchange of yours.

If, however, when you sent me your invitation, I had answered ' I won't come, I don't care about the Exchange of Bradford,' you would have been justly offended with me, not knowing the reasons of so blunt a carelessness. So I have come down, hoping that you will patiently let me tell you why, on this, and many other such occasions, I now remain silent, when formerly I should have caught at the opportunity of speaking to a gracious audience.

In a word then, I do not care about this Exchange— because *you* don't ; and because you know perfectly well I cannot make you. Look at the essential circumstances of the case, which you, as business men, know perfectly well, though perhaps you think I forget them. You are going to spend £30,000, which to you, collectively, is nothing ; the buying a new coat is, as to the cost of it, a

* Delivered in the Town Hall, Bradford.

much more important matter of consideration to me than building a new Exchange is to you. But you think you may as well have the right thing for your money. You know there are a great many odd styles of architecture about; you don't want to do anything ridiculous; you hear of me, among others, as a respectable architectural man-milliner: and you send for me, that I may tell you the leading fashion; and what is, in our shops, for the moment, the newest and sweetest thing in pinnacles.

Now, pardon me for telling you frankly, you cannot have good architecture merely by asking people's advice on occasion. All good architecture is the expression of national life and character; and it is produced by a prevalent and eager national taste, or desire for beauty. And I want you to think a little of the deep significance of this word 'taste'; for no statement of mine has been more earnestly or oftener controverted than that good taste is essentially a moral quality. 'No,' say many of my antagonists, 'taste is one thing, morality is another. Tell us what is pretty; we shall be glad to know that : but preach no sermons to us.'

Permit me, therefore, to fortify this old dogma of mine somewhat. Taste is not only a part and an index of morality—it is the ONLY morality. The first, and last, and closest trial question to any living creature is, 'What do you like?' Tell me what you like, and I'll tell you what you are. Go out into the street, and ask the first man or woman you meet, what their 'taste' is; and if they answer candidly, you know them, body and soul. 'You, my friend in the rags, with the unsteady gait, what do *you* like?' 'A pipe, and a quartern of gin.' I know you. 'You, good woman, with the quick step and tidy bonnet, what do you like?' 'A swept hearth and a clean tea-table; and my husband opposite me, and a baby at my breast.' Good, I know you also. 'You, little girl with the golden hair and the soft eyes, what do you like?'

' My canary, and a run among the wood hyacinths.' ' You, little boy with the dirty hands, and the low forehead, what do you like ? ' ' A shy at the sparrows, and a game at pitch-farthing.' Good ; we know them all now. What more need we ask ?

' Nay,' perhaps you answer ; ' we need rather to ask what these people and children do, than what they like. If they *do* right, it is no matter that they like what is wrong ; and if they *do* wrong, it is no matter that they like what is right. Doing is the great thing ; and it does not matter that the man likes drinking, so that he does not drink ; nor that the little girl likes to be kind to her canary, if she will not learn her lessons ; nor that the little boy likes throwing stones at the sparrows, if he goes to the Sunday school.' Indeed, for a short time, and in a provisional sense, this is true. For if, resolutely, people do what is right, in time they come to like doing it. But they only are in a right moral state when they *have* come to like doing it ; and as long as they don't like it, they are still in a vicious state. The man is not in health of body who is always thirsting for the bottle in the cupboard, though he bravely bears his thirst ; but the man who heartily enjoys water in the morning and wine in the evening, each in its proper quantity and time. And the entire object of true education is to make people not merely *do* the right things, but *enjoy* the right things—not merely industrious, but to love industry—not merely learned, but to love knowledge—not merely pure, but to love purity— not merely just, but to hunger and thirst after justice.

But you may answer, or think. ' Is the liking for outside ornaments—for pictures, or statues, or furniture, or architecture—a moral quality ? ' Yes, most surely, if a rightly set liking. Taste for *any* pictures or statues is not a moral quality, but taste for good ones is. Only here again we have to define the word ' good.' I don't mean by ' good,' clever—or learned—or difficult in the doing.

Take a picture by Teniers, of sots quarrelling over their dice : it is an entirely clever picture ; so clever that nothing in its kind has ever been done equal to it ; but it is also an entirely base and evil picture. It is an expression of delight in the prolonged contemplation of a vile thing, and delight in that is an ' unmannered,' or ' immoral ' quality. It is ' bad taste ' in the profoundest sense—it is the taste of the devils. On the other hand, a picture of Titian's, or a Greek statue, or a Greek coin, or a Turner landscape, expresses delight in the perpetual contemplation of a good and perfect thing. That is an entirely moral quality—it is the taste of the angels. And all delight in art, and all love of it, resolve themselves into simple love of that which deserves love. That deserving is the quality which we call ' loveliness ' (we ought to have an opposite word, hateliness, to be said of the things which deserve to be hated) ; and it is not an indifferent nor optional thing whether we love this or that ; but it is just the vital function of all our being. What we *like* determines what we *are*, and is the sign of what we are ; and to teach taste is inevitably to form character. As I was thinking over this, in walking up Fleet Street the other day, my eye caught the title of a book standing open in a bookseller's window. It was *On the necessity of the diffusion of taste among all classes.* ' Ah,' I thought to myself, ' my classifying friend, when you have diffused your taste, where will your classes be ? The man who likes what you like, belongs to the same class with you, I think. Inevitably so. You may put him to other work if you choose ; but, by the condition you have brought him into, he will dislike the other work as much as you would yourself. You get hold of a scavenger, or a costermonger, who enjoyed *The Newgate Calendar* for literature, and " Pop goes the Weasel " for music. You think you can make him like Dante and Beethoven ? I wish you joy of your lessons ; but if you do, you have made a gentleman of him: he won't like to go back to his costermongering.'

And so completely and unexceptionally is this so, that, if I had time to-night, I could show you that a nation cannot be affected by any vice, or weakness, without expressing it, legibly, and for ever, either in bad art, or by want of art; and that there is no national virtue, small or great, which is not manifestly expressed in all the art which circumstances enable the people possessing that virtue to produce. Take, for instance, your great English virtue of enduring and patient courage. You have at present in England only one art of any consequence—that is, iron-working. You know thoroughly well how to cast and hammer iron. Now, do you think in those masses of lava which you build volcanic cones to melt and which you forge at the mouths of the Infernos you have created; do you think, on those iron plates, your courage and endurance are not written for ever—not merely with an iron pen, but on iron parchment. And take also your great English vice—European vice—vice of all the world—vice of all other worlds that roll or shine in heaven, bearing with them yet the atmosphere of hell—the vice of jealousy, which brings competition into your commerce, treachery into your councils, and dishonour into your wars—that vice which has rendered for you, and for your next neighbouring nation, the daily occupations of existence no longer possible, but with the mail upon your breasts and the sword loose in its sheath; so that, at last, you have realised for all the multitudes of the two great peoples who lead the so-called civilisation of the earth—you have realised for them all, I say, in person and in policy, what was once true only of the rough Border riders of your Cheviot hills:

> They carved at the meal
> With gloves of steel.
> And they drank the red wine through the helmet barr'd;

do you think that this national shame and dastardliness of heart are not written as legibly on every rivet of your iron armour as the strength of the right hands that forged it ?  Friends, I know not whether this thing be the more ludicrous or the more melancholy.  It is quite unspeakably both.  Suppose, instead of being now sent for by you, I had been sent for by some private gentleman, living in a suburban house, with his garden separated only by a fruit-wall from his next door neighbour's ; and he had called me to consult with him on the furnishing of his drawing-room.  I begin looking about me, and find the walls rather bare ;  I think such and such a paper might be desirable—perhaps a little fresco here and there on the ceiling—a damask curtain or so at the windows.  'Ah,' says my employer, ' damask curtains, indeed !  That's all very fine, but you know I can't afford that kind of thing just now ! '  ' Yet the world credits you with a splendid income ! '  ' Ah, yes,' says my friend, 'but do you know, at present, I am obliged to spend it nearly all in steel-traps ? '  ' Steel-traps !  for whom ? '  ' Why, for that fellow on the other side the wall, you know ;  we're very good friends, capital friends ;  but we are obliged to keep our traps set on both sides of the wall ;  we could not possibly keep on friendly terms without them, and our spring guns.  The worst of it is, we are both clever fellows enough ;  and there's never a day passes that we don't find out a new trap, or a new gun-barrel, or something ;  we spend about fifteen millions a year each in our traps, take it all together ;  and I don't see how we're to do with less.'  A highly comic state of life for two private gentlemen !  but for two nations, it seems to me, not wholly comic ?  Bedlam would be comic, perhaps, if there were only one madman in it ;  and your Christmas pantomime is comic, when there is only one clown in it ;  but when the whole world turns clown, and paints itself red with its own heart's blood instead of vermilion, it is something else than comic, I think.

Mind, I know a great deal of this is play, and willingly allow for that. You don't know what to do with yourselves for a sensation ; fox-hunting and cricketing will not carry you through the whole of this unendurably long mortal life : you liked pop-guns when you were schoolboys, and rifles and Armstrongs are only the same things better made : but then the worst of it is, that what was play to you when boys, was not play to the sparrows ; and what is play to you now, is not play to the small birds of State neither ; and for the black eagles, you are somewhat shy of taking shots at them if I mistake not.

I must get back to the matter in hand, however. Believe me, without further instance, I could show you, in all time, that every nation's vice, or virtue, was written in its art : the soldiership of early Greece ; the sensuality of late Italy ; the visionary religion of Tuscany ; the splendid human energy and beauty of Venice. I have no time to do this to-night (I have done it elsewhere before now) ; but I proceed to apply the principle to ourselves in a more searching manner.

I notice that among all the new buildings which cover your once wild hills, churches and schools are mixed in due, that is to say, in large proportion, with your mills and mansions ; and I notice also that the churches and schools are almost always Gothic, and the mansions and mills are never Gothic. Will you allow me to ask precisely the meaning of this ? For, remember, it is peculiarly a modern phenomenon. When Gothic was invented, houses were Gothic as well as churches ; and when the Italian style superseded the Gothic, churches were Italian as well as houses. If there is a Gothic spire to the Cathedral of Antwerp, there is a Gothic belfry to the *Hôtel de Ville* at Brussels ; if Inigo Jones builds an Italian Whitehall, Sir Christopher Wren builds an Italian St. Paul's. But now you live under one school of architecture, and worship under another. What do you mean by doing this ? Am

I to understand that you are thinking of changing your
architecture back to Gothic ; and that you treat your
churches experimentally, because it does not matter what
mistakes you make in a church ?  Or am I to understand
that you consider Gothic a pre-eminently sacred and
beautiful mode of building, which you think, like the fine
frankincense, should be mixed for the tabernacle only,
and reserved for your religious services ?  For if this be
the feeling, though it may seem at first as if it were graceful
and reverent, you will find that, at the root of the matter,
it signifies neither more nor less than that you have
separated your religion from your life.

For consider what a wide significance this fact has ;
and remember that it is not you only, but all the people of
England, who are behaving thus just now.

You have all got into the habit of calling the church
' the house of God.'  I have seen, over the doors of many
churches, the legend actually carved ' *This* is the house
of God, and this is the gate of heaven.'  Now, note where
that legend comes from, and of what place it was first
spoken.  A boy leaves his father's house to go on a long
journey on foot, to visit his uncle :  he has to cross a wild
hill-desert ;  just as if one of your own boys had to cross
the wolds of Westmoreland, to visit an uncle at Carlisle.
The second or third day your boy finds himself somewhere
between Hawes and Brough, in the midst of the moors, at
sunset.  It is stony ground, and boggy ;  he cannot go
one foot farther that night.  Down he lies, to sleep, on
Whernside, where best he may, gathering a few of the
stones together to put under his head—so wild the place
is, he cannot get anything but stones.  And there, lying
under the broad night, he has a dream ;  and he sees a
ladder set up on the earth, and the top of it reaches to
heaven, and the angels of God are ascending and descending
upon it.  And when he wakes out of his sleep, he says,
' How dreadful is this place ;  surely, this is none other

than the house of God, and this is the gate of heaven. This PLACE, observe; not this church; not this city; not this stone, even, which he puts up for a memorial— the piece of flint on which his head has lain. But this *place*; this windy slope of Whernside; this moorland hollow, torrent-bitten, snow-blighted; this *any* place where God lets down the ladder. And how are you to know where that will be? or how are you to determine where it may be, but by being ready for it always? Do you know where the lightning is to fall next? You *do* know that, partly; you can guide the lightning; but you cannot guide the going forth of the Spirit, which is as that lightning when it shines from the east to the west.

But the perpetual and insolent warping of that strong verse to serve a merely ecclesiastical purpose, is only one of the thousand instances in which we sink back into gross Judaism. We call our churches 'temples.' Now, you know, or ought to know, they are *not* temples. They have never had, never can have, anything whatever to do with temples. They are 'synagogues,' 'gathering places,' where you gather yourselves together as an assembly; and by not calling them so, you again miss the force of another mighty text: 'Thou, when thou prayest, shalt not be as the hypocrites are; for they love to pray standing in the *churches*' [we should translate it] 'that they may be seen of men. But thou, when thou prayest, enter into thy closet, and when thou hast shut thy door, pray to thy Father'—which is, not in chancel nor in aisle, but, in secret.'

Now, you feel, as I say this to you—I know you feel— as if I were trying to take away the honour of your churches. Not so; I am trying to prove to you the honour of your houses and your hills; I am trying to show you—not that the Church is not sacred—but that the whole Earth is. I would have you feel, what careless, what constant, what infectious sin there is in all modes of thought, whereby, in calling your churches only ' holy,' you call your hearths and homes profane ; and have separated yourselves from the heathen by casting all your household gods to the ground, instead of recognising, in the places of their many and feeble Lares, the presence of your One and Mighty Lord and Lar.

' But what has all this to do with our Exchange ? ' you ask me, impatiently. My dear friends, it has just everything to do with it ; on these inner and great questions depend all the outer and little ones ; and if you have asked me down here to speak to you, because you had before been interested in anything I have written, you must know that all I have yet said about architecture was to show this. The book I called *The Seven Lamps* was to show that certain right states of temper and moral feeling were the magic powers by which all good architecture, without exception, had been produced. *The Stones of Venice* had, from beginning to end, no other aim than to show that the Gothic architecture of Venice had arisen out of, and indicated in all its features, a state of pure national faith, and of domestic virtue ; and that its Renaissance architecture had arisen out of, and in all its features indicated, a state of concealed national infidelity and of domestic corruption. And now, you ask me what style is best to build in ; and how can I answer, knowing the meaning of the two styles, but by another question— do you mean to build as Christians or as Infidels ? And still more—do you mean to build as honest Christians or as honest Infidels ? as thoroughly and confessedly either one or the other ? You don't like to be asked such rude questions. I cannot help it ; they are of much more importance than this Exchange business ; and if they can be at once answered, the Exchange business settles itself in a moment. But, before I press them farther, I must ask leave to explain one point clearly. In all my past work, my endeavour has been to show that good archi-

tecture is essentially religious—the production of a faithful
and virtuous, not of an infidel and corrupted people. But
in the course of doing this, I have had also to show that
good architecture is not *ecclesiastical*. People are so apt
to look upon religion as the business of the clergy, not
their own, that the moment they hear of anything depending on ' religion,' they think it must also have depended
on the priesthood ; and I have had to take what place was
to be occupied between these two errors, and fight both,
often with seeming contradiction. Good architecture is
the work of good and believing men ; therefore, you say,
at least some people say ' Good architecture must essentially have been the work of the clergy, not of the laity.'
No—a thousand times no ; good architecture has always
been the work of the commonalty, *not* of the clergy. What,
you say, those glorious cathedrals—the pride of Europe—
did their builders not form Gothic architecture ? No ;
they corrupted Gothic architecture. Gothic was formed
in the baron's castle, and the burgher's street. It was
formed by the thoughts, and hands, and powers of free
citizens and soldier kings. By the monk it was used as
an instrument for the aid of his superstition ; when that
superstition became a beautiful madness, and the best
hearts of Europe vainly dreamed and pined in the cloister,
and vainly raged and perished in the crusade—through
that fury of perverted faith and wasted war, the Gothic
rose also to its loveliest, most fantastic, and finally, most
foolish dreams ; and, in those dreams, was lost.

I hope, now, that there is no risk of your misunder-
standing me when I come to the gist of what I want to say
to-night ; when I repeat, that every great national architecture has been the result and exponent of a great national
religion. You can't have bits of it here, bits there—you
must have it everywhere, or nowhere. It is not the
monopoly of a clerical company—it is not the exponent of
a theological dogma—it is not the hieroglyphic writing of

an initiated priesthood ; it is the manly language of a
people inspired by resolute and common purpose, and
rendering resolute and common fidelity to the legible laws
of an undoubted God.

Now there have as yet been three distinct schools of
European architecture. I say, European, because Asiatic
and African architectures belong so entirely to other races
and climates, that there is no question of them here ; only,
in passing, I will simply assure you that whatever is good
or great in Egypt, and Syria, and India, is just good or
great for the same reasons as the buildings on our side of
the Bosphorus. We Europeans, then, have had three
great religions : the Greek, which was the worship of the
God of Wisdom and Power ; the Mediæval, which was
the worship of the God of Judgment and Consolation ; the
Renaissance, which was the worship of the God of Pride
and Beauty : these three we have had—they are past—
and now, at last, we English have got a fourth religion,
and a God of our own, about which I want to ask you.
But I must explain these three old ones first.

I repeat, first, the Greeks essentially worshipped the
God of Wisdom ; so that whatever contended against
their religion—to the Jews a stumbling block—was, to the
Greeks—*Foolishness.*

The first Greek idea of deity was that expressed in the
word, of which we keep the remnant in our words ' *Di-*
urnal ' and ' *Di-*vine '—the god of *Day*, Jupiter the
revealer. Athena is his daughter, but especially daughter
of the Intellect, springing armed from the head. We are
only with the help of recent investigation beginning to
penetrate the depth of meaning couched under the Athenaic
symbols : but I may note rapidly, that her ægis, the mantle
with the serpent fringes, in which she often, in the best
statues, is represented as folding up her left hand for
better guard, and the Gorgon on her shield, are both
representative mainly of the chilling horror and sadness

# TRAFFIC 73

(turning men to stone, as it were), of the outmost and superficial spheres of knowledge—that knowledge which separates, in bitterness, hardness, and sorrow, the heart of the full-grown man from the heart of the child. For out of imperfect knowledge spring terror, dissension, danger, and disdain; but from perfect knowledge, given by the full-revealed Athena, strength and peace, in sign of which she is crowned with the olive spray, and bears the resistless spear.

This, then, was the Greek conception of purest Deity, and every habit of life, and every form of his art developed themselves from the seeking this bright, serene, resistless wisdom; and setting himself, as a man, to do things ever-more rightly and strongly; * not with any ardent affection or ultimate hope; but with a resolute and continent energy of will, as knowing that for failure there was no consolation, and for sin there was no remission. And the Greek architecture rose unerring, bright, clearly defined, and self-contained.

Next followed in Europe the great Christian faith, which was essentially the religion of Comfort. Its great doctrine is the remission of sins; for which cause it happens, too often, in certain phases of Christianity, that sin and sickness themselves are partly glorified, as if, the more you had to be healed of, the more divine was the healing. The practical result of this doctrine, in art, is a continual contemplation of sin and disease, and of imaginary states of purification from them; thus we have an architecture

* It is an error to suppose that the Greek worship, or seeking, was chiefly of Beauty. It was essentially of Rightness and Strength, founded on Forethought: the principal character of Greek art is not beauty, but Design: and the Dorian Apollo-worship and Athenian Virgin-worship are both expressions of adoration of divine Wisdom and Purity. Next to these great deities rank, in power over the national mind, Dionysius and Ceres, the givers of human strength and life: then, for heroic example, Hercules. There is no Venus-worship among the Greeks in the great times: and the Muses are essentially teachers of Truth, and of its harmonies.

105—D

conceived in a mingled sentiment of melancholy and aspiration, partly severe, partly luxuriant, which will bend itself to every one of our needs, and every one of our fancies, and be strong or weak with us, as we are strong or weak ourselves. It is, of all architecture, the basest, when base people build it—of all, the noblest, when built by the noble.

And now note that both these religions—Greek and Mediæval—perished by falsehood in their own main purpose. The Greek religion of Wisdom perished in a false philosophy—' Oppositions of science, falsely so called.' The Mediæval religion of Consolation perished in false comfort ; in remission of sins given lyingly. It was the selling of absolution that ended the Mediæval faith ; and I can tell you more, it is the selling of absolution which, to the end of time, will mark false Christianity. Pure Christianity gives her remission of sins only by *ending* them ; but false Christianity gets her remission of sins by *compounding* for them. And there are many ways of compounding for them. We English have beautiful little quiet ways of buying absolution, whether in low Church or high, far more cunning than any of Tetzel's trading.

Then, thirdly, there followed the religion of Pleasure, in which all Europe gave itself to luxury, ending in death. First, *bals masqués* in every saloon, and then guillotines in every square. And all these three worships issue in vast temple building. Your Greek worshipped Wisdom, and built you the Parthenon—the Virgin's temple. The Mediæval worshipped Consolation, and built you Virgin temples also—but to our Lady of Salvation. Then the Revivalist worshipped beauty, of a sort, and built you Versailles, and the Vatican. Now, lastly, will you tell me what *we* worship, and what *we* build ?

You know we are speaking always of the real, active, continual, national worship ; that by which men act while

they live ; not that which they talk of when they die.
Now, we have, indeed, a nominal religion, to which we pay
tithes of property and sevenths of time ; but we have also
a practical and earnest religion, to which we devote nine-
tenths of our property and six-sevenths of our time.  And
we dispute a great deal about the nominal religion ; but
we are all unanimous about this practical one, of which
I think you will admit that the ruling goddess may be best
generally described as the ' Goddess of Getting-on,' or
' Britannia of the Market.'  The Athenians had an ' Athena
Agoraia,' or Minerva of the Market ; but she was a subordinate type of their goddess, while our Britannia Agoraia
is the principal type of ours.  And all your great architectural works are, of course, built to her.  It is long since
you built a great cathedral ; and how you would laugh at
me, if I proposed building a cathedral on the top of one of
these hills of yours, taking it for an Acropolis !  But your
railroad mounds, prolonged masses of Acropolis ;  your
railroad stations, vaster than the Parthenon, and innumerable ;  your chimneys, how much more mighty and
costly than cathedral spires !  your harbour-piers ;  your
warehouses ;  your exchanges !—all these are built to your
great Goddess of ' Getting-on ' ;  and she has formed, and
will continue to form, your architecture, as long as you
worship her ;  and it is quite vain to ask me to tell
you how to build to *her* ;  you know far better than I.

There might indeed, on some theories, be a conceivably
good architecture for Exchanges—that is to say if there
were any heroism in the fact or deed of exchange, which
might be typically carved on the outside of your building.
For, you know, all beautiful architecture must be adorned
with sculpture or painting ; and for sculpture or painting,
you must have a subject.  And hitherto it has been a
received opinion among the nations of the world that the
only right subjects for either, were *heroisms* of some sort.
Even on his pots and his flagons, the Greek put a Hercules

slaying lions, or an Apollo slaying serpents, or Bacchus slaying melancholy giants, and earth-born despondencies. On his temples, the Greek put contests of great warriors in founding states, or of gods with evil spirits. On his houses and temples alike, the Christian put carvings of angels conquering devils ; or of hero-martyrs exchanging this world for another ; subject inappropriate, I think, to our manner of exchange here. And the Master of Christians not only left his followers without any orders as to the sculpture of affairs of exchange on the outside of buildings, but gave some strong evidence of his dislike of affairs of exchange within them. And yet there might surely be a heroism in such affairs ; and all commerce became a kind of selling of doves, not impious. The wonder has always been great to me, that heroism has never been supposed to be in anywise consistent with the practice of supplying people with food, or clothes ; but rather with that of quartering oneself upon them for food, and stripping them of their clothes. Spoiling of armour is an heroic deed in all ages ; but the selling of clothes, old or new, has never taken any colour of magnanimity. Yet one does not see why feeding the hungry and clothing the naked should ever become base businesses, even when engaged in on a large scale. If one could contrive to attach the notion of conquest to them anyhow ? so that, supposing there were anywhere an obstinate race, who refused to be comforted, one might take some pride in giving them compulsory comfort ; and as it were, ' occupying a country ' with one's gifts, instead of one's armies ? If one could only consider it as much a victory to get a barren field sown, as to get an eared field stripped ; and contend who should build villages, instead of who should ' carry ' them. Are not all forms of heroism conceivable in doing these serviceable deeds ? You doubt who is strongest ? It might be ascertained by push of spade as well as push of sword. Who is wisest ? There are witty things to be thought of

in planning other business than campaigns. Who is
bravest ? There are always the elements to fight with,
stronger than men ; and nearly as merciless. The only
absolutely and unapproachably heroic element in the
soldier's work seems to be—that he is paid little for it—
and regularly : while you traffickers, and exchangers, and
others occupied in presumably benevolent business, like
to be paid much for it—and by chance. I never can make
out how it is that a knight-errant does not expect to be
paid for his trouble, but a pedlar-errant always does ;
that people are willing to take hard knocks for nothing,
but never to sell ribands cheap ; that they are ready to
go on fervent crusades to recover the tomb of a buried
God, never on any travels to fulfil the orders of a living
God ; that they will go anywhere barefoot to preach their
faith, but must be well bribed to practise it, and are
perfectly ready to give the Gospel gratis, but never the
loaves and fishes. If you chose to take the matter up
on any such soldierly principle, to do your commerce,
and your feeding of nations, for fixed salaries ; and to be
as particular about giving people the best food, and the
best cloth, as soldiers are about giving them the best gunpowder, I could carve something for you on your exchange
worth looking at. But I can only at present suggest
decorating its frieze with pendant purses ; and making its
pillars broad at the base, for the sticking of bills. And in
the innermost chambers of it there might be a statue of
Britannia of the Market, who may have, perhaps advisably,
a partridge for her crest, typical at once of her courage in
fighting for noble ideas ; and of her interest in game ; and
round its neck the inscription in golden letters ' Perdix
fovit quæ non peperit.* Then, for her spear, she might

* *Jeremiah*, xvii., 11 (best in *Septuagint* and *Vulgate*). ' As the
partridge, fostering what she brought not forth, so he that getteth
riches, not by right, shall leave them in the midst of his days, and at
his end shall be a fool.'

have a weaver's beam ; and on her shield, instead of her
Cross, the Milanese boar, semi-fleeced, with the town of
Gennesaret proper in the field, and the legend ' In the best
market,' and her corslet, of leather, folded over her heart in
the shape of a purse, with thirty slits in it for a piece of
money to go in at, on each day of the month.   And I
doubt not but that people would come to see your exchange,
and its goddess, with applause.

Nevertheless, I want to point out to you certain strange
characters in this goddess of yours.   She differs from the
great Greek and Mediæval deities essentially in two things—
first, as to the continuance of her presumed power ;
secondly, as to the extent of it.

1st, as to the Continuance.

The Greek Goddess of Wisdom gave continual increase
of wisdom, as the Christian Spirit of Comfort (or Com-
forter) continual increase of comfort.   There was no
question, with these, of any limit or cessation of function.
But with your Agora Goddess, that is just the most important question.   Getting on—but where to ?   Gathering
together—but how much ?   Do you mean to gather
always—never to spend ?   If so, I wish you joy of your
goddess, for I am just as well-off as you, without the
trouble of worshipping her at all.   But if you do not spend,
somebody else will—somebody else must.   And it is
because of this (among many other such errors) that I have
fearlessly declared your so-called science of Political
Economy to be no science ; because, namely, it has omitted
the study of exactly the most important branch of the
business—the study of *spending*.   For spend you must,
and as much as you make, ultimately.   You gather corn—
will you bury England under a heap of grain ; or will you,
when you have gathered, finally eat ?   You gather gold :
will you make your house-roofs of it, or pave your streets
with it ?   That is still one way of spending it.   But if
you keep it, that you may get more, I'll give you more ;

I'll give you all the gold you want—all you can imagine—
if you can tell me what you'll do with it. You shall have
thousands of gold pieces ; thousands of thousands—
millions—mountains, of gold : where will you keep them ?
Will you put an Olympus of silver upon a golden Pelion—
make Ossa like a wart ? Do you think the rain and dew
would then come down to you, in the streams from such
mountains, more blessedly than they will down the mountains which God has made for you, of moss and whinstone ?
But it is not gold that you want to gather ! What is it ?
greenbacks ? No ; not those neither. What is it then—
is it ciphers after a capital I ? Cannot you practise
writing ciphers, and write as many as you want ? Write
ciphers for an hour every morning, in a big book, and
say every evening, I am worth all those noughts more than
I was yesterday. Won't that do ? Well, what in the name
of Plutus is it you want ? Not gold, not greenbacks, not
ciphers after a capital I ? You will have to answer, after
all, ' No ; we want, somehow or other, money's *worth*.'
Well, what is that ? Let your Goddess of Getting-on
discover it, and let her learn to stay therein.

II. But there is yet another question to be asked respecting this Goddess of Getting-on. The first was of the
continuance of her power ; the second is of its extent.

Pallas and the Madonna were supposed to be all the
world's Pallas, and all the world's Madonna. They could
teach all men, and they could comfort all men. But, look
strictly into the nature of the power of your Goddess of
Getting-on ; and you will find she is the Goddess—not of
everybody's getting-on—but only of somebody's getting-
on. This is a vital, or rather deathful, distinction.
Examine it in your own ideal of the state of national life
which this Goddess is to evoke and maintain. I asked you
what it was, when I was last here ; you have never told
me. Now, shall I try to tell you ?

Your ideal of human life then is, I think, that it should

be passed in a pleasant undulating world, with iron and coal everywhere underneath it. On each pleasant bank of this world is to be a beautiful mansion, with two wings; and stables, and coachhouses; a moderately sized park; a large garden and hot-houses; and pleasant carriage drives through the shrubberies. In this mansion are to live the favoured votaries of the Goddess; the English gentleman, with his gracious wife, and his beautiful family; always able to have the boudoir and the jewels for the wife, and the beautiful ball dresses for the daughters and hunters for the sons, and a shooting in the Highlands for himself. At the bottom of the bank is to be the mill; not less than a quarter of a mile long, with a steam engine at each end, and two in the middle, and a chimney three hundred feet high. In this mill are to be in constant employment from eight hundred to a thousand workers, who never drink, never strike, always go to church on Sunday, and always express themselves in respectful language.

Is not that, broadly, and in the main features, the kind of thing you propose to yourselves? It is very pretty indeed, seen from above; not at all so pretty, seen from below. For, observe, while to one family this deity is indeed the Goddess of Getting-on, to a thousand families she is the Goddess of *not* Getting-on. 'Nay,' you say, ' they have all their chance.' Yes, so has every one in a lottery, but there must always be the same number of blanks. ' Ah! but in a lottery it is not skill and intelligence which take the lead, but blind chance.' What then! do you think the old practice, that ' they should take who have the power, and they should keep who can,' is less iniquitous, when the power has become power of brains instead of fist? and that, though we may not take advantage of a child's or a woman's weakness, we may of a man's foolishness? ' Nay, but finally, work must be done, and some one must be at the top, some one at the bottom.' Granted, my friends. Work must always be, and captains of work must always be ; and if you in the least remember the tone of any of my writings, you must know that they are thought unfit for this age, because they are always insisting on need of government, and speaking with scorn of liberty. But I beg you to observe that there is a wide difference between being captains or governors of work, and taking the profits of it. It does not follow, because you are general of an army, that you are to take all the treasure, or land, it wins (if it fight for treasure or land) ; neither, because you are king of a nation, that you are to consume all the profits of the nation's work. Real kings, on the contrary, are known invariably by their doing quite the reverse of this—by their taking the least possible quantity of the nation's work for themselves. There is no test of real kinghood so infallible as that. Does the crowned creature live simply, bravely, unostentatiously ? probably he *is* a King. Does he cover his body with jewels, and his table with delicates ? in all probability he is *not* a King. It is possible he may be, as Solomon was ; but that is when the nation shares his splendour with him. Solomon made gold, not only to be in his own palace as stones, but to be in Jerusalem as stones. But, even so, for the most part, these splendid kinghoods expire in ruin, and only the true kinghoods live, which are of royal labourers governing loyal labourers ; who, both leading rough lives, establish the true dynasties. Conclusively you will find that because you are king of a nation, it does not follow that you are to gather for yourself all the wealth of that nation ; neither, because you are king of a small part of the nation, and lord over the means of its maintenance—over field, or mill, or mine, are you to take all the produce of that piece of the foundation of national existence for yourself.

You will tell me I need not preach against these things, for I cannot mend them. No, good friends, I cannot ; but you can, and you will. Do you think these phenomena are to stay always in their present power or aspect ? All history shows, on the contrary, that to be the exact thing they never can do. Change *must* come ; but it is ours to determine whether change of growth, or change of death. Shall the Parthenon be in ruins on its rock, and Bolton priory in its meadow, but these mills of yours be the consummation of the buildings of the earth, and their wheels be as the wheels of eternity ? Think you that ' men may come, and men may go,' but—mills—go on for ever ? Not so ; out of these, better or worse shall come ; and it is for you to choose which.

I know that none of this wrong is done with deliberate purpose. I know, on the contrary, that you wish your workmen well ; that you do much for them, and that you desire to do more for them, if you saw your way to it, safely. I know that many of you have done, and are every day doing, whatever you feel to be in your power ; and that even all this wrong and misery are brought about by a warped sense of duty, each of you striving to do his best, without noticing that this best is essentially and centrally the best for himself, not for others. And all this has come of the spreading of that thrice accursed, thrice impious doctrine of the modern economist, that ' To do the best for yourself, is finally to do the best for others.' Friends, our great Master said not so ; and most absolutely we shall find this world is not made so. Indeed, to do the best for others, is finally to do the best for ourselves ; but it will not do to have our eyes fixed on that issue. The Pagans had got beyond that. Hear what a Pagan says of this matter ; hear what were, perhaps, the last written words of Plato—if not the last actually written (for this we cannot know), yet assuredly in fact and power his parting words—in which, endeavouring to give full crowning and harmonious close to all his thoughts, and to speak the sum of them by the imagined sentence of the Great Spirit, his strength and his heart fail him, and the words cease,

broken off for ever.  It is the close of the dialogue called
*Critias*, in which he describes, partly from real tradition,
partly in ideal dream, the early state of Athens ;  and the
genesis, and order, and religion, of the fabled isle of Atlantis ;
in which genesis he conceives the same first perfection and
final degeneracy of man, which in our own Scriptural
tradition is expressed by saying that the Sons of God
intermarried with the daughters of men, for he supposes
the earliest race to have been indeed the children of God ;
and to have corrupted themselves, until ' their spot was
not the spot of his children.'  And this, he says, was the
end ;  that indeed ' through many generations, so long as
the God's nature in them yet was full, they were submissive to the sacred laws, and carried themselves lovingly
to all that had kindred with them in divineness ;  for their
uttermost spirit was faithful and true, and in every wise
great ;  so that, in all meekness of wisdom, they dealt
with each other, and took all the chances of life ;  and
despising all things except virtue, they cared little what
happened day by day, and *bore lightly the burden* of gold
and of possessions ;  for they saw that, if only their common
love and virtue increased, all these things would be increased together with them ;  but to set their esteem and
ardent pursuit upon material possession, would be to lose
that first, and their virtue and affection together with it.
And by such reasoning, and what of the divine nature
remained in them, they gained all this greatness of which
we have already told ;  but when the God's part of them
faded and became extinct, being mixed again and again,
and effaced by the prevalent mortality ;  and the human
nature at last exceeded, they then became unable to
endure the courses of fortune ;  and fell into shapelessness
of life, and baseness in the sight of him who could see,
having lost everything that was fairest of their honour ;
while to the blind hearts which could not discern the true
life, tending to happiness, it seemed that they were then

chiefly noble and happy, being filled with all iniquity of inordinate possession and power. Whereupon, the God of Gods, whose Kinghood is in laws, beholding a once just nation thus cast into misery, and desiring to lay such punishment upon them as might make them repent into restraining, gathered together all the gods into his dwelling place, which from heaven's centre overlooks whatever has part in creation ; and having assembled them, he said——'

The rest is silence. So ended are the last words of the chief wisdom of the heathen, spoken of this idol of riches ; this idol of yours ; this golden image, high by measureless cubits, set up where your green fields of England are furnace-burnt into the likeness of the plain of Dura : this idol, forbidden to us, first of all idols, by our own Master and faith ; forbidden to us also by every human lip that has ever, in any age or people, been acounted of as able to speak according to the purposes of God. Continue to make that forbidden deity your principal one, and soon no more art, no more science, no more pleasure will be possible. Catastrophe will come ; or, worse than catastrophe, slow mouldering and withering into Hades. But if you can fix some conception of a true human state of life to be striven for—life for all men as for yourselves—if you can determine some honest and simple order of existence ; following those trodden ways of wisdom, which are pleasantness, and seeking her quiet and withdrawn paths, which are peace—then, and so sanctifying wealth into ' commonwealth,' all your art, your literature, your daily labours, your domestic affection, and citizen's duty, will join and increase into one magnificent harmony. You will know then how to build, well enough ; you will build with stone well, but with flesh better ; temples not made with hands, but riveted of hearts ; and that kind of marble, crimson-veined, is indeed eternal.

# WAR

# LECTURE III *

## WAR

YOUNG SOLDIERS, I do not doubt but that many of you came unwillingly to-night, and many in merely contemptuous curiosity, to hear what a writer on painting could possibly say, or would venture to say, respecting your great art of war. You may well think within yourselves, that a painter might, perhaps without immodesty, lecture younger painters upon painting, but not young lawyers upon law, nor young physicians upon medicine—least of all, it may seem to you, young warriors upon war. And, indeed, when I was asked to address you, I declined at first, and declined long ; for I felt that you would not be interested in my special business, and would certainly think there was small need for me to come to teach you yours. Nay, I knew that there ought to be *no* such need, for the great veteran soldiers of England are now men every way so thoughtful, so noble, and so good, that no other teaching than their knightly example, and their few words of grave and tried counsel, should be either necessary for you, or even, without assurance of due modesty in the offerer, endured by you.

But being asked, not once nor twice, I have not ventured persistently to refuse ; and I will try, in very few words, to lay before you some reason why you should accept my excuse, and hear me patiently. You may imagine that your work is wholly foreign to, and separate from mine. So far from that, all the pure and noble arts of peace are founded on war ; no great art ever yet rose on earth, but

* Delivered at the Royal Military Academy, Woolwich.

among a nation of soldiers. There is no art among a shepherd people, if it remains at peace. There is no art among an agricultural people, if it remains at peace. Commerce is barely consistent with fine art ; but cannot produce it. Manufacture not only is unable to produce it, but invariably destroys whatever seeds of it exist. There is no great art possible to a nation but that which is based on battle.

Now, though I hope you love fighting for its own sake, you must, I imagine, be surprised at my assertion that there is any such good fruit of fighting. You supposed, probably, that your office was to defend the works of peace, but certainly not to found them : nay, the common course of war, you may have thought, was only to destroy them. And truly, I, who tell you this of the use of war, should have been the last of men to tell you so, had I trusted my own experience only. Hear why : I have given a considerable part of my life to the investigation of Venetian painting ; and the result of that inquiry was my fixing upon one man as the greatest of all Venetians, and therefore, as I believed, of all painters whatsoever. I formed this faith (whether right or wrong matters at present nothing), in the supremacy of the painter Tintoret, under a roof covered with his pictures ; and of those pictures, three of the noblest were then in the form of shreds of ragged canvas, mixed up with the laths of the roof, rent through by three Austrian shells. Now, it is not every lecturer who *could* tell you that he had seen three of his favourite pictures torn to rags by bomb-shells. And after such a sight, it is not every lecturer who *would* tell you that, nevertheless, war was the foundation of all great art.

Yet the conclusion is inevitable, from any careful comparison of the states of great historic races at different periods. Merely to show you what I mean, I will sketch for you, very briefly, the broad steps of the advance of the best art of the world. The first dawn of it is in Egypt ; and the power of it is founded on the perpetual contemplation of death, and of future judgment, by the mind of a nation of which the ruling caste were priests, and the second, soldiers. The greatest works produced by them are sculptures of their kings going out to battle, or receiving the homage of conquered armies. And you must remember also, as one of the great keys to the splendour of the Egyptian nation, that the priests were not occupied in theology only. Their theology was the basis of practical government and law ; so that they were not so much priests as religious judges ; the office of Samuel, among the Jews, being as nearly as possible correspondent to theirs.

All the rudiments of art then, and much more than the rudiments of all science, are laid first by this great warrior-nation, which held in contempt all mechanical trades, and in absolute hatred the peaceful life of shepherds. From Egypt art passes directly into Greece, where all poetry, and all painting, are nothing else than the description, praise, or dramatic representation of war, or of the exercises which prepare for it, in their connection with offices of religion. All Greek institutions had first respect to war ; and their conception of it, as one necessary office of all human and divine life, is expressed simply by the images of their guiding gods. Apollo is the god of all wisdom of the intellect ; he bears the arrow and the bow, before he bears the lyre. Again, Athena is the goddess of all wisdom in conduct. It is by the helmet and the shield, oftener than by the shuttle, that she is distinguished from other deities.

There were, however, two great differences in principle between the Greek and the Egyptian theories of policy. In Greece there was no soldier caste ; every citizen was necessarily a soldier. And, again, while the Greeks rightly despised mechanical arts as much as the Egyptians, they

did not make the fatal mistake of despising agricultural
and pastoral life ; but perfectly honoured both.  These
two conditions of truer thought raise them quite into the
highest rank of wise manhood that has yet been reached ;
for all our great arts, and nearly all our great thoughts,
have been borrowed or derived from them.  Take away
from us what they have given ; and I hardly can imagine
how low the modern European would stand.

Now, you are to remember, in passing to the next phase
of history, that though you *must* have war to produce art—
you must also have much more than war ; namely, an art-
instinct or genius in the people ; and that, though all the
talent for painting in the world won't make painters of
you, unless you have a gift for fighting as well, you may
have the gift for fighting, and none for painting.  Now,
in the next great dynasty of soldiers, the art-instinct is
wholly wanting.  I have not yet investigated the Roman
character enough to tell you the causes of this ; but I
believe, paradoxical as it may seem to you, that, however
truly the Roman might say of himself that he was born of
Mars, and suckled by the wolf, he was nevertheless, at
heart, more of a farmer than a soldier.  The exercises of
war were with him practical, not poetical ; his poetry was
in domestic life only, and the object of battle, ' pacis
imponere morem.'  And the arts are extinguished in his
hands, and do not rise again, until, with Gothic chivalry,
there comes back into the mind of Europe a passionate
delight in war itself, for the sake of war.  And then, with
the romantic knighthood which can imagine no other
noble employment—under the fighting kings of France,
England, and Spain ; and under the fighting dukeships
and citizenships of Italy, art is born again, and rises to
her height in the great valleys of Lombardy and Tuscany,
through which there flows not a single stream, from all
their Alps or Apennines, that did not once run dark red
from battle : and it reaches its culminating glory in the

city which gave to history the most intense type of soldiership yet seen among men—the city whose armies were led
in their assault by their king, led through it to victory by
their king, and so led, though that king of theirs was blind,
and in the extremity of his age.

And from this time forward, as peace is established or
extended in Europe, the arts decline. They reach an
unparalleled pitch of costliness, but lose their life, enlist
themselves at last on the side of luxury and various corruption, and, among wholly tranquil nations, wither utterly
away ; remaining only in partial practice among races
who, like the French and us, have still the minds, though
we cannot all live the lives, of soldiers.

' It may be so,' I can suppose that a philanthropist might
exclaim. ' Perish then the arts, if they can flourish only
at such a cost. What worth is there in toys of canvas
and stone, if compared to the joy and peace of artless
domestic life ? ' And the answer is—truly, in themselves,
none. But as expressions of the highest state of the human
spirit, their worth is infinite. As results they may be
worthless, but, as signs, they are above price. For it is
an assured truth that, whenever the faculties of men are at
their fullness, they *must* express themselves by art ; and
to say that a state is without such expression, is to say
that it is sunk from its proper level of manly nature.
So that, when I tell you that war is the foundation of all
the arts, I mean also that it is the foundation of all the
high virtues and faculties of men.

It was very strange to me to discover this ; and very
dreadful—but I saw it to be quite an undeniable fact.
The common notion that peace and the virtues of civil life
flourished together, I found to be wholly untenable. Peace
and the *vices* of civil life only flourish together. We talk
of peace and learning, and of peace and plenty, and of
peace and civilisation ; but I found that those were not
the words which the Muse of History coupled together :

that, on her lips, the words were—peace and sensuality, peace and selfishness, peace and corruption, peace and death. I found, in brief, that all great nations learned their truth of word, and strength of thought, in war ; that they were nourished in war, and wasted by peace ; taught by war, and deceived by peace ; trained by war, and betrayed by peace—in a word, that they were born in war and expired in peace.

Yet now note carefully, in the second place, it is not *all* war of which this can be said—nor all dragon's teeth, which, sown, will start up into men.   It is not the ravage of a barbarian wolf-flock, as under Genseric or Suwarrow ; nor the habitual restlessness and rapine of mountaineers, as on the old borders of Scotland ; nor the occasional struggle of a strong peaceful nation for its life, as in the wars of the Swiss with Austria ; nor the contest of merely ambitious nations for extent of power, as in the wars of France under Napoleon, or the just terminated war in America.   None of these forms of war build anything but tombs.   But the creative or foundational war is that in which the natural restlessness and love of contest among men are disciplined, by consent, into modes of beautiful— though it may be fatal—play : in which the natural ambition and love of power of men are disciplined into the aggressive conquest of surrounding evil : and in which the natural instincts of self-defence are sanctified by the nobleness of the institutions, and purity of the households, which they are appointed to defend.   To such war as this all men are born ; in such war as this any man may happily die ; and forth from such war as this have arisen, through- out the extent of past ages, all the highest sanctities and virtues of humanity.

I shall therefore divide the war of which I would speak to you into three heads.   War for exercise or play ;  war for dominion ;  and, war for defence.

I. And first, of war for exercise or play.   I speak of it

primarily in this light, because, through all past history, manly war has been more an exercise than anything else, among the classes who cause, and proclaim it. It is not a game to the conscript, or the pressed sailor; but neither of these are the causers of it. To the governor who determines that war shall be, and to the youths who voluntarily adopt it as their profession, it has always been a grand pastime; and chiefly pursued because they had nothing else to do. And this is true without any exception. No king whose mind was fully occupied with the development of the inner resources of his kingdom, or with any other sufficing subject of thought, ever entered into war but on compulsion. No youth who was earnestly busy with any peaceful subject of study, or set on any serviceable course of action, ever voluntarily became a soldier. Occupy him, early and wisely, in agriculture or business, in science or in literature, and he will never think of war otherwise than as a calamity. But leave him idle; and, the more brave and active and capable he is by nature, the more he will thirst for some appointed field for action; and find, in the passion and peril of battle, the only satisfying fulfilment of his unoccupied being. And from the earliest incipient civilisation until now, the population of the earth divides itself, when you look at it widely, into two races; one of workers, and the other of players—one tilling the ground, manufacturing, building, and otherwise providing for the necessities of life—the other part proudly idle, and continually therefore needing recreation, in which they use the productive and laborious orders partly as their cattle, and partly as their puppets or pieces in the game of death.

Now, remember, whatever virtue or goodliness there may be in this game of war, rightly played, there is none when you thus play it with a multitude of small human pawns.

If you, the gentlemen of this or any other kingdom,

choose to make your pastime of contest, do so, and welcome ; but set not up these unhappy peasant-pieces upon the green fielded board. If the wager is to be of death, lay it on your own heads, not theirs. A goodly struggle in the Olympic dust, though it be the dust of the grave, the gods will look upon, and be with you in ; but they will not be with you, if you sit on the sides of the amphitheatre, whose steps are the mountains of earth, whose arena its valleys, to urge your peasant millions into gladiatorial war. You also, you tender and delicate women, for whom, and by whose command, all true battle has been, and must ever be ; you would perhaps shrink now, though you need not, from the thought of sitting as queens above set lists where the jousting game might be mortal. How much more, then, ought you to shrink from the thought of sitting above a theatre pit in which even a few condemned slaves were slaying each other only for your delight ! And do you *not* shrink from the *fact* of sitting above a theatre pit, where—not condemned slaves—but the best and bravest of the poor sons of your people, slay each other—not man to man—as the coupled gladiators ; but race to race, in duel of generations ? You would tell me, perhaps, that you do not sit to see this ; and it is indeed true, that the women of Europe—those who have no heart-interest of their own at peril in the contest—draw the curtains of their boxes, and muffle the openings ; so that from the pit of the circus of slaughter there may reach them only at intervals a half-heard cry and a murmur as of the wind's sighing, when myriads of souls expire. They shut out the death-cries ; and are happy, and talk wittily among themselves. That is the utter literal fact of what our ladies do in their pleasant lives.

Nay, you might answer, speaking for them : ' We do not let these wars come to pass for our play, nor by our carelessness ; we cannot help them. How can any final quarrel of nations be settled otherwise than by war ? ' I cannot now delay, to tell you how political quarrels might be otherwise settled. But grant that they cannot. Grant that no law of reason can be understood by nations ; no law of justice submitted to by them : and that, while questions of a few acres, and of petty cash, can be determined by truth and equity, the questions which are to issue in the perishing or saving of kingdoms can be determined only by the truth of the sword, and the equity of the rifle. Grant this, and even then, judge if it will always be necessary for you to put your quarrel into the hearts of your poor, and sign your treaties with peasants' blood. You would be ashamed to do this in your own private position and power. Why should you not be ashamed also to do it in public place and power ? If you quarrel with your neighbour, and the quarrel be indeterminable by law, and mortal, you and he do not send your footmen to Battersea fields to fight it out ; nor do you set fire to his tenants' cottages, nor spoil their goods. You fight out your quarrel yourselves, and at your own danger, if at all. And you do not think it materially affects the arbitrement that one of you has a larger household than the other ; so that, if the servants or tenants were brought into the field with their masters, the issue of the contest could not be doubtful ? You either refuse the private duel, or you practise it under laws of honour, not of physical force ; that so it may be, in a manner, justly concluded. Now the just or unjust conclusion of the private feud is of little moment, while the just or unjust conclusion of the public feud is of eternal moment : and yet, in this public quarrel, you take your servants' sons from their arms to fight for it, and your servants' food from their lips to support it ; and the black seals on the parchment of your treaties of peace are the deserted hearth and the fruitless field. There is a ghastly ludicrousness in this, as there is mostly in these wide and universal crimes. Hear the statement of the very fact of it in the most literal words of the greatest of our English thinkers :

What, speaking in quite unofficial language, is the net-purport and upshot of war ? To my own knowledge, for example, there dwell and toil, in the British village of Dumdrudge, usually some five hundred souls. From these, by certain ' natural enemies ' of the French, there are successively selected, during the French war, say thirty able-bodied men. Dumdrudge, at her own expense, has suckled and nursed them ; she has, not without difficulty and sorrow, fed them up to manhood, and even trained them to crafts, so that one can weave, another build, another hammer, and the weakest can stand under thirty stone avoirdupois. Nevertheless, amid much weeping and swearing, they are selected ; all dressed in red ; and shipped away, at the public charges, some two thousand miles, or say only to the south of Spain ; and fed there till wanted.

And now to that same spot in the south of Spain are thirty similar French artisans, from a French Dumdrudge, in like manner wending ; till at length, after infinite effort, the two parties come into actual juxtaposition ; and Thirty stands fronting Thirty, each with a gun in his hand.

Straightway the word ' Fire ! ' is given, and they blow the souls out of one another, and in place of sixty brisk useful craftsmen, the world has sixty dead carcases, which it must bury, and anon shed tears for. Had these men any quarrel ? Busy as the devil is, not the smallest ! They lived far enough apart ; were the entirest strangers ; nay, in so wide a universe, there was even, unconsciously, by commerce, some mutual helpfulness between them. How then ? Simpleton ! their governors had fallen out ; and instead of shooting one another, had the cunning to make these poor blockheads shoot. (*Sartor Resartus.*)

Positively, then, gentlemen, the game of battle must not, and shall not, ultimately be played this way. But should it be played any way ? Should it, if not by your servants, be practised by yourselves ? I think, yes. Both history and human instinct seem alike to say, yes. All healthy men like fighting, and like the sense of danger ; all brave women like to hear of their fighting, and of their facing danger. This is a fixed instinct in the fine race of them ; and I cannot help fancying that fair fight is the best play for them ; and that a tournament was a better game than a steeple-chase. The time may perhaps come in France as well as here, for universal hurdle-races and cricketing: but I do not think universal 'crickets' will bring out the best qualities of the nobles of either country. I use, in such question, the test which I have adopted, of the connection of war with other arts ; and I reflect how, as a sculptor, I should feel, if I were asked to design a monument for a dead knight, in Westminster Abbey, with a carving of a bat at one end, and a ball at the other. It may be the remains in me only of savage Gothic prejudices ; but I had rather carve it with a shield at one end, and a sword at the other. And this, observe, with no reference whatever to any story of duty done, or cause defended. Assume the knight merely to have ridden out occasionally to fight his neighbour for exercise ; assume him even a soldier of fortune, and to have gained his bread, and filled his purse, at the sword's point. Still, I feel as if it were, somehow, grander and worthier in him to have made his bread by sword play than any other play ; I had rather he had made it by thrusting than by batting ; much more, than by betting. Much rather that he should ride war horses, than back race horses ; and—I say it sternly and deliberately—much rather would I have him slay his neighbour, than cheat him.

But remember, so far as this may be true, the game of war is only that in which the *full personal power of the human creature* is brought out in management of its weapons. And this for three reasons :

First, the great justification of this game is that it truly, when well played, determines *who is the best man*— who is the highest bred, the most self-denying, the most fearless, the coolest of nerve, the swiftest of eye and hand. You cannot test these qualities wholly, unless there is a clear possibility of the struggle's ending in death. It is only in the fronting of that condition that the full trial of the man, soul and body, comes out. You may go to your game of wickets, or of hurdles, or of cards, and any knavery that is in you may stay unchallenged all the while. But if the play may be ended at any moment by a lance-thrust, a man will probably make up his accounts a little before he enters it. Whatever is rotten and evil in him will weaken his hand more in holding a sword hilt, than in balancing a billiard cue ; and on the whole, the habit of living lightly hearted, in daily presence of death, always has had, and must have, a tendency both to the making and testing of honest men. But for the final testing, observe, you must make the issue of battle strictly dependent on fineness of frame, and firmness of hand. You must not make it the question, which of the combatants has the longest gun, or which has got behind the biggest tree, or which has the wind in his face, or which has gunpowder made by the best chemists, or iron smelted with the best coal, or the angriest mob at his back. Decide your battle, whether of nations or individuals, on *those* terms ; and you have only multiplied confusion, and added slaughter to inquity. But decide your battle by pure trial which has the strongest arm, and steadiest heart—and you have gone far to decide a great many matters besides, and to decide them rightly.

And the other reasons for this mode of decision of cause, are the diminution both of the material destructiveness, or cost, and of the physical distress of war. For you must not think that in speaking to you in this (as you may imagine) fantastic praise of battle, I have overlooked the conditions weighing against me. I pray all of you, who have not read, to read with the most earnest attention, Mr. Helps' two essays, on War, and Government, in the first volume of the last series of *Friends in Council*. Everything that can be urged against war is there simply, exhaustively, and most graphically stated. And all, there urged, is true. But the two great counts of evil alleged against war by that most thoughtful writer, hold only against modern war. If you have to take away masses of men from all industrial employment—to feed them by the labour of others—to move them and provide them with destructive machines, varied daily in national rivalship of inventive cost; if you have to ravage the country which you attack—to destroy, for a score of future years, its roads, its woods, its cities, and its harbours; and if, finally, having brought masses of men, counted by hundreds of thousands, face to face, you tear those masses to pieces with jagged shot, and leave the fragments of living creatures, countlessly beyond all help of surgery, to starve and parch, through days of torture, down into clots of clay—what book of accounts shall record the cost of your work; what book of judgment sentence the guilt of it?

That, I say, is *modern* war—scientific war—chemical and mechanic war—worse even than the savage's poisoned arrow. And yet you will tell me, perhaps, that any other war than this is impossible now. It may be so; the progress of science cannot, perhaps, be otherwise registered than by new facilities of destruction; and the brotherly love of our enlarging Christianity be only proved by multiplication of murder. Yet hear, for a moment, what war was, in Pagan and ignorant days—what war might yet be, if we could extinguish our science in darkness, and join the heathen's practice to the Christian's theory. I read you this from a book which probably most of you know well, and all ought to know—Muller's *Dorians*;—but I have put the points I wish you to remember in closer connection than in his text.

'The chief characteristic of the warriors of Sparta was great composure and a subdued strength; the violence (λύσσα) of Aristodemus and Isadus being considered as deserving rather of blame than praise; and these qualities in general distinguished the Greeks from the northern Barbarians, whose boldness always consisted in noise and tumult. For the same reason the Spartans *sacrificed to the Muses* before an action; these goddesses being expected to produce regularity and order in battle; as they *sacrificed*

*on the same occasion in Crete to the god of love,* as the
confirmer of mutual esteem and shame.  Every man put
on a crown, when the band of flute-players gave the signal
for attack ; all the shields of the line glittered with their
high polish, and mingled their splendour with the dark
red of the purple mantles, which were meant both to adorn
the combatant, and to conceal the blood of the wounded ;
to fall well and decorously being an incentive the more
to the most heroic valour.  The conduct of the Spartans
in battle denotes a high and noble disposition which
rejected all the extremes of brutal rage.  The pursuit of
the enemy ceased when the victory was completed ; and
after the signal for retreat had been given, all hostilities
ceased.  The spoiling of arms, at least during the battle,
was also interdicted ; and the consecration of the spoils
of slain enemies to the gods, as, in general, all rejoicings
for victory, were considered as ill-omened.'

Such was the war of the greatest soldiers who prayed to
heathen gods.  What Christian war is, preached by
Christian ministers, let any one tell you, who saw the sacred
crowning, and heard the sacred flute-playing, and was
inspired and sanctified by the divinely-measured and
musical language, of any North American regiment preparing for its charge.  And what is the relative cost of
life in pagan and Christian wars, let this one fact tell you :
the Spartans won the decisive battle of Corinth with the
loss of eight men ; the victors at indecisive Gettysburg
confess to the loss of 30,000.

II. I pass now to our second order of war, the commonest
among men, that undertaken in desire of dominion.  And
let me ask you to think for a few moments what the real
meaning of this desire of dominion is—first in the minds
of kings—then in that of nations.

Now, mind you this first—that I speak either about
kings, or masses of men, with a fixed conviction that
human nature is a noble and beautiful thing ; not a foul

nor a base thing. All the sin of men I esteem as their disease, not their nature ; as a folly which may be prevented, not a necessity which must be accepted. And my wonder, even when things are at their worst, is always at the height which this human nature can attain. Thinking it high, I find it always a higher thing than I thought it ; while those who think it low, find it, and will find it, always, lower than they thought it : the fact being, that it is infinite, and capable of infinite height and infinite fall ; but the nature of it—and here is the faith which I would have you hold with me—the *nature* of it is in the nobleness, not in the catastrophe.

Take the faith in its utmost terms. When the captain of the *London* shook hands with his mate, saying ' God speed you ! I will go down with my passengers,' *that* I believe to be ' human nature.' He does not do it from any religious motive—from any hope of reward, or any fear of punishment ; he does it because he is a man. But when a mother, living among the fair fields of merry England, gives her two-year-old child to be suffocated under a mattress in her inner room, while the said mother waits and talks outside ; *that* I believe to be *not* human nature. You have the two extremes there, shortly. And you, men, and mothers, who are here face to face with me to-night, I call upon you to say which of these is human, and which inhuman—which ' natural ' and which ' unnatural ' ? Choose your creed at once, I beseech you : choose it with unshaken choice, choose it for ever. Will you take, for foundation of act and hope, the faith that this man was such as God made him, or that this woman was such as God made her ? Which of them has failed from their nature—from their present, possible, actual nature : not their nature of long ago, but their nature of now ? Which has betrayed it—falsified it ? Did the guardian who died in his trust, die inhumanly, and as a fool ; and did the murderess of her child fulfil the law of her being ?

Choose, I say ; infinitude of choices hang upon this.    You have had false prophets among you—for centuries you have had them—solemnly warned against them though you were ; false prophets, who have told you that all men are nothing but fiends or wolves, half beast, half devil. Believe that, and indeed you may sink to that.    But refuse that, and have faith that God ' made you upright,' though *you* have sought out many inventions ; so, you will strive daily to become more what your Maker meant and means you to be, and daily gives you also the power to be—and you will cling more and more to the nobleness and virtue that is in you, saying ' My righteousness I hold fast, and will not let it go.'

I have put this to you as a choice, as if you might hold either of these creeds you liked best.    But there is in reality no choice for you ;  the facts being quite easily ascertainable.    You have no business to *think* about this matter, or to choose in it.    The broad fact is, that a human creature of the highest race, and most perfect as a human thing, is invariably both kind and true ;  and that as you lower the race, you get cruelty and falseness, as you get deformity ; and this so steadily and assuredly, that the two great words which, in their first use, meant only perfection of race, have come, by consequence of the invariable connection of virtue with the fine human nature, both to signify benevolence of disposition.    The word generous, and the word gentle, both, in their origin, meant only ' of pure race,' but because charity and tenderness are inseparable from this purity of blood, the words which once stood only for pride, now stand as synonyms for virtue.

Now, this being the true power of our inherent humanity, and seeing that all the aim of education should be to develop this ;    and seeing also what magnificent self-sacrifice the higher classes of men are capable of, for any cause that they understand or feel—it is wholly inconceivable to me how well-educated princes, who ought to be of all gentlemen the gentlest, and of all nobles the most generous, and whose title or royalty means only their function of doing every man ' right '—how these, I say, throughout history, should so rarely pronounce themselves on the side of the poor and of justice, but continually maintain themselves and their own interests by oppression of the poor, and by wresting of justice ; and how this should be accepted as so natural, that the word loyalty, which means faithfulness to law, is used as if it were only the duty of a people to be loyal to their king, and not the duty of a king to be infinitely more loyal to his people. How comes it to pass that a captain will die with his passengers, and lean over the gunwale to give the parting boat its course ; but that a king will not usually die with, much less *for*, his passengers—thinks it rather incumbent on his passengers, in any number, to die for *him* ? Think, I beseech you, of the wonder of this. The sea captain, not captain by divine right, but only by company's appointment ; not a man of royal descent, but only a plebeian who can steer ; not with the eyes of the world upon him, but with feeble chance, depending on one poor boat, of his name being ever heard above the wash of the fatal waves—not with the cause of a nation resting on his act, but helpless to save so much as a child from among the lost crowd with whom he resolves to be lost—yet goes down quietly to his grave, rather than break his faith to these few emigrants. But your captain by divine right—your captain with the hues of a hundred shields of kings upon his breast—your captain whose every deed, brave or base, will be illuminated or branded for ever before unescapable eyes of men—your captain whose every thought and act are beneficent, or fatal, from sunrising to setting, blessing as the sunshine, or shadowing as the night—this captain, as you find him in history, for the most part thinks only how he may tax his passengers, and sit at most ease in his state cabin !

For observe, if there had been indeed in the hearts of the rulers of great multitudes of men any such conception of work for the good of those under their command, as there is in the good and thoughtful masters of any small company of men, not only wars for the sake of mere increase of power could never take place, but our idea of power itself would be entirely altered. Do you suppose that to think and act even for a million of men, to hear their complaints, watch their weaknesses, restrain their vices, make laws for them, lead them, day by day, to purer life, is not enough for one man's work? If any of us were absolute lord only of a district of a hundred miles square, and were resolved on doing our utmost for it; making it feed as large a number of people as possible; making every clod productive, and every rock defensive, and every human being happy; should we not have enough on our hands think you? But if the ruler has any other aim than this; if, careless of the result of his interference, he desire only the authority to interfere; and, regardless of what is ill-done or well-done, cares only that it shall be done at his bidding; if he would rather do two hundred miles' space of mischief, than one hundred miles' space of good, of course he will try to add to his territory; and to add illimitably. But does he add to his power? Do you call it power in a child, if he is allowed to play with the wheels and bands of some vast engine, pleased with their murmur and whirl, till his unwise touch, wandering where it ought not, scatters beam and wheel into ruin? Yet what machine is so vast, so incognisable, as the working of the mind of a nation; what child's touch so wanton, as the word of a selfish king? And yet, how long have we allowed the historian to speak of the extent of the calamity a man causes, as a just ground for his pride; and to extol him as the greatest prince, who is only the centre of the widest error. Follow out this thought by yourselves; and you will find that all power, properly so called, is wise and benevolent.  There may be capacity in a drifting fire-ship to destroy a fleet ; there may be venom enough in a dead body to infect a nation : but which of you, the most ambitious, would desire a drifting kinghood, robed in consuming fire, or a poison-dipped sceptre whose touch was mortal ?  There is no true potency, re-member, but that of help, nor true ambition, but ambition to save.

And then, observe farther, this true power, the power of saving, depends neither on multitude of men, nor on extent of territory.  We are continually assuming that nations become strong according to their numbers.  They indeed become so, if those numbers can be made of one mind ; but how are you sure you can stay them in one mind, and keep them from having north and south minds ?  Grant them unanimous, how know you they will be unanimous in right ?  If they are unanimous in wrong, the more they are, essentially the weaker they are.  Or, suppose that they can neither be of one mind, nor of two minds, but can only be of *no* mind ?  Suppose they are a mere helpless mob ; tottering into precipitant catastrophe, like a waggon load of stones when the wheel comes off.  Dangerous enough for their neighbours, certainly, but not ' powerful.'

Neither does strength depend on extent of territory, any more than upon number of population.  Take up your maps when you go home this evening—put the cluster of British Isles beside the mass of South America ; and then consider whether any race of men need care how much ground they stand upon.  The strength is in the men, and in their unity and virtue, not in their standing room : a little group of wise hearts is better than a wilderness full of fools ; and only that nation gains true territory, which gains itself.

And now for the brief practical outcome of all this. Remember, no government is ultimately strong, but in proportion to its kindness and justice ; and that a nation does not strengthen, by merely multiplying and diffusing itself. We have not strengthened as yet, by multiplying into America. Nay, even when it has not to encounter the separating conditions of emigration, a nation need not boast itself of multiplying on its own ground, if it multiplies only as flies or locusts do, with the god of flies for its god. It multiplies its strength only by increasing as one great family, in perfect fellowship and brotherhood. And lastly, it does not strengthen itself by seizing dominion over races whom it cannot benefit. Austria is not strengthened, but weakened, by her grasp of Lombardy ; and whatever apparent increase of majesty and of wealth may have accrued to us from the possession of India, whether these prove to us ultimately power or weakness, depends wholly on the degree in which our influence on the native race shall be benevolent and exalting. But, as it is at their own peril that any race extend their dominion in mere desire of power, so it is at their own still greater peril that they refuse to undertake aggressive war, according to their force, whenever they are assured that their authority would be helpful and protective. Nor need you listen to any sophistical objection of the impossibility of knowing when a people's help is needed, or when not. Make your national conscience clean, and your national eyes will soon be clear. No man who is truly ready to take part in a noble quarrel will ever stand long in doubt by whom, or in what cause, his aid is needed. I hold it my duty to make no political statement of any special bearing in this presence ; but I tell you broadly and boldly, that, within these last ten years, we English have, as a knightly nation, lost our spurs : we have fought where we should not have fought, for gain ; and we have been passive where we should not have been passive, for fear. I tell you that the principle of non-intervention, as now preached among us, is as selfish and cruel as the worst frenzy of conquest, and differs from it only by being not only malignant, but dastardly.

I know, however, that my opinions on this subject differ too widely from those ordinarily held, to be any farther intruded upon you ; and therefore I pass lastly to examine the conditions of the third kind of noble war—war waged simply for defence of the country in which we were born, and for the maintenance and execution of her laws, by whomsoever threatened or defied. It is to this duty that I suppose most men entering the army consider themselves in reality to be bound, and I want you now to reflect what the laws of mere defence are ; and what the soldier's duty, as now understood, or supposed to be understood. You have solemnly devoted yourselves to be English soldiers, for the guardianship of England. I want you to feel what this vow of yours indeed means, or is gradually coming to mean. You take it upon you, first, while you are senti-mental schoolboys ; you go into your military convent, or barracks, just as a girl goes into her convent while she is a sentimental schoolgirl ; neither of you then know what you are about, though both the good soldiers and good nuns make the best of it afterwards. You don't understand perhaps why I call you ' sentimental ' school-boys, when you go into the army ? Because, on the whole, it is the love of adventure, of excitement, of fine dress and of the pride of fame, all which are sentimental motives, which chiefly make a boy like going into the Guards better than into a counting-house. You fancy, perhaps, that there is a severe sense of duty mixed with these peacocky motives ? And in the best of you, there is ; but do not think that it is principal. If you cared to do your duty to your country in a prosaic and unsentimental way, depend upon it, there is now truer duty to be done in raising harvests, than in burning them ; more in building houses, than in shelling them—more in winning money by your own work, wherewith to help men, than in taxing other people's work, for money wherewith to slay men—more duty finally, in honest and unselfish living than in honest and unselfish dying, though that seems to your boys' eyes the bravest. So far then, as for your own honour, and the honour of your families, you choose brave death in a red coat before brave life in a black one, you are sentimental ; and now see what this passionate vow of yours comes to. For a little while you ride, and you hunt tigers or savages, you shoot, and are shot ; you are happy, and proud, always, and honoured and wept if you die ; and you are satisfied with your life, and with the end of it ; believing, on the whole, that good rather than harm of it comes to others, and much pleasure to you. But as the sense of duty enters into your forming minds, the vow takes another aspect. You find that you have put yourselves into the hand of your country as a weapon. You have vowed to strike, when she bids you, and to stay scabbarded when she bids you ; all that you need answer for is, that you fail not in her grasp. And there is goodness in this, and greatness, if you can trust the hand and heart of the Britomart who has braced you to her side, and are assured that when she leaves you sheathed in darkness, there is no need for your flash to the sun. But remember, good and noble as this state may be, it is a state of slavery. There are different kinds of slaves and different masters. Some slaves are scourged to their work by whips, others are scourged to it by restlessness or ambition. It does not matter what the whip is ; it is none the less a whip, because you have cut thongs for it out of your own souls : the fact, so far, of slavery, is in being driven to your work without thought, at another's bidding. Again, some slaves are bought with money, and others with praise. It matters not what the purchase-money is. The distinguishing sign of slavery is to have a price, and be bought for it. Again, it matters not what kind of work you are set on ; some slaves are set to forced diggings, others to forced marches ;

some dig furrows, others field-works, and others graves.
Some press the juice of reeds, and some the juice of vines,
and some the blood of men. The fact of the captivity is
the same whatever work we are set upon, though the
fruits of the toil may be different. But, remember, in
thus vowing ourselves to be the slaves of any master, it
ought to be some subject of forethought with us, what
work he is likely to put us upon. You may think that
the whole duty of a soldier is to be passive, that it is the
country you have left behind who is to command, and
you have only to obey. But are you sure that you have
left *all* your country behind, or that the part of it you have
so left is indeed the best part if it ? Suppose—and,
remember, it is quite conceivable—that you yourselves
are indeed the best part of England ; that you, who have
become the slaves, ought to have been the masters ; and
that those who are the masters, ought to have been the
slaves ! If it is a noble and wholehearted England, whose
bidding you are bound to do, it is well ; but if you are
yourselves the best of her heart, and the England you
have left be but a half-hearted England, how say you of
your obedience ? You were too proud to become shopkeepers : are you satisfied then to become the servants
of shopkeepers ? You were too proud to become merchants
or farmers yourselves : will you have merchants or farmers
then for your field-marshals ? You had no gifts of special
grace for Exeter Hall : will you have some gifted person
thereat for your commander-in-chief, to judge of your
work, and reward it ? You imagine yourselves to be the
army of England : how if you should find yourselves, at
last, only the police of her manufacturing towns, and the
beadles of her little Bethels ?

It is not so yet, nor will be so, I trust, for ever ; but
what I want you to see, and to be assured of, is, that the
ideal of soldiership is not mere passive obedience and
bravery ; that, so far from this, no country is in a healthy

state which has separated, even in a small degree, her civil from her military power. All states of the world, however great, fall at once when they use mercenary armies ; and, although it is a less instant form of error (because involving no national taint of cowardice), it is yet an error no less ultimately fatal—it is the error especially of modern times, of which we cannot yet know all the calamitous consequences—to take away the best blood and strength of the nation, all the soul-substance of it that is brave, and careless of reward, and scornful of pain, and faithful in trust ; and to cast that into steel, and make a mere sword of it ; taking away its voice and will ; but to keep the worst part of the nation—whatever is cowardly, avaricious, sensual, and faithless—and to give to this the voice, to this the authority, to this the chief privilege, where there is least capacity, of thought. The fulfilment of your vow for the defence of England will by no means consist in carrying out such a system. You are not true soldiers, if you only mean to stand at a shop door, to protect shop-boys who are cheating inside. A soldier's vow to his country is that he will die for the guardianship of her domestic virtue, of her righteous laws, and of her any-way challenged or endangered honour. A state without virtue, without laws, and without honour, he is bound *not* to defend ; nay, bound to redress by his own right hand that which he sees to be base in her. So sternly is this the law of Nature and life, that a nation once utterly corrupt can only be redeemed by a military despotism —never by talking, nor by its free effort. And the health of any state consists simply in this ; that in it, those who are wisest shall also be strongest ; its rulers should be also its soldiers ; or, rather, by force of intellect more than of sword, its soldiers also its rulers. Whatever the hold which the aristocracy of England has on the heart of England, in that they are still always in front of her battles, this hold will not be enough, unless they are also in front of her

thoughts. And truly her thoughts need good captain's
leading now, if ever ! Do you know what, by this beautiful
division of labour (her brave men fighting, and her cowards
thinking), she has come at last to think ? Here is a bit
of a paper in my hand,* a good one too, and an honest
one ; quite representative of the best common public
thought of England at this moment ; and it is holding
forth in one of its leaders upon our ' social welfare '—upon
our ' vivid life '—upon the ' political supremacy of Great
Britain.' And what do you think all these are owing to ?
To what our English sires have done for us, and taught us,
age after age ? No : not to that. To our honesty of
heart, or coolness of head, or steadiness of will ? No :
not to these. To our thinkers, or our statesmen, or our
poets, or our captains, or our martyrs, or the patient
labour of our poor ? No : not to these ; or at least not
to these in any chief measure. Nay, says the journal,
' more than any agency, it is the cheapness and abundance
of our coal which have made us what we are.' If it
be so, then ' ashes to ashes ' be our epitaph ! and the
sooner the better. I tell you, gentlemen of England, if
ever you would have your country breathe the pure
breath of heaven again, and receive again a soul into her
body, instead of rotting into a carcase, blown up in the

* I do not care to refer to the journal quoted, because the article
was unworthy of its general tone, though in order to enable the
audience to verify the quoted sentence, I left the number containing
it on the table, when I gave this lecture. But a saying of Baron
Liebig's, quoted at the head of a leader on the same subject in *The
Daily Telegraph* of January 11, 1866, summarily digests and presents
the maximum folly of modern thought in this respect. ' Civilisation,' says the Baron, ' is the economy of power, and English power
is coal.' Not altogether so, my chemical friend. Civilisation is the
making of civil persons, which is a kind of distillation of which
alembics are incapable, and does not at all imply the turning of a
small company of gentlemen into a large company of ironmongers.
And English power (what little of it may be left) is by no means
coal, but, indeed, of that which, ' when the whole world turns to
coal, then chiefly lives.'

belly with carbonic acid (and great *that* way), you must
think, and feel, for your England, as well as fight for her :
you must teach her that all the true greatness she ever had,
or ever can have, she won while her fields were green and
her faces ruddy—that greatness is still possible for Englishmen, even though the ground be not hollow under their
feet, nor the sky black over their heads—and that, when
the day comes for their country to lay her honours in the
dust, her crest will not rise from it more loftily because it is
dust of coal. Gentlemen, I tell you, solemnly, that the
day is coming when the soldiers of England must be her
tutors ; and the captains of her army, captains also of her
mind.

And now, remember, you soldier youths, who are thus
in all ways the hope of your country ; or must be, if she
have any hope : remember that your fitness for all future
trust depends upon what you are now. No good soldier
in his old age was ever careless or indolent in his youth.
Many a giddy and thoughtless boy has become a good
bishop, or a good lawyer, or a good merchant ; but no
such an one ever became a good general. I challenge you,
in all history, to find a record of a good soldier who was
not grave and earnest in his youth. And, in general,
I have no patience with people who talk about ' the
thoughtlessness of youth ' indulgently. I had infinitely
rather hear of thoughtless old age, and the indulgence due
to *that*. When a man has done his work, and nothing can
any way be materially altered in his fate, let him forget his
toil, and jest with his fate, if he will ; but what excuse can
you find for wilfulness of thought, at the very time when
every crisis of future fortune hangs on your decisions ?
A youth thoughtless ! when all the happiness of his home
for ever depends on the chances, or the passions, of an
hour ! A youth thoughtless ! when the career of all his
days depends on the opportunity of a moment ! A youth
thoughtless ! when his every act is a foundation-stone of

future conduct, and every imagination a fountain of life or death ! Be thoughtless in *any* after years, rather than now—though, indeed, there is only one place where a man may be nobly thoughtless—his deathbed. No thinking should ever be left to be done there.

Having, then, resolved that you will not waste recklessly, but earnestly use, these early days of yours, remember that all the duties of her children to England may be summed in two words—industry, and honour. I say first, industry, for it is in this that soldier youth are especially tempted to fail. Yet, surely, there is no reason, because your life may possibly or probably be shorter than other men's, that you should therefore waste more recklessly the portion of it that is granted you ; neither do the duties of your profession, which require you to keep your bodies strong, in any wise involve the keeping of your minds weak. So far from that, the experience, the hardship, and the activity of a soldier's life render his powers of thought more accurate than those of other men : and while, for others, all knowledge is often little more than a means of amusement, there is no form of science which a soldier may not at some time or other find bearing on business of life and death. A young mathematician may be excused for languor in studying curves to be described only with a pencil ; but not in tracing those which are to be described with a rocket. Your knowledge of a wholesome herb many involve the feeding of an army ; and acquaintance with an obscure point of geography, the success of a campaign. Never waste an instant's time, therefore ; the sin of idleness is a thousand-fold greater in you than in other youths ; for the fates of those who will one day be under your command hang upon your knowledge ; lost moments now will be lost lives then, and every instant which you carelessly take for play, you buy with blood. But there is one way of wasting time, of all the vilest, because it wastes, not time only, but the

interest and energy of your minds. Of all the ungentle-
manly habits into which you can fall, the vilest is betting,
or interesting yourselves in the issues of betting. It unites
nearly every condition of folly and vice ; you concentrate
your interest upon a matter of chance, instead upon a
subject of true knowledge ; and you back opinions which
you have no grounds for forming, merely because they are
your own. All the insolence of egotism is in this ; and so
far as the love of excitement is complicated with the hope
of winning money, you turn yourselves into the basest
sort of tradesmen—those who live by speculation. Were
there no other ground for industry, this would be a sufficient
one ; that it protected you from the temptation to so
scandalous a vice. Work faithfully, and you will put yourselves in possession of a glorious and enlarging happiness ;
not such as can be won by the speed of a horse, or marred
by the obliquity of a ball.

First, then, by industry you must fulfil your vow to your
country ; but all industry and earnestness will be useless
unless they are consecrated by your resolution to be in
all things men of honour ; not honour in the common
sense only, but in the highest. Rest on the force of the
two main words in the great verse, ' *integer* vitæ, scelerisque
*purus.*' You have vowed your life to England ; give it
her wholly—a bright, stainless, perfect life—a knightly
life. Because you have to fight with machines instead of
with lances, there may be a necessity for more ghastly
danger, but there is none for less worthiness of character,
than in olden time. You may be true knights yet, though
perhaps not *equites* ; you may have to call yourselves
' canonry ' instead of ' chivalry,' but that is no reason
why you should not call yourselves true men. So the
first thing you have to see to in becoming soldiers is that
you make yourselves wholly true. Courage is a mere
matter of course among any ordinarily well-born youths ;
but neither truth nor gentleness is matter of course. You

must bind them like shields about your necks ; you must write them on the tables of your hearts. Though it be not exacted of you, yet exact it of yourselves, this vow of stainless truth. Your hearts are, if you leave them unstirred, as tombs in which a god lies buried. Vow yourselves crusaders to redeem that sacred sepulchre. And remember, before all things—for no other memory will be so protective of you—that the highest law of this knightly truth is that under which it is vowed to women. Whomsoever else you deceive, whomsoever you injure, whomsoever you leave unaided, you must not deceive, nor injure, nor leave unaided, according to your power, any woman of whatever rank. Believe me, every virtue of the higher phases of manly character begins in this—in truth and modesty before the face of all maidens ; in truth and pity, or truth and reverence, to all womanhood.

And now let me turn for a moment to you, wives and maidens, who are the souls of soldiers ; to you, mothers, who have devoted your children to the great hierarchy of war. Let me ask you to consider what part you have to take for the aid of those who love you ; for if you fail in your part they cannot fulfil theirs ; such absolute helpmates you are that no man can stand without that help, nor labour in his own strength.

I know your hearts, and that the truth of them never fails when an hour of trial comes which you recognise for such. But you know not when the hour of trial first finds you, nor when it verily finds you. You imagine that you are only called upon to wait and to suffer ; to surrender and to mourn. You know that you must not weaken the hearts of your husbands and lovers, even by the one fear of which those hearts are capable—the fear of parting from you, or of causing you grief. Through weary years of separation ; through fearful expectancies of unknown fate ; through the tenfold bitterness of the sorrow which might so easily have been joy, and the tenfold yearning for glorious life struck down in its prime ; through all these agonies you fail not, and never will fail. But your trial is not in these. To be heroic in danger is little ; you are Englishwomen. To be heroic in change and sway of fortune is little ; for do you not love ? To be patient through the great chasm and pause of loss is little ; for do you not still love in heaven ? But to be heroic in happiness ; to bear yourselves gravely and righteously in the dazzling of the sunshine of morning ; not to forget the God in whom you trust, when He gives you most ; not to fail those who trust you, when they seem to need you least ; this is the difficult fortitude. It is not in the pining of absence, not in the peril of battle, not in the wasting of sickness, that your prayer should be most passionate, or your guardianship most tender. Pray, mothers and maidens, for your young soldiers in the bloom of their pride ; pray for them, while the only dangers round them are in their own wayward wills ; watch you, and pray, when they have to face, not death, but temptation. But it is this fortitude also for which there is the crowning reward. Believe me, the whole course and character of your lovers' lives is in your hands ; what you would have them be, they shall be, if you not only desire to have them so, but deserve to have them so ; for they are but mirrors in which you will see yourselves imaged. If you are frivolous, they will be so also ; if you have no understanding of the scope of their duty, they also will forget it ; they will listen—they *can* listen—to no other interpretation of it than that uttered from your lips. Bid them be brave ; they will be brave for you : bid them be cowards ; and, how noble soever they be, they will quail for you. Bid them be wise, and they will be wise for you ; mock at their counsel, they will be fools for you : such and so absolute is your rule over them. You fancy, perhaps, as you have been told so often, that a wife's rule should only be over her husband's house, not over his mind. Ah, no ! the true rule is just the reverse of that ; a true wife, in her husband's house, is his servant ; it is in his heart that she is queen. Whatever of best he can conceive, it is her part to be ; whatever of highest he can hope, it is hers to promise ; all that is dark in him she must purge into purity ; all that is failing in him she must strengthen into truth : from her, through all the world's clamour, he must win his praise ; in her, through all the world's warfare, he must find his peace.

And, now, but one word more. You may wonder, perhaps, that I have spoken all this night in praise of war. Yet, truly, if it might be, I, for one, would fain join in the cadence of hammer-strokes that should beat swords into ploughshares : and that this cannot be, is not the fault of us men. It is *your* fault. Wholly yours. Only by your command, or by your permission, can any contest take place among us. And the real, final, reason for all the poverty, misery, and rage of battle, throughout Europe, is simply that you women, however good, however religious, however self-sacrificing for those whom you love, are too selfish and too thoughtless to take pains for any creature out of your own immediate circles. You fancy that you are sorry for the pain of others. Now I just tell you this, that if the usual course of war, instead of unroofing peasants' houses, and ravaging peasants' fields, merely broke the china upon your own drawing-room tables, no war in civilised countries would last a week. I tell you more, that at whatever moment you chose to put a period to war, you could do it with less trouble than you take any day to go out to dinner. You know, or at least you might know if you would think, that every battle you hear of has made many widows and orphans. We have, none of us, heart enough truly to mourn with these. But at least we might put on the outer symbols of mourning with them. Let but every Christian lady who has conscience toward God, vow that she will mourn, at least outwardly, for His killed creatures. Your praying is useless, and your churchgoing mere mockery of God, if you have not plain obedience in you enough for this. Let every lady in the upper classes of civilised Europe simply vow that, while any cruel war proceeds, she will wear *black*—a mute's black—with no jewel, no ornament, no excuse for, or evasion into, prettiness. I tell you again, no war would last a week.

And lastly. You women of England are all now shrieking with one voice—you and your clergymen together— because you hear of your Bibles being attacked. If you choose to obey your Bibles, you will never care who attacks them. It is just because you never fulfil a single downright precept of the Book, that you are so careful for its credit : and just because you don't care to obey its whole words, that you are so particular about the letters of them. The Bible tells you to dress plainly, and you are mad for finery ; the Bible tells you to have pity on the poor, and you crush them under your carriage wheels ; the Bible tells you to do judgment and justice, and you do not know, nor care to know, so much as what the Bible word 'justice' means. Do but learn so much of God's truth as that comes to ; know what He means when He tells you to be just : and teach your sons, that their bravery is but a fool's boast, and their deeds but a firebrand's tossing, unless they are indeed Just men, and Perfect in the Fear of God ; and you will soon have no more war, unless it be indeed such as is willed by Him, of whom, though Prince of Peace, it is also written ' In Righteousness He doth judge, and make war.'

# INDEX

119

# THE ETHICS OF THE DUST

## TEN LECTURES
### TO
## LITTLE HOUSEWIVES
### ON
## THE ELEMENTS OF CRYSTALLIZATION

## Dedication

---

TO

### THE REAL LITTLE HOUSEWIVES

WHOSE GENTLE LISTENING

AND THOUGHTFUL QUESTIONING

ENABLED THE WRITER TO WRITE THIS BOOK

IT IS DEDICATED

WITH HIS LOVE

---

Christmas, 1865

# PREFACE

THE following Lectures were really given, in substance, at a girls' school (far in the country) ; which, in the course of various experiments on the possibility of introducing some better practice of drawing into the modern scheme of female education, I visited frequently enough to enable the children to regard me as a friend. The Lectures always fell more or less into the form of fragmentary answers to questions ; and they are allowed to retain that form, as, on the whole, likely to be more interesting than the symmetries of a continuous treatise. Many children (for the school was large) took part at different times, in the conversations ; but I have endeavoured, without confusedly multiplying the number of imaginary * speakers, to represent, as far as I could, the general tone of comment and inquiry among young people.

It will be at once seen that these Lectures were not intended for an introduction to mineralogy. Their purpose was merely to awaken in the minds of young girls, who were ready to work earnestly and systematically, a vital interest in the subject of their study. No science can be learned in play ; but it is often possible, in play, to bring good fruit out of past labour, or show sufficient reasons for the labour of the future.

The narrowness of this aim does not, indeed, justify the absence of all reference to many important principles of

* I do not mean, in saying ' imaginary,' that I have not permitted to myself, in several instances, the affectionate discourtesy of some reminiscence of personal character ; for which I must hope to be forgiven by my old pupils and their friends, as I could not otherwise have written the book at all. But only two sentences in all the dialogues, and the anecdote of ' Dotty,' are literally ' historical.'

structure, and many of the most interesting orders of minerals ; but I felt it impossible to go far into detail without illustrations ; and if readers find this book useful, I may, perhaps, endeavour to supplement it by illustrated notes of the more interesting phenomena in separate groups of familiar minerals ;—flints of the chalk ;—agates of the basalts ;—and the fantastic and exquisitely beautiful varieties of the vein-ores of the two commonest metals, lead and iron. But I have always found that the less we speak of our intentions, the more chance there is of our realising them ; and this poor little book will sufficiently have done its work, for the present, if it engages any of its young readers in study which may enable them to despise it for its shortcomings.

DENMARK HILL,
 *Christmas*, 1865.

# PERSONÆ

127

# THE VALLEY OF DIAMONDS

LECTURE I

# LECTURE I

## THE VALLEY OF DIAMONDS

*A very idle talk, by the dining-room fire, after raisin-and-almond time*

OLD LECTURER ; FLORRIE, ISABEL, MAY, LILY, *and* SIBYL

OLD LECTURER (L.). Come here, Isabel, and tell me what the make-believe was, this afternoon.

ISABEL (*arranging herself very primly on the footstool*). Such a dreadful one ! Florrie and I were lost in the Valley of Diamonds.

L. What ! Sindbad's, which nobody could get out of ?

ISABEL. Yes ; but Florrie and I got out of it.

L. So I see. At least, I see you did ; but are you sure Florrie did ?

ISABEL. Quite sure.

FLORRIE (*putting her head round from behind L.'s sofa-cushion*). Quite sure. (*Disappears again.*)

L. I think I could be made to feel surer about it.

(FLORRIE *reappears, gives* L. *a kiss, and again exit.*)

L. I suppose it's all right ; but how did you manage it ?

ISABEL. Well, you know, the eagle that took up Sindbad was very large—very, very large—the largest of all the eagles.

L. How large were the others ?

ISABEL. I don't quite know—they were so far off. But this was one, oh, so big ! and it had great wings, as wide as—twice over the ceiling. So, when it was picking up Sindbad, Florrie and I thought it wouldn't know if we

131

got on its back too : so I got up first, and then I pulled up Florrie, and we put our arms round its neck, and away it flew.

L.   But why did you want to get out of the valley ? and why haven't you brought me some diamonds ?

ISABEL.   It was because of the serpents.   I couldn't pick up even the least little bit of a diamond, I was so frightened.

L.   You should not have minded the serpents.

ISABEL.   Oh, but suppose they had minded me ?

L.   We all of us mind you a little too much, Isabel, I'm afraid.

ISABEL.   No—no—no, indeed.

L.   I tell you what, Isabel—I don't believe either Sindbad, or Florrie, or you, ever were in the Valley of Diamonds.

ISABEL.   You naughty ! when I tell you we were !

L.   Because you say you were frightened at the serpents.

ISABEL.   And wouldn't you have been ?

L.   Not at those serpents.   Nobody who really goes into the valley is ever frightened at them—they are so beautiful.

ISABEL (*suddenly serious*).   But there's no real Valley of Diamonds, is there ?

L.   Yes, Isabel ; very real indeed.

FLORRIE (*reappearing*).   Oh, where ?   Tell me about it.

L.   I cannot tell you a great deal about it ; only I know it is very different from Sindbad's.   In his valley, there was only a diamond lying here and there ; but, in the real valley, there are diamonds covering the grass in showers every morning, instead of dew : and there are clusters of trees, which look like lilac trees ; but, in spring, all their blossoms are of amethyst.

FLORRIE.   But there can't be any serpents there, then ?

L.   Why not ?

FLORRIE.   Because they don't come into such beautiful places.

L.   I never said it was a beautiful place.

FLORRIE.   What ! not with diamonds strewed about it like dew ?

L.   That's according to your fancy, Florrie.   For my- self, I like dew better.

ISABEL.   Oh, but the dew won't stay ; it all dries !

L.   Yes ;  and it would be much nicer if the diamonds dried too, for the people in the valley have to sweep them off the grass, in heaps, whenever they want to walk on it ; and then the heaps glitter so, they hurt one's eyes.

FLORRIE.   Now you're just playing, you know.

L.   So are you, you know.

FLORRIE.   Yes, but you mustn't play.

L.   That's very hard, Florrie ;  why mustn't I, if you may ?

FLORRIE.   Oh, I may, because I'm little, but you mustn't, because you're—(*hesitates for a delicate expression of magnitude*).

L. (*rudely taking the first that comes*).   Because I'm big ? No ;  that's not the way of it at all, Florrie.   Because you're little, you should have very little play ;  and because I'm big I should have a great deal.

ISABEL *and* FLORRIE (*both*).   No—no—no—no.   That isn't it at all.   (ISABEL *sola, quoting Miss Ingelow*).   ' The lambs play always—they know no better.'   (*Putting her head very much on one side*.)   Ah, now—please—please— tell us true ;  we want to know.

L.   But why do you want me to tell you true, any more than the man who wrote the *Arabian Nights* ?

ISABEL.   Because—because we like to know about real things ;  and you can tell us, and we can't ask the man who wrote the stories.

L.   What do you call real things ?

ISABEL.   Now, you know !   Things that really are.

L.   Whether you can see them or not ?

ISABEL.   Yes, if somebody else saw them.

L.   But if nobody has ever seen them ?

ISABEL (*evading the point*).   Well, but, you know, if there were a real Valley of Diamonds, somebody *must* have seen it.

L.   You cannot be so sure of that, Isabel. Many people go to real places, and never see them ; and many people pass through this valley, and never see it.

FLORRIE.   What stupid people they must be !

L.   No, Florrie.   They are much wiser than the people who do see it.

MAY.   I think I know where it is.

ISABEL.   Tell us more about it, and then we'll guess.

L.   Well.   There's a great broad road, by a riverside, leading up into it.

MAY (*gravely cunning, with emphasis on the last word*). Does the road really go *up* ?

L.   You think it should go down into a valley ?   No, it goes up ; this is a valley among the hills, and it is as high as the clouds, and is often full of them ; so that even the people who most want to see it, cannot, always.

ISABEL.   And what is the river beside the road like ?

L.   It ought to be very beautiful, because it flows over diamond sand—only the water is thick and red.

ISABEL.   Red water ?

L.   It isn't all water.

MAY.   Oh, please never mind that, Isabel, just now ; I want to hear about the valley.

L.   So the entrance to it is very wide, under a steep rock ; only such numbers of people are always trying to get in, that they keep jostling each other, and manage it but slowly.   Some weak ones are pushed back, and never get in at all ; and make great moaning as they go away : but perhaps they are none the worse in the end.

MAY.   And when one gets in, what is it like ?

L. It is up and down, broken kind of ground : the road stops directly ; and there are great dark rocks, covered all over with wild gourds and wild vines ; the gourds, if you cut them, are red, with black seeds, like water-melons, and look ever so nice ; and the people of the place make a red pottage of them : but you must take care not to eat any if you ever want to leave the valley (though I believe putting plenty of meal in it makes it wholesome). Then the wild vines have clusters of the colour of amber ; and the people of the country say they are the grapes of Eshcol : and sweeter than honey : but indeed, if anybody else tastes them, they are like gall. Then there are thickets of bramble, so thorny that they would be cut away directly, anywhere else ; but here they are covered with little cinque-foiled blossoms of pure silver ; and, for berries, they have clusters of rubies. Dark rubies, which you only see are red after gathering them. But you may fancy what blackberry parties the children have ! Only they get their frocks and hands sadly torn.

LILY. But rubies can't spot one's frocks, as blackberries do ?

L. No ; but I'll tell you what spots them—the mulberries. There are great forests of them, all up the hills, covered with silk-worms, some munching the leaves so loud that it is like mills at work ; and some spinning. But the berries are the blackest you ever saw ; and, wherever they fall, they stain a deep red ; and nothing ever washes it out again. And it is their juice, soaking through the grass, which makes the river so red, because all its springs are in this wood. And the boughs of the trees are twisted, as if in pain, like old olive branches ; and their leaves are dark. And it is in these forests that the serpents are ; but nobody is afraid of them. They have fine crimson crests, and they are wreathed about the wild branches, one in every tree, nearly ; and they are singing serpents, for the serpents are, in this forest, what birds are in ours.

FLORRIE.    Oh, I don't want to go there at all, now.

L.    You would like it very much indeed, Florrie, if you were there.    The serpents would not bite you ; the only fear would be of your turning into one !

FLORRIE.    Oh, dear, but that's worse.

L.    You wouldn't think so if you really were turned into one, Florrie ;  you would be very proud of your crest. And as long as you were yourself (not that you could get there if you remained quite the little Florrie you are now), you would like to hear the serpents sing.    They hiss a little through it, like the cicadas in Italy ; but they keep good time, and sing delightful melodies ;  and most of them have seven heads, with throats which each take a note of the octave ;  so that they can sing chords—it is very fine indeed.    And the fireflies fly round the edge of the forests all the night long ;  you wade in fireflies, they make the fields look like a lake trembling with reflection of stars ; but you must take care not to touch them, for they are not like Italian fireflies, but burn, like real sparks.

FLORRIE.    I don't like it at all ;  I'll never go there.

L.    I hope not, Florrie ;  or at least that you will get out again if you do.    And it is very difficult to get out, for beyond these serpent forests there are great cliffs of dead gold, which form a labyrinth, winding always higher and higher, till the gold is all split asunder by wedges of ice ; and glaciers, welded, half of ice seven times frozen, and half of gold seven times frozen, hang down from them, and fall in thunder, cleaving into deadly splinters, like the Cretan arrow-heads ;  and into a mixed dust of snow and gold, ponderous, yet which the mountain whirlwinds are able to lift and drive in wreaths and pillars, hiding the paths with a burial cloud, fatal at once with wintry chill, and weight of golden ashes.    So the wanderers in the labyrinth fall, one by one, and are buried there :—yet, over the drifted graves, those who are spared climb to the last, through coil on coil of the path ;—for at the end of it they see the king of the valley, sitting on his throne : and beside him (but it is only a false vision), spectra of creatures like themselves, set on thrones, from which they seem to look down on all the kingdoms of the world, and the glory of them. And on the canopy of his throne there is an inscription in fiery letters, which they strive to read, but cannot ; for it is written in words which are like the words of all languages, and yet are of none. Men say it is more like their own tongue to the English than it is to any other nation ; but the only record of it is by an Italian, who heard the king himself cry it as a war cry, ' Pape Satan, Pape Satan Aleppe.' *

SIBYL. But do they all perish there ? You said there was a way through the valley, and out of it.

L. Yes ; but few find it. If any of them keep to the grass paths, where the diamonds are swept aside ; and hold their hands over their eyes so as not to be dazzled, the grass paths lead forward gradually to a place where one sees a little opening in the golden rocks. You were at Chamouni last year, Sibyl ; did your guide chance to show you the pierced rock of the Aiguille du Midi ?

SIBYL. No, indeed, we only got up from Geneva on Monday night ; and it rained all Tuesday ; and we had to be back at Geneva again, early on Wednesday morning.

L. Of course. That is the way to see a country in a Sibylline manner, by inner consciousness : but you might have seen the pierced rock in your drive up, or down, if the clouds broke : not that there is much to see in it ; one of the crags of the aiguille-edge, on the southern slope of it, is struck sharply through, as by an awl, into a little eyelet hole ; which you may see, seven thousand feet above the valley (as the clouds flit past behind it, or leave the sky), first white, and then dark blue. Well, there's

* Dante, *Inf.* 7. 1.

just such an eyelet hole in one of the upper crags of the Diamond Valley ; and, from a distance, you think that it is no bigger than the eye of a needle. But if you get up to it, they say you may drive a loaded camel through it, and that there are fine things on the other side, but I have never spoken with anybody who had been through.

SIBYL. I think we understand it now. We will try to write it down, and think of it.

L. Meantime, Florrie, though all that I have been telling you is very true, yet you must not think the sort of diamonds that people wear in rings and necklaces are found lying about on the grass. Would you like to see how they really are found ?

FLORRIE. Oh, yes—yes.

L. Isabel—or Lily—run up to my room and fetch me the little box with a glass lid out of the top drawer of the chest of drawers. (*Race between* LILY *and* ISABEL.)

(*Re-enter* ISABEL *with the box, very much out of breath.* LILY *behind.*)

L. Why, you never can beat Lily in a race on the stairs, can you, Isabel ?

ISABEL (*panting*). Lily—beat me—ever so far—but she gave me—the box—to carry in.

L. Take off the lid, then ; gently.

FLORRIE (*after peeping in, disappointed*). There's only a great ugly brown stone !

L. Not much more than that, certainly, Florrie, if people were wise. But look, it is not a single stone ; but a knot of pebbles fastened together by gravel : and in the gravel, or compressed sand, if you look close, you will see grains of gold glittering everywhere, all through ; and then, do you see these two white beads, which shine, as if they had been covered with grease ?

FLORRIE. May I touch them ?

L. Yes ; you will find they are not greasy, only very smooth. Well, those are the fatal jewels ; native here in their dust with gold, so that you may see, cradled here together, the two great enemies of mankind—the strongest of all malignant physical powers that have tormented our race.

SIBYL. Is that really so ? I know they do gréat harm ; but do they not also do great good ?

L. My dear child, what good ? Was any woman, do you suppose, ever the better for possessing diamonds ? but how many have been made base, frivolous, and miserable by desiring them ? Was ever man the better for having coffers full of gold ? But who shall measure the guilt that is incurred to fill them ? Look into the history of any civilised nations ; analyse, with reference to this one cause of crime and misery, the lives and thoughts of their nobles, priests, merchants, and men of luxurious life. Every other temptation is at last concentrated into this ; pride, and lust, and envy, and anger all give up their strength to avarice. The sin of the whole world is essentially the sin of Judas. Men do not disbelieve their Christ ; but they sell Him.

SIBYL. But surely that is the fault of human nature ? it is not caused by the accident, as it were, of there being a pretty metal, like gold, to be found by digging. If people could not find that, would they not find something else, and quarrel for it instead ?

L. No. Wherever legislators have succeeded in excluding, for a time, jewels and precious metals from among national possessions, the national spirit has remained healthy. Covetousness is not natural to man—generosity is ; but covetousness must be excited by a special cause, as a given disease by a given miasma ; and the essential nature of a material for the excitement of covetousness is, that it shall be a beautiful thing which can be retained *without a use*. The moment we can use our possessions to any good purpose ourselves, the instinct of communicating that use to others rises side by side with our power. If you can read a book rightly, you will want others to hear it ; if you can enjoy a picture rightly, you will want others to see it : learn how to manage a horse, a plough, or a ship, and you will desire to make your subordinates good horsemen, ploughmen, or sailors : you will never be able to see the fine instrument you are master of, abused ; but, once fix your desire on anything useless, and all the purest pride and folly in your heart will mix with the desire, and make you at last wholly inhuman, a mere ugly lump of stomach and suckers, like a cuttle-fish.

SIBYL. But surely, these two beautiful things, gold and diamonds, must have been appointed to some good purpose ?

L. Quite conceivably so, my dear : as also earth-quakes and pestilences ; but of such ultimate purposes, we can have no sight. The practical, immediate office of the earthquake and pestilence is to slay us, like moths ; and, as moths, we shall be wise to live out of their way. So, the practical, immediate office of gold and diamonds is the multiplied destruction of souls (in whatever sense you have been taught to understand that phrase) ; and the paralysis of wholesome human effort and thought on the face of God's earth : and a wise nation will live out of the way of them. The money which the English habitually spend in cutting diamonds would, in ten years, if it were applied to cutting rocks instead, leave no dangerous reef nor difficult harbour round the whole island coast. Great Britain would be a diamond worth cutting, indeed, a true piece of regalia. (*Leaves this to their thoughts for a little while.*) Then, also, we poor mineralogists might sometimes have the chance of seeing a fine crystal of diamond un-hacked by the jeweller.

SIBYL. Would it be more beautiful uncut ?

L. No ; but of infinite interest. We might even come to know something about the making of diamonds.

SIBYL. I thought the chemists could make them already ?

L. In very small black crystals, yes ; but no one knows how they are formed where they are found ; or if indeed they are formed there at all. These, in my hand, look as if they had been swept down with the gravel and gold ; only we can trace the gravel and gold to their native rocks, but not the diamonds. Read the account given of the diamond in any good work on mineralogy ;—you will find nothing but lists of localities of gravel, or conglomerate rock (which is only an old indurated gravel). Some say it was once a vegetable gum ; it may have been charred wood ; but what one would like to know is, mainly, why charcoal should make itself into diamonds in India, and only into black lead in Borrowdale.

SIBYL. Are they wholly the same, then ?

L. There is a little iron mixed with our black lead ; but nothing to hinder its crystallization. Your pencils in fact are all pointed with formless diamond, though they would be H H H pencils to purpose, if it crystallized.

SIBYL. But what *is* crystallization ?

L. A pleasant question, when one's half asleep, and it has been tea time these two hours. What thoughtless things girls are !

SIBYL. Yes, we are ; but we want to know, for all that.

L. My dear, it would take a week to tell you.

SIBYL. Well, take it, and tell us.

L. But nobody knows anything about it.

SIBYL. Then tell us something that nobody knows.

L. Get along with you, and tell Dora to make tea.

(*The house rises ; but of course the* LECTURER *wanted to be forced to lecture again, and was.*)

# THE PYRAMID BUILDERS

LECTURE II

# LECTURE II

## THE PYRAMID BUILDERS

*In the large Schoolroom, to which everybody has been summoned by ringing of the great bell*

L.  So you have all actually come to hear about crystallization !  I cannot conceive why, unless the little ones think that the discussion may involve some reference to sugar-candy.

> (*Symptoms of high displeasure among the younger members of council.* Isabel *frowns severely at* L., *and shakes her head violently.*)

My dear children, if you knew it, you are yourselves, at this moment, as you sit in your ranks, nothing in the eye of a mineralogist, but a lovely group of rosy sugar-candy, arranged by atomic forces.  And even admitting you to be something more, you have certainly been crystallizing without knowing it.  Did not I hear a great hurrying and whispering, ten minutes ago, when you were late in from the playground ; and thought you would not all be quietly seated by the time I was ready :—besides some discussion about places—something about ' it's not being fair that the little ones should always be nearest ? '  Well, you were then all being crystallized.  When you ran in from the garden, and against one another in the passages, you were in what mineralogists would call a state of solution, and gradual confluence ;  when you got seated in those orderly rows, each in her proper place, you became crystalline.  That is just what the atoms of a mineral do, if they can, whenever they get disordered: they get into order again as soon as may be.

I hope you feel inclined to interrupt me, and say, ' But we know our places ; how do the atoms know theirs ? And sometimes we dispute about our places ; do the atoms—(and, besides, we don't like being compared to atoms at all)—never dispute about theirs ? ' Two wise questions these, if you had a mind to put them ! it was long before I asked them myself, of myself. And I will not call you atoms any more. May I call you—let me see— ' primary molecules ' ? (*General dissent indicated in subdued but decisive murmurs.*) No ! not even, in familiar Saxon, ' dust ' ?

> (*Pause, with expression on faces of sorrowful doubt ;*
> LILY *gives voice to the general sentiment in a timid,*
> ' *Please don't.*')

No, children, I won't call you that ; and mind, as you grow up, that you do not get into an idle and wicked habit of calling yourselves that. You are something better than dust, and have other duties to do than ever dust can do ; and the bonds of affection you will enter into are better than merely ' getting into order.' But see to it, on the other hand, that you always behave at least as well as ' dust ' ; remember, it is only on compulsion, and while it has no free permission to do as it likes, that *it* ever gets out of order : but sometimes, with some of us, the compulsion has to be the other way—hasn't it ? (*Remonstratory whispers, expressive of opinion that the* LECTURER *is becoming too personal.*) I'm not looking at anybody in particular—indeed I am not. Nay, if you blush so, Kathleen, how can one help looking ? We'll go back to the atoms.

' How do they know their places ? ' you asked, or should have asked. Yes, and they have to do much more than know them : they have to find their way to them, and that quietly and at once, without running against each other.

We may, indeed, state it briefly thus :—Suppose you

have to build a castle, with towers and roofs and buttresses, out of bricks of a given shape, and that these bricks are all lying in a huge heap at the bottom, in utter confusion, upset out of carts at random. You would have to draw a great many plans, and count all your bricks, and be sure you had enough for this and that tower, before you began, and then you would have to lay your foundation, and add layer by layer, in order, slowly.

But how would you be astonished, in these melancholy days, when children don't read children's books, nor believe any more in fairies, if suddenly a real benevolent fairy, in a bright brick-red gown, were to rise in the midst of the red bricks, and to tap the heap of them with her wand, and say : ' Bricks, bricks, to your places ! ' and then you saw in an instant the whole heap rise in the air, like a swarm of red bees, and—you have been used to see bees make a honeycomb, and to think that strange enough, but now you would see the honeycomb make itself !—You want to ask something, Florrie, by the look of your eyes.

FLORRIE. Are they turned into real bees, with stings ?

L. No, Florrie ; you are only to fancy flying bricks, as you saw the slates flying from the roof the other day in the storm ; only those slates didn't seem to know where they were going, and, besides, were going where they had no business : but my spell-bound bricks, though they have no wings, and what is worse, no heads and no eyes, yet find their way in the air just where they should settle, into towers and roofs, each flying to his place and fastening there at the right moment, so that every other one shall fit to him in his turn.

LILY. But who are the fairies, then, who build the crystals ?

L. There is one great fairy, Lily, who builds much more than crystals ; but she builds these also. I dreamed that I saw her building a pyramid, the other day, as she used to do, for the Pharaohs.

ISABEL. But that was only a dream ?

L. Some dreams are truer than some wakings, Isabel ; but I won't tell it you unless you like.

ISABEL. Oh, please, please.

L. You are all such wise children, there's no talking to you ; you won't believe anything.

LILY. No, we are not wise, and we will believe anything, when you say we ought.

L. Well, it came about this way. Sibyl, do you recollect that evening when we had been looking at your old cave by Cumæ, and wondering why you didn't live there still : and then we wondered how old you were ; and Egypt said you wouldn't tell, and nobody else could tell but she ; and you laughed—I thought very gaily for a Sibyl—and said you would harness a flock of cranes for us, and we might fly over to Egypt if we liked, and see.

SIBYL. Yes, and you went, and couldn't find out after all !

L. Why, you know, Egypt had been just doubling that third pyramid of hers ; * and making a new entrance into it ; and a fine entrance it was ! First, we had to go through an ante-room, which had both its doors blocked up with stones ; and then we had three granite portcullises to pull up, one after another ; and the moment we had got under them, Egypt signed to somebody above ; and down they came again behind us, with a roar like thunder, only louder ; then we got into a passage fit for nobody but rats, and Egypt wouldn't go any further herself, but said we might go on if we liked ; and so we came to a hole in the pavement, and then to a granite trap-door—and then we thought we had gone quite far enough, and came back, and Egypt laughed at us.

EGYPT. You would not have had me take my crown off, and stoop all the way down a passage fit only for rats ?

* See Note I.

L. It was not the crown, Egypt—you know that very well. It was the flounces that would not let you go any farther. I suppose, however, you wear them as typical of the inundation of the Nile, so it is all right.

ISABEL. Why didn't you take me with you. Where rats can go, mice can. I wouldn't have come back ?

L. No, mousie ; you would have gone on by yourself, and you might have waked one of Pasht's cats,* and it would have eaten you. I was very glad you were not there. But after all this, I suppose the imagination of the heavy granite blocks and the underground ways had troubled me, and dreams are often shaped in a strange opposition to the impressions that have caused them ; and from all that we had been reading in Bunsen about stones that couldn't be lifted with levers, I began to dream about stones that lifted themselves with wings.

SIBYL. Now you must just tell us all about it.

L. I dreamed that I was standing beside the lake, out of whose clay the bricks were made for the great pyramid of Asychis.† They had just been all finished, and were lying by the lake margin, in long ridges like waves. It was near evening ; and as I looked towards the sunset, I saw a thing like a dark pillar standing where the rock of the desert stoops to the Nile valley. I did not know there was a pillar there, and wondered at it ; and it grew larger, and glided nearer, becoming like the form of a man, but vast, and it did not move its feet, but glided, like a pillar of sand. And as it drew nearer, I looked by chance past it, towards the sun ; and saw a silver cloud, which was of all the clouds closest to the sun (and in one place crossed it), draw itself back from the sun, suddenly. And it turned, and shot towards the dark pillar ; leaping in an arch, like an arrow out of a bow. And I thought it was lightning ; but when it came near the shadowy pillar, it sank slowly down beside it, and changed into the shape of a woman,

* See Note III.　　　　† See Note II.

very beautiful, and with a strength of deep calm in her blue eyes. She was robed to the feet with a white robe; and above that, to her knees, by the cloud which I had seen across the sun; but all the golden ripples of it had become plumes, so that it had changed into two bright wings like those of a vulture, which wrapped round her to her knees. She had a weaver's shuttle hanging over her shoulder, by the thread of it, and in her left hand, arrows tipped with fire.

ISABEL (*clapping her hands*). Oh! it was Neith, it was Neith! I know now.

L. Yes; it was Neith herself; and as the two great spirits came nearer to me, I saw they were the Brother and Sister—the pillared shadow was the Greater Pthah.* And I heard them speak, and the sound of their words was like a distant singing. I could not understand the words one by one; yet their sense came to me; and so I knew that Neith had come down to see her brother's work, and the work that he had put into the mind of the king to make his servants do. And she was displeased at it; because she saw only pieces of dark clay; and no porphyry, nor marble, nor any fair stone that men might engrave the figures of the gods upon. And she blamed her brother, and said, ' O Lord of truth! is this then thy will, that men should mould only four-square pieces of clay: and the forms of the gods no more?' Then the Lord of truth sighed, and said, ' Oh! sister, in truth they do not love us; why should they set up our images? Let them do what they may, and not lie—let them make their clay four-square; and labour; and perish.'

Then Neith's dark blue eyes grew darker, and she said, ' Oh, Lord of truth! why should they love us? their love is vain; or fear us? for their fear is base. Yet let them testify of us, that they knew we lived for ever.'

But the Lord of truth answered, ' They know, and yet

* See Note III.

they know not.   Let them keep silence ; for their silence only is truth.'

But Neith answered, ' Brother, wilt thou also make league with Death, because Death is true ?   Oh ! thou potter, who hast cast these human things from thy wheel, many to dishonour, and few to honour ; wilt thou not let them so much as see my face ; but slay them in slavery ? '

But Pthah only answered, ' Let them build, sister, let them build.'

And Neith answered, ' What shall they build, if I build not with them ? '

And Pthah drew with his measuring rod upon the sand. And I saw suddenly, drawn on the sand, the outlines of great cities, and of vaults, and domes, and aqueducts, and bastions, and towers, greater than obelisks, covered with black clouds.   And the wind blew ripples of sand amidst the lines that Pthah drew, and the moving sand was like the marching of men.   But I saw that wherever Neith looked at the lines, they faded, and were effaced.

' Oh, Brother ! ' she said at last, ' what is this vanity ? If I, who am Lady of wisdom, do not mock the children of men, why shouldst thou mock them who art Lord of truth ? '   But Pthah answered, ' They thought to bind me ; and they shall be bound.   They shall labour in the fire for vanity.'

And Neith said, looking at the sand, ' Brother, there is no true labour here,—there is only weary life and wasteful death.'

And Pthah answered, ' Is it not truer labour, sister, than thy sculpture of dreams ? '

Then Neith smiled ; and stopped suddenly.

She looked to the sun ; its edge touched the horizon-edge of the desert.   Then she looked to the long heaps of pieces of clay, that lay, each with its blue shadow, by the lake shore.

' Brother,' she said, ' how long will this pyramid of thine be in building ? '

' Thoth will have sealed the scroll of the years ten times, before the summit is laid.'

' Brother, thou knowest not how to teach thy children to labour,' answered Neith. ' Look ! I must follow Phre beyond Atlas ; shall I build your pyramid for you before he goes down ? ' And Pthah answered, ' Yea, sister, if thou canst put thy winged shoulders to such work.' And Neith drew herself to her height ; and I heard a clashing pass through the plumes of her wings, and the asp stood up on her helmet, and fire gathered in her eyes. And she took one of the flaming arrows out of the sheaf in her left hand, and stretched it out over the heaps of clay. And they rose up like flights of locusts, and spread themselves in the air, so that it grew dark in a moment. Then Neith designed them places with her arrow point ; and they drew into ranks, like dark clouds laid level at morning. Then Neith pointed with her arrow to the north, and to the south, and to the east, and to the west, and the flying motes of earth drew asunder into four great ranked crowds ; and stood, one in the north, and one in the south, and one in the east, and one in the west—one against another. Then Neith spread her wings wide for an instant, and closed them with a sound like the sound of a rushing sea ; and waved her hand towards the foundation of the pyramid, where it was laid on the brow of the desert. And the four flocks drew together and sank down, like sea-birds settling to a level rock ; and when they met, there was a sudden flame as broad as the pyramid, and as high as the clouds ; and it dazzled me ; and I closed my eyes for an instant ; and when I looked again, the pyramid stood on its rock, perfect ; and purple with the light from the edge of the sinking sun.

THE YOUNGER CHILDREN (*variously pleased*). I'm so glad ! How nice ! But what did Pthah say ?

L. Neith did not wait to hear what he would say. When I turned back to look at her, she was gone ; and I only saw the level white cloud form itself again, close to the arch of the sun as it sank. And as the last edge of the sun disappeared, the form of Pthah faded into a mighty shadow, and so passed away.

EGYPT. And was Neith's pyramid left ?

L. Yes ; but you could not think, Egypt, what a strange feeling of utter loneliness came over me when the presence of the two gods passed away. It seemed as if I had never known what it was to be alone before ; and the unbroken line of the desert was terrible.

EGYPT. I used to feel that, when I was queen : sometimes I had to carve gods, for company, all over my palace. I would fain have seen real ones, if I could.

L. But listen a moment yet, for that was not quite all my dream. The twilight drew swiftly to the dark, and I could hardly see the great pyramid ; when there came a heavy murmuring sound in the air ; and a horned beetle, with terrible claws, fell on the sand at my feet, with a blow like the beat of a hammer. Then it stood up on its hind claws, and waved its pincers at me : and its fore claws became strong arms, and hands ; one grasping real iron pincers, and the other a huge hammer ; and it had a helmet on its head, without any eyelet holes, that I could see. And its two hind claws became strong crooked legs, with feet bent inwards. And so there stood by me a dwarf, in glossy black armour, ribbed and embossed like a beetle's back, leaning on his hammer. And I could not speak for wonder ; but he spoke with a murmur like the dying away of a beat upon a bell. He said, ' I will make Neith's great pyramid small. I am the lower Pthah ; and have power over fire. I can wither the strong things, and strengthen the weak : and everything that is great I can make small, and everything that is little I can make great.' Then he turned to the angle of the pyramid and limped towards it.

And the pyramid grew deep purple ; and then red like blood, and then pale rose-colour, like fire. And I saw that it glowed with fire from within. And the lower Pthah touched it with the hand that held the pincers ; and it sank down like the sand in an hour-glass,—then drew itself together, and sank, still, and became nothing, it seemed to me ; but the armed dwarf stooped down, and took it into his hand, and brought it me, saying, ' Everything that is great I can make like this pyramid ; and give into men's hands to destroy.' And I saw that he had a little pyramid in his hand, with as many courses in it as the large one ; and built like that,—only so small. And because it glowed still, I was afraid to touch it ; but Pthah said, ' Touch it—for I have bound the fire within it, so that it cannot burn.' So I touched it, and took it into my own hand ; and it was cold ; only red, like a ruby. And Pthah laughed, and became like a beetle again, and buried himself in the sand, fiercely ; throwing it back over his shoulders. And it seemed to me as if he would draw me down with him into the sand ; and I started back, and woke, holding the little pyramid so fast in my hand that it hurt me.

EGYPT.   Holding WHAT in your hand ?

L.   The little pyramid.

EGYPT.   Neith's pyramid ?

L.   Neith's, I believe ; though not built for Asychis. I know only that it is a little rosy transparent pyramid, built of more courses of bricks than I can count, it being made so small.   You don't believe me, of course, Egyptian infidel ; but there it is.   (*Giving crystal of rose Fluor.*)

(*Confused examination by crowded audience, over each other's shoulders and under each other's arms.   Disappointment begins to manifest itself.*)

SIBYL (*not quite knowing why she and others are disappointed*).   But you showed us this the other day !

L.   Yes ; but you would not look at it the other day.

SIBYL.  But was all that fine dream only about this ?

L.   What finer thing could a dream be about than this ?
It is small, if you will ; but when you begin to think of
things rightly, the ideas of smallness and largeness pass
away.   The making of this pyramid was in reality just as
wonderful as the dream I have been telling you, and just
as incomprehensible.   It was not, I suppose, as swift,
but quite as grand things are done as swiftly.   When Neith
makes crystals of snow, it needs a great deal more mar-
shalling of the atoms, by her flaming arrows, than it does
to make crystals like this one ; and that is done in a
moment.

EGYPT.   But how you *do* puzzle us !   Why do you say
Neith does it ?   You don't mean that she is a real spirit,
do you ?

L.   What *I* mean, is of little consequence.   What the
Egyptians meant, who called her ' Neith '—or Homer,
who called her ' Athena '—or Solomon, who called her by
a word which the Greeks render as ' Sophia,' you must
judge for yourselves.   But her testimony is always the
same, and all nations have received it :  ' I was by Him as
one brought up with Him, and I was daily His delight ;
rejoicing in the habitable parts of the earth, and my
delights were with the sons of men.'

MARY.   But is not that only a personification ?

L.   If it be, what will you gain by unpersonifying it, or
what right have you to do so ?   Cannot you accept the
image given you, in its life ; and listen, like children, to
the words which chiefly belong to you as children :  ' I
love them that love Me, and those that seek Me early shall
find Me ' ?

(*They are all quiet for a minute or two ; questions begin
to appear in their eyes.*)

I cannot talk to you any more to-day.  Take that
rose-crystal away with you, and think.

# THE CRYSTAL LIFE

LECTURE III

# LECTURE III

## THE CRYSTAL LIFE

*A very dull Lecture, wilfully brought upon themselves by the elder children. Some of the young ones have, however, managed to get in by mistake.* SCENE, *the Schoolroom*

L. So I am to stand up here merely to be asked questions, to-day, Miss Mary, am I?

MARY. Yes; and you must answer them plainly; without telling us any more stories. You are quite spoiling the children: the poor little things' heads are turning round like kaleidoscopes; and they don't know in the least what you mean. Nor do we old ones, either, for that matter: to-day you must really tell us nothing but facts.

L. I am sworn; but you won't like it, a bit.

MARY. Now, first of all, what do you mean by ' bricks '? —Are the smallest particles of minerals all of some accurate shape, like bricks?

L. I do not know, Miss Mary; I do not even know if anybody knows. The smallest atoms which are visibly and practically put together to make large crystals, may better be described as ' limited in fixed directions ' than as ' of fixed forms.' But I can tell you nothing clear about ultimate atoms: you will find the idea of little bricks, or, perhaps, of little spheres, available for all the uses you will have to put it to.

MARY. Well, it's very provoking; one seems always to be stopped just when one is coming to the very thing one wants to know.

L. No, Mary, for we should not wish to know anything

159

but what is easily and assuredly knowable. There's no end to it. If I could show you, or myself, a group of ultimate atoms, quite clearly, in this magnifying glass, we should both be presently vexed because we could not break them in two pieces, and see their insides.

MARY. Well then, next, what do you mean by the flying of the bricks ? What is it the atoms do, that is like flying ?

L. When they are dissolved, or uncrystallised, they are really separated from each other, like a swarm of gnats in the air, or like a shoal of fish in the sea ;—generally at about equal distances. In currents of solutions, or at different depths of them, one part may be more full of the dissolved atoms than another ; but on the whole you may think of them as equidistant, like the spots in the print of your gown. If they are separated by force of heat only, the substance is said to be melted ; if they are separated by any other substance, as particles of sugar by water, they are said to be ' dissolved.' Note this distinction carefully, all of you.

DORA. I will be very particular. When next you tell me there isn't sugar enough in your tea, I will say, ' It is not yet dissolved, sir.'

L. I tell you what shall be dissolved, Miss Dora ; and that's the present parliament, if the members get too saucy.

(DORA *folds her hands and casts down her eyes.*)

L. (*proceeds in state*). Now, Miss Mary, you know already, I believe, that nearly everything will melt, under a sufficient heat, like wax. Limestone melts (under pressure) ; sand melts ; granite melts ; the lava of a volcano is a mixed mass of many kinds of rocks melted : and any melted substance nearly always, if not always, crystallises as it cools ; the more slowly the more perfectly. Water melts at what we call the freezing, but might just as wisely, though not as conveniently, call the melting point ; and radiates as it cools into the most beautiful of all known crystals. Glass melts at a greater heat, and will crystallize, if you let it cool slowly enough, in stars, much like snow. Gold needs more heat to melt it, but crystallizes also exquisitely, as I will presently show you. Arsenic and sulphur crystallize from their vapours. Now in any of these cases, either of melted, dissolved, or vaporous bodies, the particles are usually separated from each other, either by heat, or by an intermediate substance ; and in crystallizing they are both brought nearer to each other, and packed, so as to fit as closely as possible : the essential part of the business being not the bringing together, but the packing. Who packed your trunk for you, last holidays, Isabel ?

ISABEL. Lily does, always.

L. And how much can you allow for Lily's good packing, in guessing what will go into the trunk ?

ISABEL. Oh ! I bring twice as much as the trunk holds. Lily always gets everything in.

LILY. Ah ! but, Isey, if you only knew what a time it takes ! and since you've had those great hard buttons on your frocks, I can't do anything with them. Buttons won't go anywhere, you know.

L. Yes, Lily, it would be well if she only knew what a time it takes ; and I wish any of us knew what a time crystallization takes, for that is consummately fine packing. The particles of the rock are thrown down, just as Isabel brings her things—in a heap ; and innumerable Lilies, not of the valley, but of the rock, come to pack them. But it takes such a time !

However, the best—out and out the best—way of understanding the thing, is to crystallize yourselves.

THE AUDIENCE. Ourselves !

L. Yes : not merely as you did the other day, carelessly, on the schoolroom forms ; but carefully and finely, out in the playground. You can play at crystallization there as much as you please.

KATHLEEN *and* JESSIE.   Oh ! how ?—how ?

L.   First, you must put yourselves together, as close as you can, in the middle of the grass, and form, for first practice, any figure you like.

JESSIE.   Any dancing figure, do you mean ?

L.   No ;  I mean a square, or a cross, or a diamond. Any figure you like, standing close together.  You had better outline it first on the turf with sticks, or pebbles, so as to see that it is rightly drawn ;  then get into it and enlarge or diminish it at one side, till you are all quite in it, and no empty space left.

DORA.   Crinoline and all ?

L.   The crinoline may stand eventually for rough crystalline surface, unless you pin it in ;  and then you may make a polished crystal of yourselves.

LILY.   Oh, we'll pin it in—we'll pin it in !

L.   Then, when you are all in the figure, let every one note her place, and who is next her on each side ;  and let the outsiders count how many places they stand from the corners.

KATHLEEN.   Yes, yes,—and then ?

L.   Then you must scatter all over the playground— right over it from side to side, and end to end ;  and put yourselves all at equal distances from each other, everywhere.  You needn't mind doing it very accurately, but so as to be nearly equidistant ;  not less than about three yards apart from each other, on every side.

JESSIE.   We can easily cut pieces of string of equal length, to hold.  And then ?

L.   Then at a given signal, let everybody walk, at the same rate, towards the outlined figure in the middle.  You had better sing as you walk ;  that will keep you in good time.  And as you close in towards it, let each take her place, and the next comers fit themselves in beside the first ones, till you are all in the figure again.

KATHLEEN. Oh! how we shall run against each other! What fun it will be!

L. No, no, Miss Katie; I can't allow any running against each other. The atoms never do that, whatever human creatures do. You must all know your places, and find your way to them without jostling.

LILY. But how ever shall we do that?

ISABEL. Mustn't the ones in the middle be the nearest, and the outside ones farther off—when we go away to scatter, I mean?

L. Yes; you must be very careful to keep your order; you will soon find out how to do it; it is only like soldiers forming square, except that each must stand still in her place as she reaches it, and the others come round her; and you will have much more complicated figures, afterwards, to form, than squares.

ISABEL. I'll put a stone at my place; then I shall know it.

L. You might each nail a bit of paper to the turf, at your place, with your name upon it: but it would be of no use, for if you don't know your places, you will make a fine piece of business of it, while you are looking for your names. And, Isabel, if with a little head, and eyes, and a brain (all of them very good and serviceable of their kind, as such things go), you think you cannot know your place without a stone at it, after examining it well,—how do you think each atom knows its place, when it never was there before, and there's no stone at it?

ISABEL. But does every atom know its place?

L. How else could it get there?

MARY. Are they not attracted into their places?

L. Cover a piece of paper with spots, at equal intervals; and then imagine any kind of attraction you choose, or any law of attraction to exist between the spots, and try how, on that permitted supposition, you can attract them into the figure of a Maltese cross, in the middle of the paper.

MARY (*having tried it*). Yes ; I see that I cannot :— one would need all kinds of attractions, in different ways, at different places. But you do not mean that the atoms are alive ?

L. What is it to be alive ?

DORA. There now ; you're going to be provoking, I know.

L. I do not see why it should be provoking to be asked what it is to be alive. Do you think you don't know whether you are alive or not ?

(ISABEL *skips to the end of the room and back.*)

L. Yes, Isabel, that's all very fine ; and you and I may call that being alive : but a modern philosopher calls it being in a 'mode of motion.' It requires a certain quantity of heat to take you to the sideboard ; and exactly the same quantity to bring you back again. That's all.

ISABEL. No, it isn't. And besides, I'm not hot.

L. I am, sometimes, at the way they talk. However, you know, Isabel, you might have been a particle of a mineral, and yet have been carried round the room, or anywhere else, by chemical forces, in the liveliest way.

ISABEL. Yes ; but I wasn't carried : I carried myself.

L. The fact is, mousie, the difficulty is not so much to say what makes a thing alive, as what makes it a Self. As soon as you are shut off from the rest of the universe into a Self, you begin to be alive.

VIOLET (*indignant*). Oh, surely—surely that cannot be so. Is not all the life of the soul in communion, not separation ?

L. There can be no communion where there is no distinction. But we shall be in an abyss of metaphysics presently, if we don't look out ; and besides, we must not be too grand, to-day, for the younger children. We'll be grand, some day, by ourselves, if we must. (*The younger children are not pleased, and prepare to remonstrate ; but, knowing by experience, that all conversations in which the*

*word ' communion' occurs, are unintelligible, think better of
it.*) Meantime, for broad answer about the atoms. I do
not think we should use the word 'life,' of any energy
which does not belong to a given form. A seed, or an egg,
or a young animal, are properly called ' alive ' with respect
to the force belonging to those forms, which consistently
develops that form, and no other. But the force which
crystallizes a mineral appears to be chiefly external, and
it does not produce an entirely determinate and individual
form, limited in size, but only an aggregation, in which
some limiting laws must be observed.

MARY. But I do not see much difference, that way,
between a crystal and a tree.

L. Add, then, that the mode of the energy in a living
thing implies a continual change in its elements ; and a
period for its end. So you may define life by its attached
negative, death ; and still more by its attached positive,
birth. But I won't be plagued any more about this, just
now ; if you choose to think the crystals alive, do, and
welcome. Rocks have always been called ' living ' in
their native place.

MARY. There's one question more ; then I've done.

L. Only one ?

MARY. Only one.

L. But if it is answered, won't it turn into two ?

MARY. No ; I think it will remain single, and be
comfortable.

L. Let me hear it.

MARY. You know, we are to crystallize ourselves out
of the whole playground. Now, what playground have
the minerals ? Where are they scattered before they are
crystallized ; and where are the crystals generally made ?

L. That sounds to me more like three questions than
one, Mary. If it is only one, it is a wide one.

MARY. I did not say anything about the width of it.

L. Well, I must keep it within the best compass I can.

When rocks either dry from a moist state, or cool from a heated state, they necessarily alter in bulk ; and cracks, or open spaces, form in them in all directions. These cracks must be filled up with solid matter, or the rock would eventually become a ruinous heap. So, sometimes by water, sometimes by vapour, sometimes nobody knows how, crystallizable matter is brought from somewhere, and fastens itself in these open spaces, so as to bind the rock together again, with crystal cement. A vast quantity of hollows are formed in lavas by bubbles of gas, just as the holes are left in bread well baked. In process of time these cavities are generally filled with various crystals.

MARY. But where does the crystallizing substance come from ?

L. Sometimes out of the rock itself ; sometimes from below or above, through the veins. The entire substance of the contracting rock may be filled with liquid, pressed into it so as to fill every pore ;—or with mineral vapour ;— or it may be so charged at one place and empty at another. There's no end to the 'may be's.' But all that you need fancy, for our present purpose, is that hollows in the rocks, like the caves in Derbyshire, are traversed by liquids or vapour containing certain elements in a more or less free or separate state, which crystallize on the cave walls.

SIBYL. There now ;—Mary has had all her questions answered : it's my turn to have mine.

L. Ah, there's a conspiracy among you, I see. I might have guessed as much.

DORA. I'm sure you ask us questions enough ! How can you have the heart, when you dislike so to be asked them yourself ?

L. My dear child, if people do not answer questions, it does not matter how many they are asked, because they've no trouble with them. Now, when I ask you questions, I never expect to be answered ; but when you ask me, you always do ; and it's not fair.

DORA. Very well, we shall understand, next time.

SIBYL. No, but seriously, we all want to ask one thing more, quite dreadfully.

L. And I don't want to be asked it, quite dreadfully; but you'll have your own way, of course.

SIBYL. We none of us understand about the lower Pthah. It was not merely yesterday; but in all we have read about him in Wilkinson, or in any book, we cannot understand what the Egyptians put their god into that ugly little deformed shape for.

L. Well, I'm glad it's that sort of question; because I can answer anything I like, to that.

EGYPT. Anything you like will do quite well for us; we shall be pleased with the answer, if you are.

L. I am not so sure of that, most gracious queen; for I must begin by the statement that queens seem to have disliked all sorts of work, in those days, as much as some queens dislike sewing to-day.

EGYPT. Now, it's too bad! and just when I was trying to say the civillest thing I could!

L. But, Egypt, why did you tell me you disliked sewing so!

EGYPT. Did not I show you how the thread cuts my fingers? and I always get cramp, somehow, in my neck, if I sew long.

L. Well, I suppose the Egyptian queens thought everybody got cramp in their neck, if they sewed long; and that thread always cut people's fingers. At all events, every kind of manual labour was despised both by them, and the Greeks; and, while they owned the real good and fruit of it, they yet held it a degradation to all who practised it. Also, knowing the laws of life thoroughly, they perceived that the special practice necessary to bring any manual art to perfection strengthened the body distortedly; one energy or member gaining at the expense of the rest. They especially dreaded and despised any kind of work that had to be done near fire : yet, feeling what they owed to it in metal-work, as the basis of all other work, they expressed this mixed reverence and scorn in the varied types of the lame Hephæstus, and the lower Pthah.

SIBYL.  But what did you mean by making him say, 'Everything great I can make small, and everything small great'?

L.  I had my own separate meaning in that.  We have seen in modern times the power of the lower Pthah developed in a separate way, which no Greek nor Egyptian could have conceived.  It is the character of pure and eyeless manual labour to conceive everything as subjected to it : and, in reality, to disgrace and diminish all that is so subjected ; aggrandising itself, and the thought of itself, at the expense of all noble things.  I heard an orator, and a good one too, at the Working Men's College, the other day, make a great point in a description of our railroads ; saying, with grandly conducted emphasis, 'They have made man greater, and the world less.'  His working audience were mightily pleased ; they thought it so very fine a thing to be made bigger themselves ; and all the rest of the world less.  I should have enjoyed asking them (but it would have been a pity—they were so pleased), how much less they would like to have the world made ;— and whether, at present, those of them really felt themselves the biggest men, who lived in the least houses.

SIBYL.  But then, why did you make Pthah say that he could make weak things strong, and small things great ?

L.  My dear, he is a boaster and self-assertor, by nature ; but it is so far true.  For instance, we used to have a fair in our neighbourhood—a very fine fair we thought it. You never saw such an one ; but if you look at the engraving of Turner's 'St. Catherine's Hill,' you will see what it was like.  There were curious booths, carried on poles ; and peep-shows ; and music, with plenty of drums and cymbals ; and much barley-sugar and gingerbread, and the like : and in the alleys of this fair the London populace would enjoy themselves, after their fashion, very thoroughly. Well, the little Pthah set to work upon it one day ; he made the wooden poles into iron ones, and put them across, like his own crooked legs, so that you always fall over them if you don't look where you are going ; and he turned all the canvas into panes of glass, and put it up on his iron cross-poles ; and made all the little booths into one great booth ;—and people said it was very fine, and a new style of architecture ; and Mr. Dickens said nothing was ever like it in Fairy-land, which was very true. And then the little Pthah set to work to put fine fairings in it ; and he painted the Nineveh bulls afresh, with the blackest eyes he could paint (because he had none himself), and he got the angels down from Lincoln choir, and gilded their wings like his gingerbread of old times ; and he sent for everything else he could think of, and put it in his booth. There are the casts of Niobe and her children ; and the Chimpanzee ; and the wooden Caffres and New-Zealanders ; and the Shakespeare House ; and Le Grand Blondin, and Le Petit Blondin ; and Handel ; and Mozart ; and no end of shops, and buns, and beer ; and all the little-Pthah-worshippers say, never was anything so sublime !

SIBYL. Now, do you mean to say you never go to these Crystal Palace concerts ? They're as good as good can be.

L. I don't go to the thundering things with a million of bad voices in them. When I want a song, I get Julia Mannering and Lucy Bertram and Counsellor Pleydell to sing ' We be three poor Mariners ' to me ; then I've no headache next morning. But I do go to the smaller concerts, when I can ; for they are very good, as you say, Sibyl : and I always get a reserved seat somewhere near the orchestra, where I am sure I can see the kettle-drummer drum.

105—G

SIBYL. Now *do* be serious, for one minute.

L. I am serious—never was more so. You know one can't see the modulation of violinists' fingers, but one can see the vibration of the drummer's hand ; and it's lovely.

SIBYL. But fancy going to a concert, not to hear, but to see !

L. Yes, it is very absurd. The quite right thing, I believe, is to go there to talk. I confess, however, that in most music, when very well done, the doing of it is to me the chiefly interesting part of the business. I'm always thinking how good it would be for the fat, supercilious people, who care so little for their half-crown's worth, to be set to try and do a half-crown's worth of anything like it.

MARY. But surely that Crystal Palace is a great good and help to the people of London ?

L. The fresh air of the Norwood hills is, or was, my dear ; but they are spoiling that with smoke as fast as they can. And the palace (as they call it) is a better place for them, by much, than the old fair ; and it is always there, instead of for three days only ; and it shuts up at proper hours of night. And good use may be made of the things in it, if you know how : but as for its teaching the people, it will teach them nothing but the lowest of the lower Pthah's work—nothing but hammer and tongs. I saw a wonderful piece, of his doing, in the place, only the other day. Some unhappy metal-worker—I am not sure if it was not a metal-working firm—had taken three years to make a Golden eagle.

SIBYL. Of real gold ?

L. No ; of bronze, or copper, or some of their foul patent metals—it is no matter what. I meant a model of our chief British eagle. Every feather was made separately ; and every filament of every feather separately, and so joined on ; and all the quills modelled of the right length and right section, and at last the whole cluster of them fastened together. You know, children, I don't think much of my own drawing ; but take my proud word for once, that when I go to the Zoological Gardens, and happen to have a bit of chalk in my pocket, and the Grey Harpy will sit, without screwing his head round, for thirty seconds,—I can do a better thing of him in that time than the three years' work of this industrious firm. For, during the thirty seconds, the eagle is my object,—not myself ; and during the three years, the firm's object, in every fibre of bronze it made, was itself, and not the eagle. That is the true meaning of the little Pthah's having no eyes—he can see only himself. The Egyptian beetle was not quite the full type of him ; our northern ground beetle is a truer one. It is beautiful to see it at work, gathering its treasures (such as they are) into little round balls ; and pushing them home with the strong wrong end of it—head downmost all the way—like a modern political economist with his ball of capital, declaring that a nation can stand on its vices better than on its virtues. But away with you, children, now, for I'm getting cross.

DORA. I'm going downstairs ; I shall take care, at any rate, that there are no little Pthahs in the kitchen cupboards.

# THE CRYSTAL ORDERS

LECTURE IV

# LECTURE IV

## THE CRYSTAL ORDERS

*A working Lecture, in the large Schoolroom; with experimental Interludes. The great bell has rung unexpectedly*

KATHLEEN (*entering disconsolate, though first at the summons*). Oh dear, oh dear, what a day! Was ever anything so provoking! just when we wanted to crystallize ourselves;—and I'm sure it's going to rain all day long.

L. So am I, Kate. The sky has quite an Irish way with it. But I don't see why Irish girls should also look so dismal. Fancy that you don't want to crystallize yourselves: you didn't, the day before yesterday, and you were not unhappy when it rained then.

FLORRIE. Ah! but we do want to-day; and the rain's so tiresome.

L. That is to say, children, that because you are all the richer by the expectation of playing at a new game, you choose to make yourselves unhappier than when you had nothing to look forward to, but the old ones.

ISABEL. But then, to have to wait—wait—wait; and before we've tried it;—and perhaps it will rain to-morrow, too!

L. It may also rain the day after to-morrow. We can make ourselves uncomfortable to any extent with perhapses, Isabel. You may stick perhapses into your little minds, like pins, till you are as uncomfortable as the Lilliputians made Gulliver with their arrows, when he would not lie quiet.

175

ISABEL.  But what *are* we to do to-day ?

L.  To be quiet, for one thing, like Gulliver when he saw there was nothing better to be done.  And to practise patience.  I can tell you, children, *that* requires nearly as much practising as music ;  and we are continually losing our lessons when the master comes.  Now, to-day, here's a nice little adagio lesson for us, if we play it properly.

ISABEL.  But I don't like that sort of lesson.  I can't play it properly.

L.  Can you play a Mozart sonata yet, Isabel ?  The more need to practise.  All one's life is a music, if one touches the notes rightly, and in time.  But there must be no hurry.

KATHLEEN.  I'm sure there's no music in stopping in on a rainy day.

L.  There's no music in a ' rest,' Katie, that I know of : but there's the making of music in it.  And people are always missing that part of the life-melody ;  and scrambling on without counting—not that it's easy to count ;  but nothing on which so much depends ever *is* easy.  People are always talking of perseverance, and courage, and fortitude ;  but patience is the finest and worthiest part of fortitude,—and the rarest, too.  I know twenty persevering girls for one patient one :  but it is only that twenty-first who can do her work, out and out, or enjoy it. For patience lies at the root of all pleasures, as well as of all powers.  Hope herself ceases to be happiness, when Impatience companions her.

(ISABEL *and* LILY *sit down on the floor, and fold their hands.  The others follow their example.*)

Good children !  but that's not quite the way of it, neither.  Folded hands are not necessarily resigned ones. The Patience who really smiles at grief usually stands, or walks, or even runs :  she seldom sits ;  though she may sometimes have to do it, for many a day, poor thing, by monuments ;  or like Chaucer's, ' with face pale, upon a hill of sand.' But we are not reduced to that to-day. Suppose we use this calamitous forenoon to choose the shapes we are to crystallize into ? we know nothing about them yet.

(*The pictures of resignation rise from the floor, not in the patientest manner. General applause.*)

MARY (*with one or two others*). The very thing we wanted to ask you about !

LILY. We looked at the books about crystals, but they are so dreadful.

L. Well, Lily, we must go through a little dreadfulness, that's a fact : no road to any good knowledge is wholly among the lilies and the grass ; there is rough climbing to be done always. But the crystal-books are a little *too* dreadful, most of them, I admit ; and we shall have to be content with very little of their help. You know, as you cannot stand on each other's heads, you can only make yourselves into the sections of crystals,—the figures they show when they are cut through ; and we will choose some that will be quite easy. You shall make diamonds of yourselves——

ISABEL. Oh, no, no ! we won't be diamonds, please.

L. Yes, you shall, Isabel ; they are very pretty things, if the jewellers, and the kings and queens, would only let them alone. You shall make diamonds of yourselves, and rubies of yourselves, and emeralds ; and Irish diamonds ; two of those—with Lily in the middle of one, which will be very orderly, of course ; and Kathleen in the middle of the other, for which we will hope the best ;—and you shall make Derbyshire spar of yourselves, and Iceland spar, and gold, and silver, and—Quicksilver there's enough of in you, without any making.

MARY. Now, you know, the children will be getting quite wild : we must really get pencils and paper, and begin properly.

L. Wait a minute, Miss Mary ; I think as we've the

schoolroom clear to-day, I'll try to give you some notion
of the three great orders or ranks of crystals, into which
all the others seem more or less to fall. We shall only
want one figure a day, in the playground ; and that can
be drawn in a minute : but the general ideas had better
be fastened first. I must show you a great many minerals ;
so let me have three tables wheeled into the three windows,
that we may keep our specimens separate ;—we will keep
the three orders of crystals on separate tables.

*(First Interlude, of pushing and pulling, and spreading
of baize covers. VIOLET, not particularly minding
what she is about, gets herself jammed into a corner,
and bid to stand out of the way ; on which she devotes
herself to meditation.)*

VIOLET *(after interval of meditation).* How strange it is
that everything seems to divide into threes !

L. Everything doesn't divide into threes. Ivy won't,
though shamrock will ; and daisies won't, though lilies
will.

VIOLET. But all the nicest things seem to divide into
threes.

L. Violets won't.

VIOLET. No ; I should think not, indeed ! But I mean
the great things.

L. I've always heard the globe had four quarters.

ISABEL. Well ; but you know you said it hadn't any
quarters at all. So mayn't it really be divided into three ?

L. If it were divided into no more than three, on the
outside of it, Isabel, it would be a fine world to live in ;
and if it were divided into three in the inside of it, it would
soon be no world to live in at all.

DORA. We shall never get to the crystals, at this rate.
*(Aside to MARY.)* He will get off into political economy
before we know where we are. *(Aloud.)* But the crystals
are divided into three, then ?

L. No ; but there are three general notions by which

we may best get hold of them.   Then between these notions there are other notions.

LILY (*alarmed*).   A great many ?   And shall we have to learn them all ?

L.   More than a great many—a quite infinite many. So you cannot learn them all.

LILY (*greatly relieved*).   Then may we only learn the three ?

L.   Certainly ; unless, when you have got those three notions, you want to have some more notions ;—which would not surprise me.   But we'll try for the three, first. Katie, you broke your coral necklace this morning ?

KATHLEEN.   Oh ! who told you ?   It was in jumping. I'm so sorry !

L.   I'm very glad.   Can you fetch me the beads of it ?

KATHLEEN.   I've lost some ; here are the rest in my pocket, if I can only get them out.

L.   You mean to get them out some day, I suppose ; so try now.   I want them.

(KATHLEEN *empties her pocket on the floor.   The beads disperse.   The School disperses also.   Second Interlude—hunting piece.*)

L. (*after waiting patiently for a quarter of an hour, to* ISABEL, *who comes up from under the table with her hair all about her ears, and the last findable beads in her hand*). Mice are useful little things sometimes.   Now, mousie, I want all those beads crystallized.   How many ways are there of putting them in order ?

ISABEL.   Well, first one would string them, I suppose ?

L.   Yes, that's the first way.   You cannot string ultimate atoms ; but you can put them in a row, and then they fasten themselves together, somehow, into a long rod or needle.   We will call these ' *Needle*-crystals.'   What would be the next way ?

ISABEL.   I suppose, as we are to get together in the playground, when it stops raining, in different shapes ?

L. Yes; put the beads together, then, in the simplest form you can, to begin with. Put them into a square, and pack them close.

ISABEL (*after careful endeavour*). I can't get them closer.

L. That will do. Now you may see, beforehand, that if you try to throw yourselves into square in this confused way, you will never know your places; so you had better consider every square as made of rods, put side by side. Take four beads of equal size, first, Isabel; put them into a little square. That, you may consider as made up of two rods of two beads each. Then you can make a square a size larger, out of three rods of three. Then the next square may be a size larger. How many rods, Lily?

LILY. Four rods of four beads each, I suppose.

L. Yes, and then five rods of five, and so on. But now, look here; make another square of four beads again. You see they leave a little opening in the centre.

ISABEL (*pushing two opposite ones closer together*). Now they don't.

L. No; but now it isn't a square; and by pushing the two together you have pushed the two others farther apart.

ISABEL. And yet, somehow, they all seem closer than they were!

L. Yes; for before, each of them only touched two of the others, but now each of the two in the middle touches the other three. Take away one of the outsiders, Isabel: now you have three in a triangle—the smallest triangle you can make out of the beads. Now put a rod of three beads on at one side. So, you have a triangle of six beads; but just the shape of the first one. Next a rod of four on the side of that; and you have a triangle of ten beads: then a rod of five on the side of that; and you have a triangle of fifteen. Thus you have a square with five beads on the side, and a triangle with five beads on the side ; equal-sided, therefore, like the square. So, however few or many you may be, you may soon learn how to crystallize quickly into these two figures, which are the foundation of form in the commonest, and therefore actually the most important, as well as in the rarest, and therefore, by our esteem, the most important, minerals of the world. Look at this in my hand.

VIOLET. Why, it is leaf gold !

L. Yes ; but beaten by no man's hammer ; or rather, not beaten at all, but woven. Besides, feel the weight of it. There is gold enough there to gild the walls and ceiling, if it were beaten thin.

VIOLET. How beautiful ! And it glitters like a leaf covered with frost.

L. You only think it so beautiful because you know it is gold. It is not prettier, in reality, than a bit of brass : for it is Transylvanian gold ; and they say there is a foolish gnome in the mines there, who is always wanting to live in the moon, and so alloys all the gold with a little silver. I don't know how that may be : but the silver always *is* in the gold ; and if he does it, it's very provoking of him, for no gold is woven so fine anywhere else.

MARY (*who has been looking through her magnifying glass*). But this is not woven. This is all made of little triangles.

L. Say ' patched,' then, if you must be so particular. But if you fancy all those triangles, small as they are (and many of them are infinitely small), made up again of rods, and those of grains, as we built our great triangle of the beads, what word will you take for the manufacture ?

MAY. There's no word—it is beyond words.

L. Yes ; and that would matter little, were it not beyond thoughts too. But, at all events, this yellow leaf of dead gold, shed, not from the ruined woodlands, but the ruined rocks, will help you to remember the second kind of crystals, *Leaf*-crystals, or *Foliated* crystals ; though

I show you the form in gold first only to make a strong impression on you, for gold is not generally, or characteristically, crystallized in leaves; the real type of foliated crystals is this thing, Mica; which if you once feel well, and break well, you will always know again; and you will often have occasion to know it, for you will find it everywhere, nearly, in hill countries.

KATHLEEN. If we break it well! May we break it?

L. To powder, if you like.

(*Surrenders plate of brown mica to public investigation. Third Interlude. It sustains severely philosophical treatment at all hands.*)

FLORRIE (*to whom the last fragments have descended*). Always leaves, and leaves, and nothing but leaves, or white dust!

L. That dust itself is nothing but finer leaves.

(*Shows them to* FLORRIE *through magnifying glass.*)

ISABEL (*peeping over* FLORRIE'S *shoulder*). But then this bit under the glass looks like that bit out of the glass! If we could break this bit under the glass, what would it be like?

L. It would be all leaves still.

ISABEL. And then if we broke those again?

L. All less leaves still.

ISABEL (*impatiently*). And if we broke them again, and again, and again, and again, and again?

L. Well, I suppose you would come to a limit, if you could only see it. Notice that the little flakes already differ somewhat from the large ones: because I can bend them up and down, and they stay bent; while the large flake, though it bent easily a little way, sprang back when you let it go, and broke, when you tried to bend it far. And a large mass would not bend at all.

MARY. Would that leaf gold separate into finer leaves, in the same way?

L. No; and therefore, as I told you, it is not a

characteristic specimen of a foliated crystallization. The little triangles are portions of solid crystals, and so they are in this, which looks like a black mica ; but you see it is made up of triangles, like the gold, and stands, almost accurately, as an intermediate link, in crystals, between mica and gold. Yet this is the commonest, as gold the rarest, of metals.

MARY. Is it iron ? I never saw iron so bright.

L. It is rust of iron, finely crystallized : from its resemblance to mica, it is often called micaceous iron.

KATHLEEN. May we break this, too ?

L. No, for I could not easily get such another crystal ; besides, it would not break like the mica ; it is much harder. But take the glass again, and look at the fineness of the jagged edges of the triangles where they lap over each other. The gold has the same : but you see them better here, terrace above terrace, countless, and in successive angles, like superb fortified bastions.

MAY. But all foliated crystals are not made of triangles ?

L. Far from it ; mica is occasionally so, but usually of hexagons ; and here is a foliated crystal made of squares, which will show you that the leaves of the rock-land have their summer green, as well as their autumnal gold.

FLORRIE. Oh ! oh ! oh ! (jumps for joy).

L. Did you never see a bit of green leaf before, Florrie ?

FLORRIE. Yes, but never so bright as that, and not in a stone.

L. If you will look at the leaves of the trees in sunshine after a shower, you will find they are much brighter than that ; and surely they are none the worse for being on stalks instead of in stones ?

FLORRIE. Yes, but then there are so many of them, one never looks, I suppose.

L. Now you have it, Florrie.

VIOLET (sighing). There are so many beautiful things we never see !

L. You need not sigh for that, Violet ; but I will tell

you what we should all sigh for,—that there are so many ugly things we never see.

VIOLET. But we don't want to see ugly things!

L. You had better say, 'We don't want to suffer them.' You ought to be glad in thinking how much more beauty God has made, than human eyes can ever see; but not glad in thinking how much more evil man has made, than his own soul can ever conceive, much more than his hands can ever heal.

VIOLET. I don't understand;—how is that like the leaves?

L. The same law holds in our neglect of multiplied pain, as in our neglect of multiplied beauty. Florrie jumps for joy at sight of half an inch of a green leaf in a brown stone; and takes more notice of it than of all the green in the wood; and you, or I, or any of us, would be unhappy if any single human creature beside us were in sharp pain; but we can read, at breakfast, day after day, of men being killed, and of women and children dying of hunger, faster than the leaves strew the brooks in Vallombrosa;—and then go out to play croquet, as if nothing had happened.

MAY. But we do not see the people being killed or dying.

L. You did not see your brother, when you got the telegram the other day, saying he was ill, May; but you cried for him; and played no croquet. But we cannot talk of these things now; and what is more, you must let me talk straight on, for a little while; and ask no questions till I've done: for we branch ('exfoliate,' I should say, mineralogically) always into something else, though that's my fault more than yours; but I must go straight on now. You have got a distinct notion, I hope, of leaf-crystals; and you see the sort of look they have: you can easily remember that 'folium' is Latin for a leaf, and that the separate flakes of mica, or any other such stones, are called 'folia'; but, because mica is the most characteristic of these stones, other things that are like it in structure are called 'mica'; thus we have Uran-mica, which is the green leaf I showed you; and Copper-mica, which is another like it, made chiefly of copper; and this foliated iron is called 'micaceous iron.' You have then these two great orders, Needle-crystals, made (probably) of grains in rows; and Leaf-crystals, made (probably) of needles interwoven; now, lastly, there are crystals of a third order, in heaps, or knots, or masses, which may be made, either of leaves laid one upon another, or of needles bound like Roman fasces; and mica itself, when it is well crystallized, puts itself into such masses, as if to show us how others are made. Here is a brown six-sided crystal, quite as beautifully chiselled at the sides as any castle tower; but you see it is entirely built of folia of mica, one laid above another, which break away the moment I touch the edge with my knife. Now, here is another hexagonal tower, of just the same size and colour, which I want you to compare with the mica carefully; but as I cannot wait for you to do it just now, I must tell you quickly what main differences to look for. First, you will feel it is far heavier than the mica. Then, though its surface looks quite micaceous in the folia of it, when you try them with a knife, you will find you cannot break them away——

KATHLEEN. May I try?

L. Yes, you mistrusting Katie. Here's my strong knife for you. (*Experimental pause.* KATHLEEN *doing her best.*) You'll have that knife shutting on your finger presently, Katie; and I don't know a girl who would like less to have her hand tied up for a week.

KATHLEEN (*who also does not like to be beaten,—giving up the knife despondently*). What *can* the nasty hard thing be?

L. It is nothing but indurated clay, Kate: very hard set certainly, yet not so hard as it might be. If it were thoroughly well crystallized, you would see none of those micaceous fractures ; and the stone would be quite red and clear, all through.

KATHLEEN.    Oh, cannot you show us one ?

L.    Egypt can, if you ask her ; she has a beautiful one in the clasp of her favourite bracelet.

KATHLEEN.    Why, that's a ruby !

L.    Well, so is that thing you've been scratching at.

KATHLEEN.    My goodness !

   (*Takes up the stone again, very delicately ; and drops it.    General consternation.*)

L.    Never mind, Katie, you might drop it from the top of the house, and do it no harm.    But though you really are a very good girl, and as good-natured as anybody can possibly be, remember, you have your faults, like other people ; and, if I were you, the next time I wanted to assert anything energetically, I would assert it by ' my badness,' not ' my goodness.'

KATHLEEN.    Ah, now, it's too bad of you !

L.    Well, then, I'll invoke, on occasion, my ' too-badness.'    But you may as well pick up the ruby, now you have dropped it ; and look carefully at the beautiful hexagonal lines which gleam on its surface : and here is a pretty white sapphire (essentially the same stone as the ruby), in which you will see the same lovely structure, like the threads of the finest white cobweb.    I do not know what is the exact method of a ruby's construction ; but you see by these lines, what fine construction there *is*, even in this hardest of stones (after the diamond), which usually appears as a massive lump or knot.    There is therefore no real mineralogical distinction between needle crystals and knotted crystals, but, practically, crystallized masses throw themselves into one of the three groups we have been examining to-day ; and appear either as Needles, as Folia, or as Knots ; when they are in needles (or fibres), they make the stones or rocks formed out of them ' *fibrous* ' ;

when they are in folia, they make them ' *foliated* ' ; when they are in knots (or grains), ' *granular.*' Fibrous rocks are comparatively rare, in mass ; but fibrous minerals are innumerable ; and it is often a question which really no one but a young lady could possibly settle, whether one should call the fibres composing them 'threads' or ' needles.' Here is amianthus, for instance, which is quite as fine and soft as any cotton thread you ever sewed with ; and here is sulphide of bismuth, with sharper points and brighter lustre than your finest needles have ; and fastened in white webs of quartz more delicate than your finest lace ; and here is sulphide of antimony, which looks like mere purple wool, but it is all of purple needle crystals ; and here is red oxide of copper (you must not breathe on it as you look, or you may blow some of the films of it off the stone), which is simply a woven tissue of scarlet silk. However, these finer thread forms are comparatively rare, while the bolder and needle-like crystals occur constantly ; so that, I believe, ' Needle-crystals ' is the best word (the grand one is ' Acicular crystal,' but Sibyl will tell you it is all the same, only less easily understood ; and therefore more scientific). Then the Leaf-crystals, as I said, form an immense mass of foliated rocks ; and the Granular crystals, which are of many kinds, form essentially granular, or granitic and porphyritic rocks : and it is always a point of more interest to me (and I think will ultimately be to you), to consider the causes which force a given mineral to take any one of these three general forms, than what the peculiar geometrical limitations are, belonging to its own crystals.* It is more interesting to me, for instance, to try and find out why the red oxide of copper, usually crystallizing in cubes or octahedrons, makes itself exquisitely, out of its cubes, into this red silk in one particular Cornish mine, than what are the absolutely necessary angles of the octahedron, which is its

* See Note IV.

common form. At all events, that mathematical part of crystallography is quite beyond girls' strength; but these questions of the various tempers and manners of crystals are not only comprehensible by you, but full of the most curious teaching for you. For in the fulfilment, to the best of their power, if their adopted form under given circumstances, there are conditions entirely resembling those of human virtue; and indeed expressible under no term so proper as that of the Virtue, or Courage of crystals: —which, if you are not afraid of the crystals making you ashamed of yourselves, we will try to get some notion of, to-morrow. But it will be a bye-lecture, and more about yourselves than the minerals. Don't come unless you like.

MARY. I'm sure the crystals will make us ashamed of ourselves; but we'll come, for all that.

L. Meantime, look well and quietly over these needle, or thread crystals, and those on the other two tables, with magnifying glasses; and see what thoughts will come into your little heads about them. For the best thoughts are generally those which come without being forced, one does not know how. And so I hope you will get through your wet day patiently.

# CRYSTAL VIRTUES




LECTURE V

# LECTURE V

## CRYSTAL VIRTUES

*A quiet talk, in the afternoon, by the sunniest window of the
Drawing-room. Present,* FLORRIE, ISABEL, MAY,
LUCILLA, KATHLEEN, DORA, MARY, *and some others,
who have saved time for the bye-Lecture*

L. So you have really come, like good girls, to be made
ashamed of yourselves ?

DORA (*very meekly*). No, we needn't be made so ; we
always are.

L. Well, I believe that's truer than most pretty
speeches : but you know, you saucy girl, some people
have more reason to be so than others. Are you sure
everybody is, as well as you ?

THE GENERAL VOICE. Yes, yes ; everybody.

L. What ! Florrie ashamed of herself ?

(FLORRIE *hides behind the curtain.*)

L. And Isabel ?

(ISABEL *hides under the table.*)

L. And May ?

(MAY *runs into the corner behind the piano.*)

L. And Lucilla ?

(LUCILLA *hides her face in her hands.*)

L. Dear, dear ; but this will never do. I shall have
to tell you of the faults of the crystals, instead of virtues,
to put you in heart again.

MAY (*coming out of her corner*). Oh ! have the crystals
faults, like us ?

L. Certainly, May. Their best virtues are shown in
191

fighting their faults. And some have a great many faults ;
and some are very naughty crystals indeed.

FLORRIE (*from behind her curtain*). As naughty as me ?

ISABEL (*peeping from under the table-cloth*). Or me ?

L. Well, I don't know. They never forget their syntax,
children, when once they've been taught it. But I think
some of them are, on the whole, worse than any of you.
Not that it's amiable of you to look so radiant, all in a
minute, on that account.

DORA. Oh ! but it's so much more comfortable.

(*Everybody seems to recover their spirits. Eclipse of*
FLORRIE *and* ISABEL *terminates.*)

L. What kindly creatures girls are, after all, to their
neighbours' failings ! I think you may be ashamed of
yourselves indeed, now, children ! I can tell you, you
shall hear of the highest crystalline merits that I can think
of, to-day : and I wish there were more of them ; but
crystals have a limited, though a stern, code of morals ;
and their essential virtues are but two ;—the first is to be
pure, and the second to be well shaped.

MARY. Pure ! Does that mean clear—transparent ?

L. No ; unless in the case of a transparent substance.
You cannot have a transparent crystal of gold ; but you
may have a perfectly pure one.

ISABEL. But you said that it was the shape that made
things be crystals ; therefore, oughtn't their shape to be
their first virtue, not their second ?

L. Right, you troublesome mousie. But I call their
shape only their second virtue, because it depends on time
and accident, and things which the crystal cannot help.
If it is cooled too quickly, or shaken, it must take what
shape it can ; but it seems as if, even then, it had in itself
the power of rejecting impurity, if it has crystalline life
enough. Here is a crystal of quartz, well enough shaped
in its way ; but it seems to have been languid and sick
at heart ; and some white milky substance has got into it,

and mixed itself up with it, all through. It makes the quartz quite yellow, if you hold it up to the light, and milky blue on the surface. Here is another, broken into a thousand separate facets, and out of all traceable shape ; but as pure as a mountain spring. I like this one best.

THE AUDIENCE. So do I—and I—and I.

MARY. Would a crystallographer ?

L. I think so. He would find many more laws curiously exemplified in the irregularly grouped but pure crystal. But it is a futile question, this of first or second. Purity is in most cases a prior, if not a nobler, virtue ; at all events it is most convenient to think about it first.

MARY. But what ought we to think about it ? Is there much to be thought—I mean, much to puzzle one ?

L. I don't know what you call ' much.' It is a long time since I met with anything in which there was little. There's not much in this, perhaps. The crystal must be either dirty or clean,—and there's an end. So it is with one's hands, and with one's heart—only you can wash your hands without changing them, but not hearts, nor crystals. On the whole, while you are young, it will be as well to take care that your hearts don't want much washing ; for they may perhaps need wringing also, when they do.

(*Audience doubtful and uncomfortable.* LUCILLA *at last takes courage.*)

LUCILLA. Oh ! but surely, sir, we cannot make our hearts clean ?

L. Not easily, Lucilla ; so you had better keep them so, when they are.

LUCILLA. When they are ! But, sir——

L. Well ?

LUCILLA. Sir—surely—are we not told that they are all evil ?

L. Wait a little, Lucilla : that is difficult ground you are getting upon ; and we must keep to our crystals till at least we understand what *their* good and evil consist in ; they may help us afterwards to some useful hints about our own. I said that their goodness consisted chiefly in purity of substance, and perfectness of form : but those are rather the *effects* of their goodness, than the goodness itself. The inherent virtues of the crystals, resulting in these outer conditions, might really seem to be best described in the words we should use respecting living creatures—' force of heart ' and ' steadiness of purpose.' There seem to be in some crystals, from the beginning, an unconquerable purity of vital power, and strength of crystal spirit. Whatever dead substance, unacceptant of this energy, comes in their way, is either rejected, or forced to take some beautiful subordinate form ; the purity of the crystal remains unsullied, and every atom of it bright with coherent energy. Then the second condition is, that from the beginning of its whole structure, a fine crystal seems to have determined that it will be of a certain size and of a certain shape ; it persists in this plan, and completes it. Here is a perfect crystal of quartz for you. It is of an unusual form, and one which it might seem very difficult to build—a pyramid with convex sides, composed of other minor pyramids. But there is not a flaw in its contour throughout; not one of its myriads of component sides but is as bright as a jeweller's facetted work (and far finer, if you saw it close). The crystal points are as sharp as javelins ; their edges will cut glass with a touch. Anything more resolute, consummate, determinate in form, cannot be conceived. Here, on the other hand, is a crystal of the same substance, in a perfectly simple type of form —a plain six-sided prism ; but from its base to its point— and it is nine inches long—it has never for one instant made up its mind what thickness it will have. It seems to have begun by making itself as thick as it thought possible with the quantity of material at command. Still not being as thick as it would like to be, it has clumsily

# pixel

glued on more substance at one of its sides. Then it has thinned itself, in a panic of economy; then puffed itself out again; then starved one side to enlarge another; then warped itself quite out of its first line. Opaque, rough-surfaced, jagged on the edge, distorted in the spine, it exhibits a quite human image of decrepitude and dishonour; but the worst of all the signs of its decay and helplessness, is that half-way up, a parasite crystal, smaller, but just as sickly, has rooted itself in the side of the larger one, eating out a cavity round its root, and then growing backwards, or downwards, contrary to the direction of the main crystal. Yet I cannot trace the least difference in purity of substance between the first most noble stone, and this ignoble and dissolute one. The impurity of the last is in its will, or want of will.

MARY. Oh, if we could but understand the meaning of it all!

L. We can understand all that is good for us. It is just as true for us, as for the crystal, that the nobleness of life depends on its consistency,—clearness of purpose,—quiet and ceaseless energy. All doubt, and repenting, and botching, and retouching, and wondering what it will be best to do next, are vice, as well as misery.

MARY (*much wondering*). But must not one repent when one does wrong, and hesitate when one can't see one's way?

L. You have no business at all to do wrong; nor to get into any way that you cannot see. Your intelligence should always be far in advance of your act. Whenever you do not know what you are about, you are sure to be doing wrong.

KATHLEEN. Oh, dear, but I never know what I am about!

L. Very true, Katie, but it is a great deal to know, if you know that. And you find that you have done wrong afterwards; and perhaps some day you may begin to know, or at least, think, what you are about.

ISABEL. But surely people can't do very wrong if they don't know, can they ? I mean, they can't be very naughty. They can be wrong, like Kathleen or me, when we make mistakes ; but not wrong in the dreadful way. I can't express what I mean ; but there are two sorts of wrong, are there not ?

L. Yes, Isabel ; but you will find that the great difference is between kind and unkind wrongs, not between meant and unmeant wrong. Very few people really mean to do wrong,—in a deep sense, none. They only don't know what they are about. Cain did not mean to do wrong when he killed Abel.

(ISABEL *draws a deep breath, and opens her eyes very wide.*)

L. No, Isabel ; and there are countless Cains among us now, who kill their brothers by the score a day, not only for less provocation than Cain had, but for *no* provocation —and merely for what they can make of their bones—yet do not think they are doing wrong in the least. Then sometimes you have the business reversed, as over in America these last years, where you have seen Abel resolutely killing Cain, and not thinking he is doing wrong. The great difficulty is always to open people's eyes : to touch their feelings, and break their hearts, is easy ; the difficult thing is to break their heads. What does it matter, as long as they remain stupid, whether you change their feelings or not ? You cannot be always at their elbow to tell them what is right : and they may just do as wrong as before, or worse ; and their best intentions merely make the road smooth for them,—you know where, children. For it is not the place itself that is paved with them, as people say so often. You can't pave the bottomless pit ; but you may the road to it.

MAY. Well, but if people do as well as they can see how, surely that is the right for them, isn't it ?

L. No, May, not a bit of it ; right is right, and wrong

is wrong. It is only the fool who does wrong, and says he
' did it for the best.' And if there's one sort of person in
the world that the Bible speaks harder of than another,
it is fools. Their particular and chief way of saying
' There is no God ' is this, of declaring that whatever their
' public opinion ' may be, is right ; and that God's opinion
is of no consequence.

MAY. But surely nobody can always know what is
right ?

L. Yes, you always can, for to-day ; and if you do
what you see of it to-day, you will see more of it, and
more clearly, to-morrow. Here, for instance, you children
are at school, and have to learn French, and arithmetic,
and music, and several other such things. That is your
' right ' for the present ; the ' right ' for us, your teachers,
is to see that you learn as much as you can, without spoiling
your dinner, your sleep, or your play ; and that what you
do learn, you learn well. You all know when you learn
with a will, and when you dawdle. There's no doubt of
conscience about that, I suppose ?

VIOLET. No ; but if one wants to read an amusing book,
instead of learning one's lesson ?

L. You don't call that a ' question,' seriously, Violet ?
You are then merely deciding whether you will resolutely
do wrong or not.

MARY. But, in after life, how many fearful difficulties
may arise, however one tries to know or to do what is
right !

L. You are much too sensible a girl, Mary, to have
felt that, whatever you may have seen. A great many of
young ladies' difficulties arise from their falling in love
with a wrong person : but they have no business to let
themselves fall in love, till they know he is the right one.

DORA. How many thousands ought he to have a year ?

L. (disdaining reply). There are, of course, certain
crises of fortune when one has to take care of oneself ; and

mind shrewdly what one is about. There is never any real doubt about the path, but you may have to walk very slowly.

MARY.  And if one is forced to do a wrong thing by some one who has authority over you ?

L.  My dear, no one can be forced to do a wrong thing, for the guilt is in the will : but you may any day be forced to do a fatal thing, as you might be forced to take poison ; the remarkable law of nature in such cases being, that it is always unfortunately *you* who are poisoned, and not the person who gives you the dose.  It is a very strange law, but it *is* a law.  Nature merely sees to the carrying out of the normal operation of arsenic.  She never troubles herself to ask who gave it you.  So also you may be starved to death, morally as well as physically, by other people's faults.  You are, on the whole, very good children sitting here to-day :—do you think that your goodness comes all by your own contriving ? or that you are gentle and kind because your dispositions are naturally more angelic than those of the poor girls who are playing, with wild eyes, on the dustheaps in the alleys of our great towns ; and who will one day fill their prisons—or, better, their graves ?  Heaven only knows where they, and we who have cast them there, shall stand at last.  But the main judgment question will be, I suppose, for all of us, ' Did you keep a good heart through it ? '  What you were, others may answer for ;—what you tried to be, you must answer for, yourself.  Was the heart pure and true—tell us that ?

And so we come back to your sorrowful question, Lucilla, which I put aside a little ago.  You would be afraid to answer that your heart *was* pure and true, would not you ?

LUCILLA.  Yes, indeed, sir.

L.  Because you have been taught that it is all evil— ' only evil continually.'  Somehow, often as people say that, they never seem, to me, to believe it. Do you really believe it?

LUCILLA. Yes, sir; I hope so.

L. That you have an entirely bad heart?

LUCILLA (*a little uncomfortable at the substitution of the monosyllable for the dissyllable, nevertheless persisting in her orthodoxy*). Yes, sir.

L. Florrie, I am sure you are tired; I never like you to stay when you are tired; but, you know, you must not play with the kitten while we are talking.

FLORRIE. Oh! but I'm not tired; and I'm only nursing her. She'll be asleep in my lap, directly.

L. Stop! that puts me in mind of something I had to show you, about minerals that are like hair. I want a hair out of Tittie's tail.

FLORRIE (*quite rude, in her surprise, even to the point of repeating expressions*). Out of Tittie's tail!

L. Yes; a brown one: Lucilla, you can get at the tip of it nicely, under Florrie's arm; just pull one out for me.

LUCILLA. Oh! but, sir, it will hurt her so!

L. Never mind; she can't scratch you while Florrie is holding her. Now that I think of it, you had better pull out two.

LUCILLA. But then she may scratch Florrie! and it will hurt her so, sir! if you only want brown hairs, wouldn't two of mine do?

L. Would you really rather pull out your own than Tittie's?

LUCILLA. Oh, of course, if mine will do.

L. But that's very wicked, Lucilla!

LUCILLA. Wicked, sir?

L. Yes; if your heart was not so bad, you would much rather pull all the cat's hairs out, than one of your own.

LUCILLA. Oh! but sir, I didn't mean bad, like that.

L. I believe, if the truth were told, Lucilla, you would

like to tie a kettle to Tittie's tail, and hunt her round the playground.

LUCILLA. Indeed, I should not, sir.

L. That's not true, Lucilla ; you know it cannot be.

LUCILLA. Sir ?

L. Certainly it is not ;—how can you possibly speak any truth out of such a heart as you have. It is wholly deceitful.

LUCILLA. Oh ! no, no ; I don't mean that way ; I don't mean that it makes me tell lies, quite out.

L. Only that it tells lies within you ?

LUCILLA. Yes.

L. Then, outside of it, you know what is true, and say so ; and I may trust the outside of your heart ; but within, it is all foul and false. Is that the way ?

LUCILLA. I suppose so : I don't understand it, quite.

L. There is no occasion for understanding it ; but do you feel it ? Are you sure that your heart is deceitful above all things, and desperately wicked ?

LUCILLA (*much relieved by finding herself among phrases with which she is acquainted*). Yes, sir. I'm sure of that.

L. (*pensively*). I'm sorry for it, Lucilla.

LUCILLA. So am I, indeed.

L. What are you sorry with, Lucilla ?

LUCILLA. Sorry with, sir ?

L. Yes ; I mean, where do you feel sorry ? in your feet ?

LUCILLA (*laughing a little*). No, sir, of course.

L. In your shoulders, then ?

LUCILLA. No, sir.

L. You are sure of that ? Because, I fear, sorrow in the shoulders would not be worth much.

LUCILLA. I suppose I feel it in my heart, if I really am sorry.

L. If you really are ! Do you mean to say that you are sure you are utterly wicked, and yet do not care ?

LUCILLA. No, indeed ; I have cried about it often.

L. Well, then, you are sorry in your heart ?

LUCILLA. Yes, when the sorrow is worth anything.

L. Even if it be not, it cannot be anywhere else but there. It is not the crystalline lens of your eyes which is sorry, when you cry ?

LUCILLA. No, sir, of course.

L. Then, have you two hearts ; one of which is wicked, and the other grieved ? or is one side of it sorry for the other side ?

LUCILLA (*weary of cross-examination, and a little vexed*). Indeed, sir, you know I can't understand it ; but you know how it is written—' another law in my members warring against the law of my mind.'

L. Yes, Lucilla, I know how it is written ; but I do not see that it will help us to know that, if we neither understand what is written, nor feel it. And you will not get nearer to the meaning of one verse, if, as soon as you are puzzled by it, you escape to another, introducing three new words—' law,' ' members,' and ' mind ' ; not one of which you at present know the meaning of ; and respecting which, you probably never will be much wiser ; since men like Montesquieu and Locke have spent great part of their lives in endeavouring to explain two of them.

LUCILLA. Oh ! please, sir, ask somebody else.

L. If I thought any one else could answer better than you, Lucilla, I would : but suppose I try, instead, myself, to explain your feelings to you ?

LUCILLA. Oh, yes ; please do.

L. Mind, I say your ' feelings,' not your ' belief.' For I cannot undertake to explain anybody's beliefs. Still I must try a little, first, to explain the belief also, because I want to draw it to some issue. As far as I understand what you say, or any one else taught as you have been taught, says, on this matter,—you think that there is an external goodness, a whited-sepulchre kind of goodness, which appears beautiful outwardly, but is within full of uncleanness : a deep secret guilt, of which we ourselves are not sensible ; and which can only be seen by the Maker of us all.  (*Approving murmurs from audience.*)

L.   Is it not so with the body as well as the soul ?
(*Looked notes of interrogation.*)

L.   A skull, for instance, is not a beautiful thing ?
(*Grave faces, signifying ' Certainly not,' and ' What next ? '*)

L.   And if you all could see in each other, with clear eyes, whatever God sees beneath those fair faces of yours, you would not like it ?
(*Murmured ' No's.'*)

L.   Nor would it be good for you ?
(*Silence.*)

L.   The probability being that what God does not allow you to see, He does not wish you to see ; nor even to think of ?
(*Silence prolonged.*)

L.   It would not at all be good for you, for instance, whenever you were washing your faces, and braiding your hair, to be thinking of the shapes of the jawbones, and of the cartilage of the nose, and of the jagged sutures of the scalp ?
(*Resolutely whispered ' No's.'*)

L.   Still less, to see through a clear glass the daily processes of nourishment and decay ?
(*No.*)

L.   Still less if instead of merely inferior and preparatory conditions of structure, as in the skeleton—or inferior offices of structure, as in operations of life and death—there were actual disease in the body ; ghastly and dreadful. You would try to cure it ; but having taken such measures as were necessary, you would not think the cure likely to be promoted by perpetually watching the wounds, or thinking of them.  On the contrary, you would be thankful for every moment of forgetfulness : as, in daily health, you must be thankful that your Maker has veiled whatever is fearful in your frame under a sweet and manifest beauty ; and has made it your duty, and your only safety, to rejoice in that, both in yourself and in others :—not indeed concealing, or refusing to believe in sickness, if it come ; but never dwelling on it.

Now, your wisdom and duty touching soul-sickness are just the same. Ascertain clearly what is wrong with you ; and so far as you know any means of mending it, take those means, and have done : when you are examining yourself, never call yourself merely a ' sinner,' that is very cheap abuse ; and utterly useless. You may even get to like it, and be proud of it. But call yourself a liar, a coward, a sluggard, a glutton, or an evil-eyed, jealous wretch, if you indeed find yourself to be in any wise any of these. Take steady means to check yourself in whatever fault you have ascertained, and justly accused yourself of. And as soon as you are in active way of mending, you will be no more inclined to moan over an undefined corruption. For the rest, you will find it less easy to uproot faults, than to choke them by gaining virtues. Do not think of your faults ; still less of others' faults : in every person who comes near you, look for what is good and strong : honour that ; rejoice in it ; and, as you can, try to imitate it : and your faults will drop off, like dead leaves, when their time comes. If, on looking back, your whole life should seem rugged as a palm-tree stem ; still, never mind, so long as it has been growing ; and has its grand green shade of leaves, and weight of honied fruit, at top. And even if you cannot find much good in yourself at last, think that it does not much matter to the universe either what you were, or are ; think how many people are noble, if you cannot be ; and rejoice in *their* nobleness. An immense quantity of modern confession of sin, even when honest, is merely a sickly egotism ; which will rather gloat over its own evil, than lose the centralisation of its interest in itself.

MARY. But then, if we ought to forget ourselves so much, how did the old Greek proverb 'Know thyself' come to be so highly esteemed?

L. My dear, it is the proverb of proverbs;—Apollo's proverb, and the sun's;—but do you think you can know yourself by looking *into* yourself? Never. You can know what you are, only by looking *out* of yourself. Measure your own powers with those of others; compare your own interests with those of others; try to understand what you appear to them, as well as what they appear to you; and judge of yourselves, in all things, relatively and subordinately; not positively: starting always with a wholesome conviction of the probability that there is nothing particular about you. For instance, some of you perhaps think you can write poetry. Dwell on your own feelings and doings; —and you will soon think yourselves Tenth Muses; but forget your own feelings; and try, instead, to understand a line or two of Chaucer or Dante: and you will soon begin to feel yourselves very foolish girls—which is much like the fact.

So, something which befalls you may seem a great misfortune;—you meditate over its effects on you personally; and begin to think that it is a chastisement, or a warning, or a this or that or the other of profound significance; and that all the angels in heaven have left their business for a little while, that they may watch its effects on your mind. But give up this egotistic indulgence of your fancy; examine a little what misfortunes, greater a thousandfold, are happening, every second, to twenty times worthier persons: and your self-consciousness will change into pity and humility; and you will know yourself, so far as to understand that 'there hath nothing taken thee but what is common to man.'

Now, Lucilla, these are the practical conclusions which

any person of sense would arrive at, supposing the texts which relate to the inner evil of the heart were as many, and as prominent, as they are often supposed to be by careless readers. But the way in which common people read their Bibles is just like the way that the old monks thought hedgehogs ate grapes. They rolled themselves (it was said), over and over, where the grapes lay on the ground. What fruit stuck to their spines, they carried off, and ate. So your hedgehoggy readers roll themselves over and over their Bibles, and declare that whatever sticks to their own spines is Scripture ; and that nothing else is. But you can only get the skins of the texts that way. If you want their juice, you must press them in cluster. Now, the clustered texts about the human heart, insist, as a body, not on any inherent corruption in all hearts, but on the terrific distinction between the bad and the good ones. ' A good man, out of the good treasure of his heart, bringeth forth that which is good ; and an evil man, out of the evil treasure, bringeth forth that which is evil.' ' They on the rock are they which, in an honest and good heart, having heard the word, keep it.' ' Delight thyself in the Lord, and He shall give thee the desires of thine heart.' ' The wicked have bent their bow, that they may privily shoot at him that is upright in heart.' And so on ; they are countless, to the same effect. And, for all of us, the question is not at all to ascertain how much or how little corruption there is in human nature ; but to ascertain whether, out of all the mass of that nature, we are of the sheep or the goat breed ; whether we are people of upright heart, being shot at, or people of crooked heart, shooting. And, of all the texts bearing on the subject, this, which is a quite simple and practical order, is the one you have chiefly to hold in mind. ' Keep thy heart with all diligence, for out of it are the issues of life.'

LUCILLA. And yet, how inconsistent the texts seem !

L. Nonsense, Lucilla ! do you think the universe is

bound to look consistent to a girl of fifteen ?   Look up at your own room window ;—you can just see it from where you sit.   I'm glad that it is left open, as it ought to be, in so fine a day.   But do you see what a black spot it looks, in the sun-lighted wall ?

LUCILLA.   Yes, it looks as black as ink.

L.   Yet you know it is a very bright room when you are inside of it ; quite as bright as there is any occasion for it to be, that its little lady may see to keep it tidy.   Well, it is very probable, also, that if you could look into your heart from the sun's point of view, it might appear a very black hole to you indeed : nay, the sun may sometimes think good to tell you that it looks so to Him ; but He will come into it, and make it very cheerful for you, for all that, if you don't put the shutters up.   And the one question for *you*, remember, is not ' dark or light ? ' but ' tidy or untidy ? '   Look well to your sweeping and garnishing ; and be sure it is only the banished spirit, or some of the seven wickeder ones at his back, who will still whisper to you that it is all black.

# CRYSTAL QUARRELS

# LECTURE VI

## CRYSTAL QUARRELS

*Full conclave, in Schoolroom. There has been a game at crystallization in the morning, of which various account has to be rendered. In particular, everybody has to explain why they were always where they were not intended to be*

L. (*having received and considered the report*). You have got on pretty well, children : but you know these were easy figures you have been trying. Wait till I have drawn you out the plans of some crystals of snow !

MARY. I don't think those will be the most difficult :— they are so beautiful that we shall remember our places better ; and then they are all regular, and in stars : it is those twisty oblique ones we are afraid of.

L. Read Carlyle's account of the Battle of Leuthen, and learn Friedrich's ' oblique order.' You will ' get it done for once, I think, provided you *can* march as a pair of compasses would.' But remember, when you can construct the most difficult single figures, you have only learned half the game—nothing so much as the half, indeed, as the crystals themselves play it.

MARY. Indeed ; what else is there ?

L. It is seldom that any mineral crystallizes alone. Usually two or three, under quite different crystalline laws, form together. They do this absolutely without flaw or fault, when they are in fine temper : and observe what this signifies. It signifies that the two, or more, minerals of different natures agree, somehow, between themselves, how much space each will want ;—agree

which of them shall give way to the other at their junction ;
or in what measure each will accommodate itself to the
other's shape ! And then each takes its permitted shape,
and allotted share of space ; yielding, or being yielded to,
as it builds, till each crystal has fitted itself perfectly and
gracefully to its differently-natured neighbour. So that,
in order to practise this, in even the simplest terms, you
must divide into two parties, wearing different colours ;
each must choose a different figure to construct ; and you
must form one of these figures through the other, both
going on at the same time.

MARY. I think *we* may, perhaps, manage it ; but I
cannot at all understand how the crystals do. It seems to
imply so much preconcerting of plan, and so much giving
way to each other, as if they really were living.

L. Yes, it implies both concurrence and compromise,
regulating all wilfulness of design : and, more curiously
still, the crystals do *not* always give way to each other.
They show exactly the same varieties of temper that
human creatures might. Sometimes they yield the required place with perfect grace and courtesy ; forming
fantastic, but exquisitely finished, groups : and sometimes
they will not yield at all ; but fight furiously for their
places, losing all shape and honour, and even their own
likeness, in the contest.

MARY. But is not that wholly wonderful ? How is it
that one never sees it spoken of in books ?

L. The scientific men are all busy in determining the
constant laws under which the struggle takes place ; these
indefinite humours of the elements are of no interest to
them. And unscientific people rarely give themselves the
trouble of thinking at all, when they look at stones. Not
that it is of much use to think ; the more one thinks, the
more one is puzzled.

MARY. Surely it is more wonderful than anything in
botany ?

L. Everything has its own wonders ; but, given the nature of the plant, it is easier to understand what a flower will do, and why it does it, than, given anything we as yet know of stone-nature, to understand what a crystal will do, and why it does it. You at once admit a kind of volition and choice, in the flower ; but we are not accustomed to attribute anything of the kind to the crystal. Yet there is, in reality, more likeness to some conditions of human feeling among stones than among plants. There is a far greater difference between kindly-tempered and ill-tempered crystals of the same mineral, than between any two specimens of the same flower : and the friendships and wars of crystals depend more definitely and curiously on their varieties of disposition, than any associations of flowers. Here, for instance, is a good garnet, living with good mica ; one rich red, and the other silver white : the mica leaves exactly room enough for the garnet to crystallize comfortably in ; and the garnet lives happily in its little white house ; fitted to it, like a pholas in its cell. But here are wicked garnets living with wicked mica. See what ruin they make of each other ! You cannot tell which is which ; the garnets look like dull red stains on the crumbling stone. By the way, I never could understand, if St. Gothard is a real saint, why he can't keep his garnets in better order. These are all under his care ; but I suppose there are too many of them for him to look after. The streets of Airolo are paved with them.

MAY. Paved with garnets ?

L. With mica-slate and garnets ; I broke this bit out of a paving stone. Now garnets and mica are natural friends, and generally fond of each other ; but you see how they quarrel when they are ill brought up. So it is always. Good crystals are friendly with almost all other good crystals, however little they chance to see of each other, or however opposite their habits may be ; while wicked crystals quarrel with one another, though they may be exactly alike in habits, and see each other continually. And of course the wicked crystals quarrel with the good ones.

ISABEL. Then do the good ones get angry?

L. No, never: they attend to their own work and life; and live it as well as they can, though they are always the sufferers. Here, for instance, is a rock-crystal of the purest race and finest temper, who was born, unhappily for him, in a bad neighbourhood, near Beaufort in Savoy; and he has had to fight with vile calcareous mud all his life. See here, when he was but a child, it came down on him, and nearly buried him; a weaker crystal would have died in despair; but he only gathered himself together, like Hercules against the serpents, and threw a layer of crystal over the clay; conquered it—imprisoned it—and lived on. Then, when he was a little older, came more clay; and poured itself upon him here, at the side; and he has laid crystal over that, and lived on, in his purity. Then the clay came on at his angles, and tried to cover them, and round them away; but upon that he threw out buttress-crystals at his angles, all as true to his own central line as chapels round a cathedral apse; and clustered them round the clay; and conquered it again. At last the clay came on at his summit, and tried to blunt his summit; but he could not endure that for an instant; and left his flanks all rough, but pure; and fought the clay at his crest, and built crest over crest, and peak over peak, till the clay surrendered at last: and here is his summit, smooth and pure, terminating a pyramid of alternate clay and crystal, half a foot high!

LILY. Oh, how nice of him! What a dear, brave crystal! But I can't bear to see his flanks all broken, and the clay within them.

L. Yes; it was an evil chance for him, the being born to such contention; there are some enemies so base that even to hold them captive is a kind of dishonour. But look, here has been quite a different kind of struggle : the adverse power has been more orderly, and has fought the pure crystal in ranks as firm as its own.  This is not mere rage and impediment of crowded evil : here is a disciplined hostility ;  army against army.

LILY.  Oh, but this is much more beautiful !

L.  Yes, for both the elements have true virtue in them ; it is a pity they are at war, but they war grandly.

MARY.  But is this the same clay as in the other crystal ?

L.  I used the word clay for shortness.  In both, the enemy is really limestone ; but in the first, disordered, and mixed with true clay ; while, here, it is nearly pure, and crystallizes into its own primitive form, the oblique six-sided one, which you know : and out of these it makes regiments ;  and then squares of the regiments, and so charges the rock crystal, literally in square against column.

ISABEL.  Please, please, let me see.  And what does the rock crystal do ?

L.  The rock crystal seems able to do nothing.  The calcite cuts it through at every charge.  Look here,—and here !  The loveliest crystal in the whole group is hewn fairly into two pieces.

ISABEL.  Oh, dear ; but is the calcite harder than the crystal then ?

L.  No, softer.  Very much softer.

MARY.  But then, how can it possibly cut the crystal ?

L.  It did not really cut it, though it passes through it. The two were formed together, as I told you ; but no one knows how.  Still, it is strange that this hard quartz has in all cases a good-natured way with it, of yielding to every-thing else.  All sorts of soft things make nests for them-selves in it ;  and it never makes a nest for itself in any-thing.  It has all the rough outside work ; and every sort of cowardly and weak mineral can shelter itself within it. Look ; these are hexagonal plates of mica ; if they were outside of this crystal they would break, like burnt paper ;

but they are inside of it—nothing can hurt them—the crystal has taken them into its very heart, keeping all their delicate edges as sharp as if they were under water, instead of bathed in rock. Here is a piece of branched silver : you can bend it with a touch of your finger, but the stamp of its fibre is on the rock in which it lay, as if the quartz had been as soft as wool.

LILY.   Oh, the good, good quartz ! But does it never get inside of anything ?

L.   As it is a little Irish girl who asks, I may perhaps answer, without being laughed at, that it gets inside of itself sometimes. But I don't remember seeing quartz make a nest for itself in anything else.

ISABEL.   Please, there was something I heard you talking about, last term, with Miss Mary.   I was at my lessons, but I heard something about nests ; and I thought it was birds' nests ; and I couldn't help listening ; and then, I remember, it was about 'nests of quartz in granite.' I remember, because I was so disappointed !

L.   Yes, mousie, you remember quite rightly ; but I can't tell you about those nests to-day, nor perhaps to-morrow : but there's no contradiction between my saying then, and now ; I will show you that there is not, some day.   Will you trust me meanwhile ?

ISABEL.   Won't I !

L.   Well, then, look, lastly, at this piece of courtesy in quartz ; it is on a small scale, but wonderfully pretty. Here is nobly born quartz living with a green mineral, called epidote ; and they are immense friends.   Now, you see, a comparatively large and strong quartz-crystal, and a very weak and slender little one of epidote, have begun to grow, close by each other, and sloping unluckily towards each other, so that at last they meet.   They cannot go on growing together ; the quartz crystal is five times as thick, and more than twenty times as strong,* as the epidote ; but

* Quartz is not much harder than epidote ; the strength is only

he stops at once, just in the very crowning moment of his life, when he is building his own summit ! He lets the pale little film of epidote grow right past him ; stopping his own summit for it ; and he never himself grows any more.

LILY (*after some silence of wonder*). But is the quartz *never* wicked then ?

L. Yes, but the wickedest quartz seems good-natured, compared to other things. Here are two very characteristic examples ; one is good quartz, living with good pearlspar, and the other, wicked quartz, living with wicked pearlspar. In both, the quartz yields to the soft carbonate of iron : but, in the first piece, the iron takes only what it needs of room ; and is inserted into the planes of the rock crystal with such precision, that you must break it away before you can tell whether it really penetrates the quartz or not ; while the crystals of iron are perfectly formed, and have a lovely bloom on their surface besides. But here, when the two minerals quarrel, the unhappy quartz has all its surfaces jagged and torn to pieces ; and there is not a single iron crystal whose shape you can completely trace. But the quartz has the worst of it, in both instances.

VIOLET. Might we look at that piece of broken quartz again, with the weak little film across it ? it seems such a strange lovely thing, like the self-sacrifice of a human being.

L. The self-sacrifice of a human being is not a lovely thing, Violet. It is often a necessary and noble thing ; but no form nor degree of suicide can be ever lovely.

VIOLET. But self-sacrifice is not suicide !

L. What is it then ?

VIOLET. Giving up one's self for another.

L. Well ; and what do you mean by ' giving up one's self ' ?

supposed to be in some proportion to the squares of the diameters.

VIOLET. Giving up one's tastes, one's feelings, one's time, one's happiness, and so on, to make others happy.

L. I hope you will never marry anybody, Violet, who expects you to make him happy in that way.

VIOLET (*hesitating*). In what way?

L. By giving up your tastes, and sacrificing your feelings, and happiness.

VIOLET. No, no, I don't mean that; but you know, for other people, one must.

L. For people who don't love you, and whom you know nothing about? Be it so; but how does this ' giving up ' differ from suicide then?

VIOLET. Why, giving up one's pleasures is not killing one's self?

L. Giving up wrong pleasure is not; neither is it self-sacrifice, but self-culture. But giving up right pleasure is. If you surrender the pleasure of walking, your foot will wither; you may as well cut it off; if you surrender the pleasure of seeing, your eyes will soon be unable to bear the light; you may as well pluck them out. And to maim yourself is partly to kill yourself. Do but go on maiming, and you will soon slay.

VIOLET. But why do you make me think of that verse then, about the foot and the eye?

L. You are indeed commanded to cut off and to pluck out, if foot or eye offend you; but why *should* they offend you?

VIOLET. I don't know; I never quite understood that.

L. Yet it is a sharp order; one needing to be well understood if it is to be well obeyed! When Helen sprained her ankle the other day, you saw how strongly it had to be bandaged; that is to say, prevented from all work, to recover it. But the bandage was not ' lovely.'

VIOLET. No, indeed.

L. And if her foot had been crushed, or diseased, or snake-bitten, instead of sprained, it might have been needful to cut it off. But the amputation would not have been ' lovely.'

VIOLET. No.

L. Well, if eye and foot are dead already, and betray you ;—if the light that is in you be darkness, and your feet run into mischief, or are taken in the snare,—it is indeed time to pluck out, and cut off, I think : but, so crippled, you can never be what you might have been otherwise. You enter into life, at best, halt or maimed ; and the sacrifice is not beautiful, though necessary.

VIOLET (*after a pause*). But when one sacrifices one's self for others ?

L. Why not rather others for you ?

VIOLET. Oh ! but I couldn't bear that.

L. Then why should they bear it ?

DORA (*bursting in, indignant*). And Thermopylæ, and Protesilaus, and Marcus Curtius, and Arnold de Winkelried, and Iphigenia, and Jephthah's daughter ?

L. (*sustaining the indignation unmoved*). And the Samaritan woman's son ?

DORA. Which Samaritan woman's ?

L. Read 2 *Kings* vi. 29.

DORA (*obeys*). How horrid ! As if we meant anything like that !

L. You don't seem to me to know in the least what you do mean, children. What practical difference is there between ' that,' and what you are talking about ? The Samaritan children had no voice of their own in the business, it is true ; but neither had Iphigenia : the Greek girl was certainly neither boiled, nor eaten ; but that only makes a difference in the dramatic effect ; not in the principle.

DORA (*biting her lip*). Well, then, tell us what we ought to mean. As if you didn't teach it all to us, and mean it yourself, at this moment, more than we do, if you wouldn't be tiresome !

L. I mean, and always have meant, simply this, Dora ;

—that the will of God respecting us is that we shall live by
each other's happiness, and life ; not by each other's
misery, or death.   I made you read that verse which so
shocked you just now, because the relations of parent and
child are typical of all beautiful human help.   A child
may have to die for its parents ; but the purpose of Heaven
is that it shall rather live for them ;—that, not by its sacrifice, but by its strength, its joy, its force of being, it shall
be to them renewal of strength ; and as the arrow in the
hand of the giant.   So it is in all other right relations.   Men
help each other by their joy, not by their sorrow.   They
are not intended to slay themselves for each other, but to
strengthen themselves for each other.   And among the
many apparently beautiful things which turn, through mis-
taken use, to utter evil, I am not sure but that the thought-
lessly meek and self-sacrificing spirit of good men must be
named as one of the fatallest.   They have so often been
taught that there is a virtue in mere suffering, as such ; and
foolishly to hope that good may be brought by Heaven
out of all on which Heaven itself has set the stamp of evil,
that we may avoid it—that they accept pain and defeat
as if these were their appointed portion ; never understanding that their defeat is not the less to be mourned
because it is more fatal to their enemies than to them.   The
one thing that a good man has to do, and to see done, is
justice ; he is neither to slay himself nor others causelessly :
so far from denying himself, since he is pleased by good,
he is to do his utmost to get his pleasure accomplished.
And I only wish there were strength, fidelity, and sense
enough, among the good Englishmen of this day, to render
it possible for them to band together in a vowed brotherhood, to enforce, by strength of heart and hand, the doing
of human justice among all who came within their sphere.
And finally, for your own teaching, observe, although there
may be need for much self-sacrifice and self-denial in the
correction of faults of character, the moment the character

is formed, the self-denial ceases. Nothing is really well done, which it costs you pain to do.

VIOLET. But surely, sir, you are always pleased with us when we try to please others, and not ourselves ?

L. My dear child, in the daily course and discipline of right life, we must continually and reciprocally submit and surrender in all kind and courteous and affectionate ways : and the submissions and ministries to each other, of which you all know (none better) the practice and the preciousness, are as good for the yielder as the receiver : they strengthen and perfect as much as they soften and refine. But the real sacrifice of all our strength, or life, or happiness to others (though it may be needed, and though all brave creatures hold their lives in their hand, to be given when such need comes, as frankly as a soldier gives his life in battle), is yet always a mournful and momentary necessity ; not the fulfilment of the continuous law of being. Self-sacrifice which is sought after, and triumphed in, is usually foolish ; and calamitous in its issue : and by the sentimental proclamation and pursuit of it, good people have not only made most of their own lives useless, but the whole framework of their religion so hollow, that at this moment, while the English nation, with its lips, pretends to teach every man to ' love his neighbour as himself,' with its hands and feet it clutches and tramples like a wild beast ; and practically lives, every soul of it that can, on other people's labour. Briefly, the constant duty of every man to his fellows is to ascertain his own powers and special gifts ; and to strengthen them for the help of others. Do you think Titian would have helped the world better by denying himself, and not painting ; or Casella by denying himself, and not singing ? The real virtue is to be ready to sing the moment people ask us ; as he was, even in purgatory. The very word ' virtue ' means not ' conduct ' but 'strength,' vital energy in the heart. Were not you reading about that group of words beginning with V—vital, virtuous, vigorous, and so on—in Max Müller, the other day, Sibyl ? Can't you tell the others about it ?

SIBYL. No, I can't ; will you tell us, please ?

L. Not now, it is too late. Come to me some idle time to-morrow, and I'll tell you about it, if all's well. But the gist of it is, children, that you should at least know two Latin words ; recollect that ' mors ' means death and delaying ; and ' vita ' means life, and growing : and try always, not to mortify yourselves, but to vivify yourselves.

VIOLET. But, then, are we not to mortify our earthly affections ? and surely we are to sacrifice ourselves, at least in God's service, it not in man's ?

L. Really, Violet, we are getting too serious. I've given you enough ethics for one talk, I think ! Do let us have a little play. Lily, what were you so busy about, at the ant-hill in the wood, this morning ?

LILY. Oh, it was the ants who were busy, not I ; I was only trying to help them a little.

L. And they wouldn't be helped, I suppose ?

LILY. No, indeed. I can't think why ants are always so tiresome, when one tries to help them ! They were carrying bits of stick, as fast as they could, through a piece of grass ; and pulling and pushing, so hard ; and tumbling over and over,—it made one quite pity them ; so I took some of the bits of stick and carried them forward a little, where I thought they wanted to put them ; but instead of being pleased, they left them directly, and ran about looking quite angry and frightened ; and at last ever so many of them got up my sleeves, and bit me all over, and I had to come away.

L. I couldn't think what you were about. I saw your French grammar lying on the grass behind you, and thought perhaps you had gone to ask the ants to hear you a French verb.

ISABEL. Ah ! but you didn't, though !

L. Why not, Isabel ? I knew, well enough, Lily couldn't learn that verb by herself.

ISABEL. No ; but the ants couldn't help her.

L. Are you sure the ants could not have helped you, Lily ?

LILY (*thinking*). I ought to have learned something from them, perhaps.

L. But none of them left their sticks to help you through the irregular verb ?

LILY. No, indeed. (*Laughing, with some others.*)

L. What are you laughing at, children ? I cannot see why the ants should not have left their tasks to help Lily in hers. Since here is Violet thinking she ought to leave *her* tasks, to help God in His. Perhaps, however, she takes Lily's more modest view, and thinks only that ' He ought to learn something from her.'

(*Tears in* VIOLET'S *eyes.*)

DORA (*scarlet*). It's too bad—it's a shame :—poor Violet !

L. My dear children, there's no reason why one should be so red, and the other so pale, merely because you are made for a moment to feel the absurdity of a phrase which you have been taught to use, in common with half the religious world. There is but one way in which man can ever help God—that is, by letting God help him : and there is no way in which His name is more guiltily taken in vain, than by calling the abandonment of our own work, the performance of His.

God is a kind Father. He sets us all in the places where He wishes us to be employed ; and that employment is truly ' our Father's business.' He chooses work for every creature which will be delightful to them, if they do it simply and humbly. He gives us always strength enough, and sense enough, for what He wants us to do ; if we either tire ourselves or puzzle ourselves, it is our own fault. And we may always be sure, whatever we are doing, that we cannot be pleasing Him if we are not happy ourselves. Now, away with you, children ; and be as happy as you can. And when you cannot, at least don't plume yourselves upon pouting.

# HOME VIRTUES

LECTURE VII

# LECTURE VII

## HOME VIRTUES

*By the fireside, in the Drawing-room.   Evening*

DORA.  Now, the curtains are drawn, and the fire's bright, and here's your armchair—and you're to tell us all about what you promised.

L.  All about what ?

DORA.  All about virtue.

KATHLEEN.  Yes, and about the words that begin with V.

L.  I heard you singing about a word that begins with V, in the playground, this morning, Miss Katie.

KATHLEEN.  Me singing !

MAY.  Oh tell us—tell us.

L.  ' Vilikens and his——'

KATHLEEN (*stopping his mouth*).  Oh !  please don't. Where were you ?

ISABEL.  I'm sure I wish I had known where he was ! We lost him among the rhododendrons, and I don't know where he got to ;  oh, you naughty—naughty—(*climbs on his knee*).

DORA.  Now, Isabel, we really want to talk.

L.  *I* don't.

DORA.  Oh, but you must.   You promised, you know.

L.  Yes, if all was well ;  but all's ill.   I'm tired, and cross ;  and I won't.

DORA.  You're not a bit tired, and you're not crosser than two sticks ;  and we'll make you talk, if you were crosser than six.   Come here, Egypt, and get on the other side of him.

(EGYPT *takes up a commanding position near the hearth brush.*)

DORA (*reviewing her forces*). Now, Lily, come and sit on the rug in front.

(LILY *does as she is bid.*)

L. (*seeing he has no chance against the odds*). Well, well; but I'm really tired. Go and dance a little, first; and let me think.

DORA. No; you mustn't think. You will be wanting to make us think next; that will be tiresome.

L. Well, go and dance first, to get quit of thinking: and then I'll talk as long as you like.

DORA. Oh, but we can't dance to-night. There isn't time; and we want to hear about virtue.

L. Let me see a little of it first. Dancing is the first of girls' virtues.

EGYPT. Indeed! And the second?

L. Dressing.

EGYPT. Now, you needn't say that! I mended that tear the first thing before breakfast this morning.

L. I cannot otherwise express the ethical principle, Egypt; whether you have mended your gown or not.

DORA. Now don't be tiresome. We really must hear about virtue, please; seriously.

L. Well. I'm telling you about it, as fast as I can.

DORA. What! the first of girls' virtues is dancing?

L. More accurately, it is wishing to dance, and not wishing to tease, nor to hear about virtue.

DORA (*to* EGYPT). Isn't he cross?

EGYPT. How many balls must we go to in the season, to be perfectly virtuous?

L. As many as you can without losing your colour. But I did not say you should wish to go to balls. I said you should be always wanting to dance.

EGYPT. So we do; but everybody says it is very wrong.

L. Why, Egypt, I thought—

'There was a lady once,
That would not be a queen—that would she not,
For all the mud in Egypt.'

You were complaining the other day of having to go out
a great deal oftener than you liked.

EGYPT. Yes, so I was; but then, it isn't to dance.
There's no room to dance: it's—(*Pausing to consider what
it is for*).

L. It is only to be seen, I suppose. Well, there's no
harm in that. Girls ought to like to be seen.

DORA (*her eyes flashing*). Now, you don't mean that;
and you're too provoking; and we won't dance again, for
a month.

L. It will answer every purpose of revenge, Dora, if
you only banish me to the library; and dance by yourselves; but I don't think Jessie and Lily will agree to that.
You like me to see you dancing, don't you, Lily?

LILY. Yes, certainly,—when we do it rightly.

L. And besides, Miss Dora, if young ladies really do not
want to be seen, they should take care not to let their eyes
flash when they dislike what people say; and, more than
that, it is all nonsense from beginning to end, about not
wanting to be seen. I don't know any more tiresome
flower in the borders than your especially 'modest' snow-
drop; which one always has to stoop down and take all
sorts of tiresome trouble with, and nearly break its poor
little head off, before you can see it; and then, half of
it is not worth seeing. Girls should be like daisies; nice
and white, with an edge of red, if you look close; making
the ground bright wherever they are; knowing simply and
quietly that they do it, and are meant to do it, and that
it would be very wrong if they didn't do it. Not want to
be seen, indeed! How long were you in doing your back
hair, this afternoon, Jessie?

(JESSIE *not immediately answering*, DORA *comes to her
assistance.*)

DORA.  Not above three-quarters of an hour, I think, Jess ?

JESSIE (*putting her finger up*).  Now, Dorothy, *you* needn't talk, you know !

L.  I know she needn't, Jessie ; I shall ask her about those dark plaits presently. (DORA *looks round to see if there is any way open for retreat.*)  But never mind ; it was worth the time, whatever it was ; and nobody will ever mistake that golden wreath for a chignon : but if you don't want it to be seen, you had better wear a cap.

JESSIE.  Ah, now, are you really going to do nothing but play ?  And we all have been thinking, and thinking, all day ; and hoping you would tell us things ; and now— !

L.  And now I am telling you things, and true things, and things good for you ; and you won't believe me.  You might as well have let me go to sleep at once, as I wanted to. (*Endeavours again to make himself comfortable.*)

ISABEL.  Oh, no, no, you sha'n't go to sleep, you naughty !—Kathleen, come here.

L. (*knowing what he has to expect if* KATHLEEN *comes*). Get away, Isabel, you're too heavy. (*Sitting up.*)  What have I been saying ?

DORA.  I do believe he has been asleep all the time ! You never heard anything like the things you've been saying.

L.  Perhaps not.  If you have heard them, and anything like them, it is all I want.

EGYPT.  Yes, but we don't understand, and you know we don't ; and we want to.

L.  What did I say first ?

DORA.  That the first virtue of girls was wanting to go to balls.

L.  I said nothing of the kind.

JESSIE.  ' Always wanting to dance,' you said.

L.  Yes, and that's true.  Their first virtue is to be intensely happy ;—so happy that they don't know what to do with themselves for happiness,—and dance, instead of walking.  Don't you recollect ' Louisa ' ?

> ' No fountain from a rocky cave
>    E'er tripped with foot so free ;
> She seemed as happy as a wave
>    That dances on the sea.'

A girl is always like that, when everything's right with her.

VIOLET.   But, surely, one must be sad sometimes ?

L.   Yes, Violet ;  and dull sometimes, and stupid sometimes, and cross sometimes.   What must be, must ;  but it is always either our own fault, or somebody else's.   The last and worst thing that can be said of a nation is, that it has made its young girls sad, and weary.

MAY.   But I am sure I have heard a great many good people speak against dancing ?

L.   Yes, May ;  but it does not follow they were wise as well as good.   I suppose they think Jeremiah liked better to have to write Lamentations for his people, than to have to write that promise for them, which everybody seems to hurry past, that they may get on quickly to the verse about Rachel weeping for her children ;  though the verse they pass is the counter blessing to that one :  ' Then shall the virgin rejoice in the dance ;  and both young men and old together ;  and I will turn their mourning into joy.'

   (*The children get very serious, but look at each other, as if pleased.*)

MARY.   They understand now :  but, do you know what you said next ?

L.   Yes ;  I was not more than half asleep.   I said their second virtue was dressing.

MARY.   Well ! what did you mean by that ?

L.   What do *you* mean by dressing ?

MARY.   Wearing fine clothes.

L.   Ah ! there's the mistake.   *I* mean wearing plain ones.

MARY. Yes, I dare say! but that's not what girls understand by dressing, you know.

L. I can't help that. If they understand by dressing, buying dresses, perhaps they also understand by drawing, buying pictures. But when I hear them say they can draw, I understand that they can make a drawing; and when I hear them say they can dress, I understand that they can make a dress; and—which is quite as difficult—wear one.

DORA. I'm not sure about the making, for the wearing, we can all wear them—out, before anybody expects it.

EGYPT (*aside, to* L., *piteously*). Indeed I have mended that torn flounce quite neatly; look if I haven't!

L. (*aside, to* EGYPT). All right; don't be afraid. (*Aloud, to* DORA.) Yes, doubtless; but you know that is only a slow way of undressing.

DORA. Then, we are all to learn dressmaking, are we?

L. Yes; and always to dress yourselves beautifully—not finely, unless on occasion; but then very finely and beautifully too. Also, you are to dress as many other people as you can; and to teach them how to dress, if they don't know; and to consider every ill-dressed woman or child whom you see anywhere, as a personal disgrace; and to get at them, somehow, until everybody is as beautifully dressed as birds.

(*Silence; the children drawing their breaths hard, as if they had come from under a shower bath.*)

L. (*seeing objections begin to express themselves in the eyes.*) Now you needn't say you can't; for you can: and it's what you were meant to do, always; and to dress your houses, and your gardens, too; and to do very little else, I believe, except singing; and dancing, as we said, of course: and—one thing more.

DORA. Our third and last virtue, I suppose?

L. Yes; on Violet's system of triplicities.

Dora. Well, we are prepared for anything now. What is it ?

L. Cooking.

Dora. Cardinal, indeed ! If only Beatrice were here with her seven handmaids, that she might see what a fine eighth we had found for her !

Mary. And the interpretation ? What does ' cooking' mean ?

L. It means the knowledge of Medea, and of Circe, and of Calypso, and of Helen, and of Rebekah and of the Queen of Sheba. It means the knowledge of all herbs, and fruits, and balms, and spices ; and of all that is healing and sweet in fields and groves, and savoury in meats ; it means carefulness, and inventiveness, and watchfulness, and willingness, and readiness of appliance ; it means the economy of your great-grandmothers, and the science of modern chemists ; it means much tasting, and no wasting ; it means English thoroughness, and French art, and Arabian hospitality ; and it means, in fine, that you are to be perfectly and always, ' ladies '—' loaf-givers ' ; and, as you are to see, imperatively, that everybody has something pretty to put on,—so you are to see, yet more imperatively, that everybody has something nice to eat.

(*Another pause, and long-drawn breath.*)

Dora (*slowly recovering herself*) *to* Egypt. We had better have let him go to sleep, I think, after all !

L. You had better let the younger ones go to sleep, now : for I haven't half done.

Isabel (*panic-struck*). Oh ! please, please ! just one quarter of an hour.

L. No, Isabel ; I cannot say what I've got to say, in a quarter of an hour ; and it is too hard for you, besides :— you would be lying awake, and trying to make it out, half the night. That will never do.

Isabel. Oh, please !

L. It would please me exceedingly, mousie : but there

are times when we must both be displeased ; more's the pity.   Lily may stay for half an hour, if she likes.

LILY.   I can't ; because Isey never goes to sleep, if she is waiting for me to come.

ISABEL.   Oh, yes, Lily ; I'll go to sleep to-night, I will, indeed.

LILY.   Yes, it's very likely, Isey, with those fine round eyes !   (*To* L.)   You'll tell me something of what you've been saying, to-morrow, won't you ?

L.   No, I won't, Lily.   You must choose.   It's only in Miss Edgeworth's novels that one can do right, and have one's cake and sugar afterwards, as well (not that I consider the dilemma, to-night, so grave).

(LILY, *sighing, takes* ISABEL'*s hand.*)

Yes, Lily dear, it will be better, in the outcome of it, so, than if you were to hear all the talks that ever were talked, and all the stories that ever were told.   Good night.

(*The door leading to the condemned cells of the Dormitory closes on* LILY, ISABEL, FLORRIE, *and other diminutive and submissive victims.*)

JESSIE (*after a pause*).   Why, I thought you were so fond of Miss Edgeworth !

L.   So I am ; and so you ought all to be.   I can read her over and over again, without ever tiring : there's no one whose every page is so full, and so delightful ; no one who brings you into the company of pleasanter or wiser people ; no one who tells you more truly how to do right. And it is very nice, in the midst of a wild world, to have the very ideal of poetical justice done always to one's hand :—to have everybody found out, who tells lies ; and everybody decorated with a red riband, who doesn't ; and to see the good Laura, who gave away her half sovereign, receiving a grand ovation from an entire dinner party disturbed for the purpose ; and poor, dear, little Rosamond, who chooses purple jars instead of new shoes, left at last without either her shoes or her bottle.   But it

isn't life : and, in the way children might easily understand
it, it isn't morals.

JESSIE.   How do you mean we might understand it ?

L.   You might think Miss Edgeworth meant that the
right was to be done mainly because one was always
rewarded for doing it.   It is an injustice to her to say
that : her heroines always do right simply for its own
sake, as they should ;   and her examples of conduct and
motive are wholly admirable.   But her representation of
events is false and misleading.   Her good characters never
are brought into the deadly trial of goodness—the doing
right, and suffering for it, quite finally.   And that is life,
as God arranges it.   ' Taking up one's cross ' does not at
all mean having ovations at dinner parties, and being
put over everybody else's head.

DORA.   But what *does* it mean then ?   That is just
what we couldn't understand, when you were telling us
about not sacrificing ourselves, yesterday.

L.   My dear, it means simply that you are to go the
road which you see to be the straight one ;   carrying whatever you find is given you to carry, as well and stoutly as
you can ;   without making faces, or calling people to come
and look at you.   Above all, you are neither to load, nor
unload, yourself ;   nor cut your cross to your own liking.
Some people think it would be better for them to have it
large ;   and many, that they could carry it much faster
if it were small ;   and even those who like it largest are
usually very particular about its being ornamental, and
made of the best ebony.   But all that you have really to
do is to keep your back as straight as you can ;   and not
think about what is upon it—above all, not to boast of
what is upon it.   The real and essential meaning of
' virtue ' is in that straightness of back.   Yes ;   you may
laugh, children, but it is.   You know I was to tell you
about the words that began with V.   Sibyl, what does
' virtue ' mean, literally.

SIBYL. Does it mean courage ?

L. Yes ; but a particular kind of courage. It means courage of the nerve ; vital courage. That first syllable of it, if you look in Max Müller, you will find really means 'nerve,' and from it come 'vis,' and 'vir,' and 'virgin' (through vireo), and the connected word 'virga'—'a rod' ;—the green rod, or springing bough of a tree, being the type of perfect human strength, both in the use of it in the Mosaic story, when it becomes a serpent, or strikes the rock ; or when Aaron's bears its almonds ; and in the metaphorical expressions, the 'Rod out of the stem of Jesse,' and the 'Man whose name is the Branch,' and so on. And the essential idea of real virtue is that of a vital human strength, which instinctively, constantly, and without motive, does what is right. You must train men to this by habit, as you would the branch of a tree ; and give them instincts and manners (or morals) of purity, justice, kindness, and courage. Once rightly trained, they act as they should, irrespectively of all motive, of fear, or of reward. It is the blackest sign of putrescence in a national religion, when men speak as if it were the only safeguard of conduct ; and assume that, but for the fear of being burned, or for the hope of being rewarded, everybody would pass their lives in lying, stealing, and murdering. I think quite one of the notablest historical events of this century (perhaps the very notablest), was that council of clergymen, horror-struck at the idea of any diminution in our dread of hell, at which the last of English clergymen whom one would have expected to see in such a function, rose as the 'devil's advocate ; to tell us how impossible it was we could get on without him.

VIOLET (after a pause). But, surely, if people weren't afraid—(hesitates again).

L. They should be afraid of doing wrong, and of that only, my dear. Otherwise, if they only don't do wrong for fear of being punished, they *have* done wrong in their hearts, already.

VIOLET. Well, but surely, at least one ought to be afraid of displeasing God ; and one's desire to please Him should be one's first motive ?

L. He never would be pleased with us, if it were, my dear. When a father sends his son out into the world— suppose as an apprentice—fancy the boy's coming home at night, and saying, ' Father, I could have robbed the till to-day ; but I didn't, because I thought you wouldn't like it.' Do you think the father would be particularly pleased ?

(VIOLET *is silent.*)

He would answer, would he not, if he were wise and good, ' My boy, though you had no father, you must not rob tills ' ? And nothing is ever done so as really to please our Great Father, unless we would also have done it, though we had had no Father to know of it.

VIOLET (*after long pause*). But, then, what continual threatenings, and promises of reward there are !

L. And how vain both ! with the Jews, and with all of us. But the fact is, that the threat and promise are simply statements of the Divine law, and of its consequences. The fact is truly told you,—make what use you may of it : and as collateral warning, or encouragement, or comfort, the knowledge of future consequences may often be helpful to us ; but helpful chiefly to the better state when we can act without reference to them. And there's no measuring the poisoned influence of that notion of future reward on the mind of Christian Europe, in the early ages. Half the monastic system rose out of that, acting on the occult pride and ambition of good people (as the other half of it came of their follies and misfortunes). There is always a considerable quantity of pride, to begin with, in what is called ' giving one's self ' to God. As if one had ever belonged to anybody else !

DORA. But, surely, great good has come out of the monastic system—our books,—our sciences—all saved by the monks ?

L. Saved from what, my dear ? From the abyss of misery and ruin which that false Christianity allowed the whole active world to live in. When it had become the principal amusement, and the most admired art, of Christian men, to cut one another's throats, and burn one another's towns ; of course the few feeble or reasonable persons left, who desired quiet, safety, and kind fellowship, got into cloisters ; and the gentlest, thoughtfullest, noblest men and women shut themselves up, precisely where they could be of least use. They are very fine things, for us painters, now,—the towers and white arches upon the tops of the rocks ; always in places where it takes a day's climbing to get at them : but the intense tragi-comedy of the thing, when one thinks of it, is unspeakable. All the good people of the world getting themselves hung up out of the way of mischief, like Bailie Nicol Jarvie ;—poor little lambs, as it were, dangling there for the sign of the Golden Fleece ; or like Socrates in his basket in the *Clouds* ! (I must read you that bit of Aristophanes again, by the way.) And believe me, children, I am no warped witness, as far as regards monasteries ; or if I am, it is in their favour. I have always had a strong leaning that way ; and have pensively shivered with Augustines at St. Bernard ; and happily made hay with Franciscans at Fesolé ; and sat silent with Carthusians in their little gardens, south of Florence ; and mourned through many a day-dream, at Melrose and Bolton. But the wonder is always to me, not how much, but how little, the monks have, on the whole done, with all that leisure, and all that good-will ! What nonsense monks characteristically wrote ; —what little progress they made in the sciences to which they devoted themselves as a duty,—medicine especially ;— and, last and worst, what depths of degradation they can sometimes see one another, and the population round them, sink into ; without either doubting their system, or reforming it !

(*Seeing questions rising to lips.*) Hold your little tongues, children ; it's very late, and you'll make me forget what I've to say. Fancy yourselves in pews, for five minutes. There's one point of possible good in the conventual system, which is always attractive to young girls ; and the idea is a very dangerous one ;—the notion of a merit, or exalting virtue, consisting in a habit of meditation on the ' things above,' or things of the next world. Now it is quite true, that a person of beautiful mind, dwelling on whatever appears to them most desirable and lovely in a possible future, will not only pass their time pleasantly, but will even acquire, at last, a vague and wildly gentle charm of manner and feature, which will give them an air of peculiar sanctity in the eyes of others. Whatever real or apparent good there may be in this result, I want you to observe, children, that we have no real authority for the reveries to which it is owing. We are told nothing distinctly of the heavenly world ; except that it will be free from sorrow, and pure from sin. What is said of pearl gates, golden floors, and the like, is accepted as merely figurative by religious enthusiasts themselves : and whatever they pass their time in conceiving, whether of the happiness of risen souls, of their intercourse, or of the appearance and employment of the heavenly powers, is entirely the product of their own imagination ; and as completely and distinctly a work of fiction, or romantic invention, as any novel of Sir Walter Scott's. That the romance is founded on religious theory or doctrine ;— that no disagreeable or wicked persons are admitted into the story ;—and that the inventor fervently hopes that some portion of it may hereafter come true, does not in the least alter the real nature of the effort or enjoyment.

Now, whatever indulgence may be granted to amiable

people for pleasing themselves in this innocent way, it is beyond question, that to seclude themselves from the rough duties of life, merely to write religious romances, or, as in most cases, merely to dream them, without taking so much trouble as is implied in writing, ought not to be received as an act of heroic virtue.    But, observe, even in admitting thus much, I have assumed that the fancies are just and beautiful, though fictitious.    Now, what right have any of us to assume that our own fancies will assuredly be either the one or the other ?    That they delight us, and appear lovely to us, is no real proof of its not being wasted time to form them :  and we may surely be led somewhat to distrust our judgment of them by observing what ignoble imaginations have sometimes sufficiently, or even enthusiastically, occupied the hearts of others.    The principal source of the spirit of religious contemplation is the East ; now I have here in my hand a Byzantine image of Christ, which, if you will look at it seriously, may, I think, at once and for ever render you cautious in the indulgence of a merely contemplative habit of mind.    Observe, it is the fashion to look at such a thing only as a piece of barbarous art ;  that is the smallest part of its interest.    What I want you to see, is the baseness and falseness of a religious state of enthusiasm, in which such a work could be dwelt upon with pious pleasure.    That a figure, with two small round black beads for eyes ;  a gilded face, deep cut into horrible wrinkles ;  an open gash for a mouth, and a distorted skeleton for a body, wrapped about, to make it fine, with striped enamel of blue and gold ;—that such a figure, I say, should ever have been thought helpful towards the conception of a Redeeming Deity, may make you, I think, very doubtful, even of the Divine approval —much more of the Divine inspiration—or religious reverie in general.    You feel, doubtless, that your own idea of Christ would be something very different from this ;  but in what does the difference consist ?    Not in any more divine authority in your imagination; but in the intellectual work of six intervening centuries; which, simply, by artistic discipline, has refined this crude conception for you, and filled you, partly with an innate sensation, partly with an acquired knowledge, of higher forms,—which render this Byzantine crucifix as horrible to you, as it was pleasing to its maker. More is required to excite your fancy; but your fancy is of no more authority than his was: and a point of national art-skill is quite conceivable, in which the best we can do now will be as offensive to the religious dreamers of the more highly cultivated time, as this Byzantine crucifix is to you.

MARY. But surely, Angelico will always retain his power over everybody?

L. Yes, I should think, always; as the gentle words of a child will: but you would be much surprised, Mary, if you thoroughly took the pains to analyse, and had the perfect means of analysing, that power of Angelico—to discover its real sources. Of course it is natural, at first, to attribute it to the pure religious fervour by which he was inspired; but do you suppose Angelico was really the only monk, in all the Christian world of the Middle Ages, who laboured in art, with a sincere religious enthusiasm?

MARY. No, certainly not.

L. Anything more frightful, more destructive of all religious faith whatever, than such a supposition, could not be. And yet, what other monk ever produced such work? I have myself examined carefully upwards of two thousand illuminated missals, with especial view to the discovery of any evidence of a similar result upon the art, from the monkish devotion; and utterly in vain.

MARY. But then, was not Fra Angelico a man of entirely separate and exalted genius?

L. Unquestionably; and granting him to be that, the peculiar phenomenon in his art is, to me, not its loveliness, but its weakness. The effect of 'inspiration,' had it been real, on a man of consummate genius, should have been, one would have thought, to make everything that he did faultless and strong, no less than lovely. But of all men, deserving to be called ' great,' Fra Angelico permits to himself the least pardonable faults, and the most palpable follies. There is evidently within him a sense of grace, and power of invention, as great as Ghiberti's :—we are in the habit of attributing those high qualities to his religious enthusiasm ; but, if they were produced by that enthusiasm in him, they ought to be produced by the same feelings in others ; and we see they are not. Whereas, comparing him with contemporary great artists, of equal grace and invention, one peculiar character remains notable in him—which, logically, we ought therefore to attribute to the religious fervour ;—and that distinctive character is, the contented indulgence of his own weaknesses, and perseverance in his own ignorances.

MARY. But that's dreadful ! And what *is* the source of the peculiar charm which we all feel in his work ?

L. There are many sources of it, Mary ; united and seeming like one. You would never feel that charm but in the work of an entirely good man ; be sure of that : but the goodness is only the recipient and modifying element, not the creative one. Consider carefully what delights you in any original picture of Angelico's. You will find, for one minor thing, an exquisite variety and brightness of ornamental work. That is not Angelico's inspiration. It is the final result of the labour and thought of millions of artists, of all nations ; from the earliest Egyptian potters downwards—Greeks, Byzantines, Hindoos, Arabs, Gauls, and Northmen—all joining in the toil ; and con- summating it in Florence, in that century, with such embroidery of robe and inlaying of armour as had never been seen till then ; nor, probably, ever will be seen more. Angelico merely takes his share of this inheritance, and applies it in the tenderest way to subjects which are peculiarly acceptant of it. But the inspiration, if it exist anywhere, flashes on the knight's shield quite as radiantly as on the monk's picture. Examining farther into the sources of your emotion in the Angelico work, you will find much of the impression of sanctity dependent on a singular repose and grace of gesture, consummating itself in the floating, flying, and above all, in the dancing groups. That is not Angelico's inspiration. It is only a peculiarly tender use of systems of grouping which had been long before developed by Giotto, Memmi, and Orcagna ; and the real root of it all is simply—What do you think, children ? The beautiful dancing of the Florentine maidens !

DORA (*indignant again*). Now, I wonder what next ! Why not say it all depended on Herodias' daughter, at once ?

L. Yes ; it is certainly a great argument against singing, that there were once sirens.

DORA. Well, it may be all very fine and philosophical ; but shouldn't I just like to read you the end of the second volume of *Modern Painters* !

L. My dear, do you think any teacher could be worth your listening to, or anybody else's listening to, who had learned nothing, and altered his mind in nothing, from seven and twenty to seven and forty ? But that second volume is very good for you as far as it goes. It is a great advance, and a thoroughly straight and swift one, to be led, as it is the main business of that second volume to lead you, from Dutch cattle-pieces, and ruffian-pieces, to Fra Angelico. And it is right for you also, as you grow older, to be strengthened in the general sense and judgment which may enable you to distinguish the weaknesses from the virtues of what you love : else you might come to love both alike ; or even the weaknesses without the virtues. You might end by liking Overbeck and Cornelius as well as Angelico. However, I have perhaps been leaning a

105—I *

little too much to the merely practical side of things, in to-night's talk ; and you are always to remember, children, that I do not deny, though I cannot affirm, the spiritual advantages resulting, in certain cases, from enthusiastic religious reverie, and from the other practices of saints and anchorites.   The evidence respecting them has never yet been honestly collected, much less dispassionately examined : but assuredly, there is in that direction a probability, and more than a probability, of dangerous error, while there is none whatever in the practice of an active, cheerful, and benevolent life.   The hope of attaining a higher religious position, which induces us to encounter, for its exalted alternative, the risk of unhealthy error, is often, as I said, founded more on pride than piety ; and those who, in modest usefulness, have accepted what seemed to them here the lowliest place in the kingdom of their Father, are not, I believe, the least likely to receive hereafter the command, then unmistakable, ' Friend, go up higher.'

# CRYSTAL  CAPRICE

# LECTURE VIII

## CRYSTAL CAPRICE

*Formal Lecture in Schoolroom, after some practical examination of minerals*

L.  We have seen enough, children, though very little of what might be seen if we had more time, of mineral structures produced by visible opposition, or contest among elements ;  structures of which the variety, however great, need not surprise us :  for we quarrel, ourselves, for many and slight causes ;—much more, one should think, may crystals, who can only feel the antagonism, not argue about it.   But there is a yet more singular mimicry of our human ways in the varieties of form which appear owing to no antagonistic force ;  but merely to the variable humour and caprice of the crystals themselves :  and I have asked you all to come into the schoolroom to-day, because, of course, this is a part of the crystal mind which must be peculiarly interesting to a feminine audience.  (*Great symptoms of disapproval on the part of said audience.*)  Now, you need not pretend that it will not interest you ;  why should it not ?   It is true that we men are never capricious ; but that only makes us the more dull and disagreeable. You, who are crystalline in brightness, as well as in caprice, charm infinitely, by infinitude of change.  (*Audible murmurs of ' Worse and worse ! '   ' As if we could be got over that way ! '   etc.   The* LECTURER, *however, observing the expression of the features to be more complacent, proceeds.*) And the most curious mimicry, if not of your changes of fashion, at least of your various modes (in healthy periods) of national costume, takes place among the crystals of different countries. With a little experience, it is quite possible to say at a glance, in what districts certain crystals have been found ; and although, if we had knowledge extended and accurate enough, we might of course ascertain the law and circumstances which have necessarily produced the form peculiar to each locality, this would be just as true of the fancies of the human mind. If we could know the exact circumstances which affect it, we could foretell what now seems to us only caprice of thought, as well as what now seems to us only caprice of crystal : nay, so far as our knowledge reaches, it is on the whole easier to find some reason why the peasant girls of Berne should wear their caps in the shape of butterflies ; and the peasant girls of Munich theirs in the shape of shells, than to say why the rock-crystals of Dauphiné should all have their summits of the shape of lip-pieces of flageolets, while those of St. Gothard are symmetrical ; or why the fluor of Chamouni is rose-coloured, and in octahedrons, while the fluor of Weardale is green, and in cubes. Still farther removed is the hope, at present, of accounting for minor differences in modes of grouping and construction. Take, for instance, the caprices of this single mineral, quartz ;—variations upon a single theme. It has many forms ; but see what it will make out of this *one*, the six-sided prism. For shortness' sake, I shall call the body of the prism its ' column,' and the pyramid at the extremities its ' cap.' Now, here, first you have a straight column, as long and thin as a stalk of asparagus, with two little caps at the ends ; and here you have a short thick column, as solid as a haystack, with two fat caps at the ends ; and here you have two caps fastened together, and no column at all between them ! Then here is a crystal with its column fat in the middle, and tapering to a little cap ; and here is one stalked like a mushroom, with a huge cap put on the top of a slender column ! Then here is a column built wholly out of little caps, with a large smooth cap at the top. And here is a column built of columns and caps ; the caps all truncated about half way to their points. And in both these last the little crystals are set anyhow, and build the large one in a disorderly way; but here is a crystal made of columns and truncated caps, set in regular terraces all the way up.

MARY. But are not these, groups of crystals, rather than one crystal ?

L. What do you mean by a group, and what by one crystal ?

DORA (*audibly aside, to* MARY, *who is brought to pause*). You know you are never expected to answer, Mary.

L. I'm sure this is easy enough. What do you mean by a group of people ?

MARY. Three or four together, or a good many together, 'ike the caps in these crystals.

L. But when a great many persons get together they don't take the shape of one person ?

(MARY *still at pause.*)

ISABEL. No, because they can't ; but, you know the crystals can ; so why shouldn't they ?

L. Well, they don't ; that is to say, they don't always, nor even often. Look here, Isabel.

ISABEL. What a nasty ugly thing !

L. I'm glad you think it so ugly. Yet it is made of beautiful crystals ; they are a little grey and cold in colour, but most of them are clear.

ISABEL. But they're in such horrid, horrid disorder !

L. Yes ; all disorder is horrid, when it is among things that are naturally orderly. Some little girls' rooms are naturally *dis*-orderly, I suppose ; or I don't know how they could live in them, if they cry out so when they only see quartz crystals in confusion.

ISABEL. Oh ! but how come they to be like that ?

L. You may well ask. And yet you will always hear people talking as if they thought order more wonderful than disorder ! It *is* wonderful—as we have seen ; but to me,

as to you, child, the supremely wonderful thing is that
nature should ever be ruinous or wasteful, or deathful!   I
look at this wild piece of crystallization with endless
astonishment.

MARY.   Where does it come from ?

L.   The Tête Noire of Chamonix.   What makes it more
strange is that it should be in a vein of fine quartz rock.   If
if were in a mouldering rock, it would be natural enough ;
but in the midst of so fine substance, here are the crystals
tossed in a heap ;  some large, myriads small (almost as
small as dust), tumbling over each other like a terrified
crowd, and glued together by the sides, and edges, and backs,
and heads ;  some warped, and some pushed out and in, and
all spoiled, and each spoiling the rest.

MARY.   And how flat they all are !

L.   Yes ;  that's the fashion at the Tête Noire.

MARY.   But surely this is ruin, not caprice ?

L.   I believe it is in great part misfortune ;  and we will
examine these crystal troubles in next lecture.   But if you
want to see the gracefullest and happiest caprices of which
dust is capable, you must go to the Hartz ;  not that I ever
mean to go there myself, for I want to retain the romantic
feeling about the name ;  and I have done myself some
harm already by seeing the monotonous and heavy form
of the Brocken from the suburbs of Brunswick.   But
whether the mountains be picturesque or not, the tricks
which the goblins (as I am told) teach the crystals in them,
are incomparably pretty.   They work chiefly on the mind
of a docile, bluish-coloured, carbonate of lime ;  which comes
out of a grey limestone.   The goblins take the greatest
possible care of its education, and see that nothing happens
to it to hurt its temper :  and when it may be supposed to
have arrived at the crisis which is, to a well brought up
mineral, what presentation at court is to a young lady—
after which it is expected to set fashions—there's no end
to its pretty ways of behaving.   First it will make itself

into pointed darts as fine as hoar-frost ; here it is changed
into a white fur as fine as silk ; here into little crowns and
circlets, as bright as silver ; as if for the gnome princesses
to wear ; here it is in beautiful little plates, for them to eat
off ; presently it is in towers, which they might be imprisoned in ; presently in caves and cells, where they may
make nun-gnomes of themselves, and no gnome ever hear
of them more ; here is some of it in sheaves, like corn ; here,
some in drifts, like snow ; here, some in rays, like stars :
and, though these are, all of them, necessarily, shapes that
the mineral takes in other places, they are all taken here
with such a grace that you recognise the high caste and
breeding of the crystals wherever you meet them ; and
know at once they are Hartz-born.

Of course, such fine things are these are only done by
crystals which are perfectly good, and good-humoured ;
and of course, also, there are ill-humoured crystals who
torment each other, and annoy quieter crystals, yet without
coming to anything like serious war. Here (for once) is
some ill-disposed quartz, tormenting a peaceable octahedron
of fluor, in mere caprice. I looked at it the other night so
long, and so wonderingly, just before putting my candle
out, that I fell into another strange dream. But you don't
care about dreams.

DORA. No ; we didn't, yesterday ; but you know we
are made up of caprice ; so we do, to-day : and you must
tell it us directly.

L. Well, you see, Neith and her work were still much
in my mind ; and then, I had been looking over these
Hartz things for you, and thinking of the sort of grotesque
sympathy there seemed to be in them with the beautiful
fringe and pinnacle work of Northern architecture. So,
when I fell asleep, I thought I saw Neith and St. Barbara
talking together.

DORA. But what had St. Barbara to do with it ? *

* See Note V.

L.  My dear, I am quite sure St. Barbara is the patroness of good architects : not St. Thomas, whatever the old builders thought.  It might be very fine, according to the monks' notions, in St. Thomas, to give all his employer's money away to the poor : but breaches of contract are bad foundations ; and I believe, it was not he, but St. Barbara, who overlooked the work in all the buildings you and I care about.  However that may be, it was certainly she whom I saw in my dream with Neith.  Neith was sitting weaving, and I thought she looked sad, and threw her shuttle slowly ; and St. Barbara was standing at her side, in a stiff little gown, all ins and outs, and angles ; but so bright with embroidery that it dazzled me whenever she moved ; the train of it was just like a heap of broken jewels, it was so stiff, and full of corners, and so many-coloured, and bright.  Her hair fell over her shoulders in long, delicate waves, from under a little three-pinnacled crown, like a tower.  She was asking Neith about the laws of architecture in Egypt and Greece ; and when Neith told her the measures of the pyramids, St. Barbara said she thought they would have been better three-cornered : and when Neith told her the measures of the Parthenon, St. Barbara said she thought it ought to have had two transepts.  But she was pleased when Neith told her of the temple of the dew, and of the Caryan maidens bearing its frieze : and then she thought that perhaps Neith would like to hear what sort of temples she was building herself, in the French valleys, and on the crags of the Rhine.  So she began gossiping, just as one of you might to an old lady : and certainly she talked in the sweetest way in the world to Neith ; and explained to her all about crockets and pinnacles : and Neith sat, looking very grave ; and always graver as St. Barbara went on ; till at last, I'm sorry to say, St. Barbara lost her temper a little.

MAY (*very grave herself*).  ' St. Barbara ? '

L.  Yes, May.  Why shouldn't she ?  It was very tiresome of Neith to sit looking like that.

MAY. But, then, St. Barbara was a saint !

L. What's that, May ?

MAY. A saint ! A saint is—I'm sure you know !

L. If I did, it would not make me sure that you knew too, May : but I don't.

VIOLET (*expressing the incredulity of the audience*). Oh—sir ?

L. That is to say, I know that people are called saints who are supposed to be better than others : but I don't know how much better they must be, in order to be saints ; nor how nearly anybody may be a saint, and yet not be quite one ; nor whether everybody who is called a saint was one ; nor whether everybody who isn't called a saint, isn't one.

(*General silence ; the audience feeling themselves on the verge of the Infinities—and a little shocked—and much puzzled by so many questions at once.*)

L. Besides, did you never hear that verse about being ' called to be saints ' ?

MAY (*repeats Rom.* i. 7).

L. Quite right, May. Well, then, who are called to be that ? People in Rome only ?

MAY. Everybody, I suppose, whom God loves.

L. What ! little girls as well as other people ?

MAY. All grown-up people, I mean.

L. Why not little girls ? Are they wickeder when they are little ?

MAY. Oh, I hope not.

L. Why not little girls, then ?

(*Pause.*)

LILY. Because, you know, we can't be worth anything if we're ever so good ;—I mean, if we try to be ever so good ; and we can't do difficult things—like saints.

L. I am afraid, my dear, that old people are not more able or willing for their difficulties than you children are for yours. All I can say is, that if ever I see any of you, when you are seven or eight and twenty, knitting your brows over any work you want to do or to understand, as I saw you, Lily, knitting your brows over your slate this morning, I should think you very noble women. But—to come back to my dream—St. Barbara *did* lose her temper a little ; and I was not surprised. For you can't think how provoking Neith looked, sitting there just like a statue of sandstone ; only going on weaving, like a machine ; and never quickening the cast of her shuttle ; while St. Barbara was telling her so eagerly all about the most beautiful things, and chattering away, as fast as bells ring on Christmas Eve, till she saw that Neith didn't care ; and then St. Barbara got as red as a rose, and stopped, just in time ;—or I think she would really have said something naughty.

ISABEL. Oh, please, but didn't Neith say anything then ?

L. Yes. She said, quite quietly, ' It may be very pretty, my love ; but it is all nonsense.'

ISABEL. Oh dear, oh dear ; and then ?

L. Well ; then I was a little angry myself, and hoped St. Barbara would be quite angry ; but she wasn't. She bit her lips first ; and then gave a great sigh—such a wild, sweet sigh—and then she knelt down and hid her face on Neith's knees. Then Neith smiled a little, and was moved.

ISABEL. Oh, I am so glad !

L. And she touched St. Barbara's forehead with a flower of white lotus ; and St. Barbara sobbed once or twice, and then said : ' If you only could see how beautiful it is, and how much it makes people feel what is good and lovely ; and if you could only hear the children singing in the Lady chapels !' And Neith smiled—but still sadly— and said, ' How do you know what I have seen, or heard, my love ? Do you think all those vaults and towers of yours have been built without me ? There was not a pillar in your Giotto's Santa Maria del Fiore which I did not set true by my spearshaft as it rose. But this pinnacle and flame work which has set your little heart on fire, is all vanity; and you will see what it will come to, and that soon; and none will grieve for it more than I. And then every one will disbelieve your pretty symbols and types. Men must be spoken simply to, my dear, if you would guide them kindly, and long.' But St. Barbara answered, that, ' Indeed she thought every one liked her work,' and that ' the people of different towns were as eager about their cathedral towers as about their privileges or their markets; ' and then she asked Neith to come and build something with her, wall against tower; and ' see whether the people will be as much pleased with your building as with mine.' But Neith answered, ' I will not contend with you, my dear. I strive not with those who love me; and for those who hate me, it is not well to strive with me, as weaver Arachne knows. And remember, child, that nothing is ever done beautifully, which is done in rivalship; nor nobly, which is done in pride.'

Then St. Barbara hung her head quite down, and said she was very sorry she had been so foolish; and kissed Neith; and stood thinking a minute: and then her eyes got bright again, and she said, she would go directly and build a chapel with fine windows in it; four for the four cardinal virtues, and one for humility, in the middle, bigger than the rest. And Neith very nearly laughed quite out, I thought; certainly her beautiful lips lost all their sternness for an instant; then she said, ' Well, love, build it, but do not put so many colours into your windows as you usually do; else no one will be able to see to read, inside: and when it is built, let a poor village priest consecrate it, and not an archbishop.' St. Barbara started a little, I thought, and turned as if to say something; but changed her mind, and gathered up her train, and went out. And Neith bent herself again to her loom, in which she was weaving a web of strange dark colours, I thought; but perhaps it was only after the glittering of St. Barbara's embroidered train : and I tried to make out the figures in Neith's web, and confused myself among them, as one always does in dreams ; and then the dream changed altogether, and I found myself, all at once, among a crowd of little Gothic and Egyptian spirits, who were quarrelling : at least the Gothic ones were trying to quarrel ; for the Egyptian ones only sat with their hands on their knees, and their aprons sticking out very stiffly ; and stared.     And after a while I began to understand what the matter was.     It seemed that some of the troublesome building imps, who meddle and make continually, even in the best Gothic work, had been listening to St. Barbara's talk with Neith ; and had made up their minds that Neith had no workpeople who could build against them.     They were but dull imps, as you may fancy, by their thinking that ; and never had done much, except disturbing the great Gothic building angels at their work, and playing tricks to each other ; indeed, of late they had been living years and years, like bats, up under the cornices of Strasbourg and Cologne cathedrals, with nothing to do but to make mouths at the people below.     However, they thought they knew everything about tower building ; and those who had heard what Neith said, told the rest ; and they all flew down directly, chattering in German, like jackdaws, to show Neith's people what they could do. And they had found some of Neith's old work people somewhere near Sais, sitting in the sun, with their hands on their knees ; and abused them heartily : and Neith's people did not mind, at first, but, after a while, they seemed to get tired of the noise ; and one or two rose up slowly, and laid hold of their measuring rods, and said, ' If St. Barbara's people liked to build with them, tower against pyramid, they would show them how to lay stones.'     Then the Gothic little spirits threw a great many double somersaults for joy ; and put the tips of their tongues out slily to each other, on one side ; and I heard the Egyptians say,

' they must be some new kind of frog—they didn't think there was much building in *them*.' However, the stiff old workers took their rods, as I said, and measured out a square space of sand ; but as soon as the German spirits saw that, they declared they wanted exactly that bit of ground to build on, themselves. Then the Egyptian builders offered to go farther off, and the German ones said, ' Ja wohl.' But as soon as the Egyptians had measured out another square, the little Germans said they must have some of that too. Then Neith's people laughed ; and said, ' they might take as much as they liked, but they would not move the plan of their pyramid again.' Then the little Germans took three pieces, and began to build three spires directly ; one large, and two little. And when the Egyptians saw they had fairly begun, they laid their foundation all round, of large square stones : and began to build, so steadily that they had like to have swallowed up the three little German spires. So when the Gothic spirits saw that, they built their spires leaning, like the tower of Pisa, that they might stick out at the side of the pyramid. And Neith's people stared at them ; and thought it very clever, but very wrong ; and on they went, in their own way, and said nothing. Then the little Gothic spirits were terribly provoked because they could not spoil the shape of the pyramid ; and they sat down all along the ledges of it to make faces ; but that did no good. Then they ran to the corners, and put their elbows on their knees, and stuck themselves out as far as they could, and made more faces ; but that did not good, neither. Then they looked up to the sky, and opened their mouths wide, and gobbled, and said it was too hot for work, and wondered when it would rain ; but that did no good, neither. And all the while the Egyptian spirits were laying step above step, patiently. But when the Gothic ones looked, and saw how high they had got, they said, ' Ach, Himmel ! ' and flew down in a great black cluster to the bottom ; and swept out a level spot in the sand with their wings, in no time, and began building a tower straight up, as fast as they could. And the Egyptians stood still again to stare at them ; for the Gothic spirits had got quite into a passion, and were really working very wonderfully. They cut the sandstone into strips as fine as reeds ; and put one reed on the top of another, so that you could not see where they fitted ; and they twisted them in and out like basket work, and knotted them into likenesses of ugly faces, and of strange beasts biting each other : and up they went, and up still, and they made spiral staircases at the corners, for the loaded workers to come up by (for I saw they were but weak imps, and could not fly with stones on their backs), and then they made traceried galleries for them to run round by ; and so up again ; with finer and finer work, till the Egyptians wondered whether they meant the thing for a tower or a pillar : and I heard them saying to one another, ' It was nearly as pretty as lotus stalks ; and if it were not for the ugly faces, there would be a fine temple, if they were going to build it all with pillars as big as that ! ' But in a minute afterwards—just as the Gothic spirits had carried their work as high as the upper course, but three or four, of the pyramid—the Egyptians called out to them to ' mind what they were about, for the sand was running away from under one of their tower corners.' But it was too late to mind what they were about ; for, in another instant, the whole tower sloped aside ; and the Gothic imps rose out of it like a flight of puffins, in a single cloud ; but screaming worse than any puffins you ever heard : and down came the tower, all in a piece, like a falling poplar, with its head right on the flank of the pyramid ; against which it snapped short off. And of course that waked me !

MARY. What a shame of you to have such a dream, after all you have told us about Gothic architecture !

L. If you have understood anything I ever told you about it, you know that no architecture was ever corrupted more miserably ; or abolished more justly by the accomplishment of its own follies.  Besides, even in its days of power, it was subject to catastrophes of this kind.  I have stood too often, mourning, by the grand fragment of the apse of Beauvais, not to have that fact well burnt into me. Still, you must have seen, surely, that these imps were of the Flamboyant school ; or, at least, of the German schools corresponding with it in extravagance.

MARY.  But, then, where is the crystal about which you dreamed all this ?

L.  Here ; but I suppose little Pthah has touched it again, for it is very small.  But, you see, here is the pyramid, built of great square stones of fluor spar, straight up ; and here are the three little pinnacles of mischievous quartz, which have set themselves, at the same time, on the same foundation ;  only they lean like the tower of Pisa, and come out obliquely at the side :  and here is one great spire of quartz which seems as if it had been meant to stand straight up, a little way off ;  and then had fallen down against the pyramid base, breaking its pinnacle away.  In reality, it has crystallized horizontally, and terminated imperfectly :  but, then, by what caprice does one crystal form horizontally, when all the rest stand upright ?  But this is nothing to the phantasies of fluor, and quartz, and some other such companions, when they get leave to do anything they like.  I could show you fifty specimens, about every one of which you might fancy a new fairy tale. Not that, in truth, any crystals get leave to do quite what they like ;  and many of them are sadly tried, and have little time for caprices—poor things !

MARY.  I thought they always looked as if they were either in play or in mischief ?  What trials have they ?

L.  Trials much like our own.  Sickness, and starvation ; fevers, and agues, and palsy ;  oppression ;  and old age, and the necessity of passing away in their time, like all else.

If there's any pity in you, you must come to-morrow, and take some part in these crystal griefs.

DORA.  I am sure we shall cry till our eyes are red.

L.  Ah, you may laugh, Dora: but I've been made grave, not once, nor twice, to see that even crystals ' cannot choose but be old ' at last.  It may be but a shallow proverb of the Justice's ; but it is a shrewdly wide one.

DORA (*pensive, for once*).  I suppose it *is* very dreadful to be old !  But then (*brightening again*), what should we do without our dear old friends, and our nice old lecturers ?

L.  If all nice old lecturers were minded as little as one I know of——

DORA.  And if they all meant as little what they say, would they not deserve it ?  But we'll come—we'll come, and cry.

# CRYSTAL SORROWS

# LECTURE IX

## CRYSTAL SORROWS

### *Working Lecture in Schoolroom*

L.   We have been hitherto talking, children, as if crystals might live, and play, and quarrel, and behave ill or well, according to their characters, without interruption from anything else.   But so far from this being so, nearly all crystals, whatever their characters, have to live a hard life of it, and meet with many misfortunes.   If we could see far enough, we should find, indeed, that, at the root, all their vices were misfortunes : but to-day I want you to see what sort of troubles the best crystals have to go through, occasionally, by no fault of their own.

This black thing, which is one of the prettiest of the very few pretty black things in the world, is called ' Tourmaline.'   It may be transparent, and green, or red, as well as black ;   and then no stone can be prettier (only, all the light that gets into it, I believe, comes out a good deal the worse ;   and is not itself again for a long while).   But this is the commonest state of it,—opaque, and as black as jet.

MARY.   What does ' Tourmaline ' mean ?

L.   They say it is Ceylanese, and I don't know Ceylanese ; but we may always be thankful for a graceful word, whatever it means.

MARY.   And what is it made of ?

L.   A little of everything ;   there's always flint, and clay, and magnesia in it ;   and the black is iron, according to its fancy ;   and there's boracic acid, if you know what that is ; and if you don't, I cannot tell you to-day, and it doesn't signify: and there's potash, and soda; and, on the whole, the chemistry of it is more like a mediæval doctor's prescription, than the making of a respectable mineral: but it may, perhaps, be owing to the strange complexity of its make, that it has a notable habit which makes it, to me, one of the most interesting of minerals. You see these two crystals are broken right across, in many places, just as if they had been shafts of black marble fallen from a ruinous temple; and here they lie, imbedded in white quartz, fragment succeeding fragment, keeping the line of the original crystal, while the quartz fills up the intervening spaces. Now tourmaline has a trick of doing this, more than any other mineral I know: here is another bit which I picked up on the glacier of Macugnaga; it is broken, like a pillar built of very flat broad stones, into about thirty joints, and all these are heaved and warped away from each other sideways, almost into a line of steps; and then all is filled up with quartz paste. And here, lastly, is a green Indian piece, in which the pillar is first disjointed, and then wrung round into the shape of an S.

MARY. How *can* this have been done?

L. There are a thousand ways in which it may have been done; the difficulty is not to account for the doing of it; but for the showing of it in some crystals, and not in others. You never by any chance get a quartz crystal broken or twisted in this way. If it break or twist at all, which it does sometimes, like the spire of Dijon, it is by its own will or fault; it never seems to have been passively crushed. But, for the forces which cause this passive ruin of the tourmaline—here is a stone which will show you multitudes of them in operation at once. It is known as ' brecciated agate,' beautiful, as you see; and highly valued as a pebble: yet, so far as I can read or hear, no one has ever looked at it with the least attention. At the first glance, you see it is made of very fine red striped agates, which have been broken into small pieces, and fastened together again by paste, also of agate.  There would be nothing wonderful in this, if this were all.  It is well known that by the movements of strata, portions of rock are often shattered to pieces :—well known also that agate is a deposit of flint by water under certain conditions of heat and pressure : there is, therefore, nothing wonderful in an agate's being broken ; and nothing wonderful in its being mended with the solution out of which it was itself originally congealed.  And with this explanation, most people, looking at a brecciated agate, or brecciated any-thing, seem to be satisfied.  I was so myself, for twenty years ; but, lately happening to stay for some time at the Swiss Baden, where the beach of the Limmat is almost wholly composed of brecciated limestones, I began to examine them thoughtfully ; and perceived, in the end, that they were, one and all, knots of as rich mystery as any poor little human brain was ever lost in.  That piece of agate in your hand, Mary, will show you many of the com-mon phenomena of breccias : but you need not knit your brows over it in that way ; depend upon it, neither you nor I shall ever know anything about the way it was made, as long as we live.

DORA.  That does not seem much to depend upon.

L.  Pardon me, puss.  When once we gain some real notion of the extent and the unconquerableness of our ignorance, it is a very broad and restful thing to depend upon ; you can throw yourself upon it at ease, as on a cloud, to feast with the gods.  You do not thenceforward trouble yourself—nor any one else—with theories, or the contradiction of theories ; you neither get headache nor heartburning ; and you never more waste your poor little store of strength, or allowance of time.

However, there are certain facts, about this agate-making, which I can tell you ; and then you may look at it in a pleasant wonder as long as you like ; pleasant wonder is no loss of time.

First, then, it is not broken freely by a blow ; it is slowly wrung, or ground, to pieces. You can only with extreme dimness conceive the force exerted on mountains in transitional states of movement. You have all read a little geology ; and you know how coolly geologists talk of mountains being raised or depressed. They talk coolly of it, because they are accustomed to the fact ; but the very universality of the fact prevents us from ever conceiving distinctly the conditions of force involved. You know I was living last year in Savoy : my house was on the back of a sloping mountain, which rose gradually for two miles, behind it ; and then fell at once in a great precipice towards Geneva, going down three thousand feet in four or five cliffs, or steps. Now that whole group of cliffs had simply been torn away by sheer strength from the rocks below, as if the whole mass had been as soft as biscuit. Put four or five captain's biscuits on the floor, on the top of one another ; and try to break them all in half, not by bending, but by holding one half down, and tearing the other halves straight up ;—of course you will not be able to do it, but you will feel and comprehend the sort of force needed. Then, fancy each captain's biscuit a bed of rock, six or seven hundred feet thick ; and the whole mass torn straight through ; and one half heaved up three thousand feet, grinding against the other as it rose,—and you will have some idea of the making of the Mont Saléve.

MAY. But it must crush the rocks all to dust !

L. No ; for there is no room for dust. The pressure is too great ; probably the heat developed also so great that the rock is made partly ductile ; but the worst of it is, that we never can see these parts of mountains in the state they were left in at the time of their elevation ; for it is precisely in these rents and dislocations that the crystalline power principally exerts itself. It is essentially a styptic power, and wherever the earth is torn, it heals and binds ; nay, the torture and grieving of the earth seem necessary to bring out its full energy ; for you only find the crystalline living power fully in action, where the rents and faults are deep and many.

DORA. If you please, sir—would you tell us—what are ' faults ' ?

L. You never heard of such things ?

DORA. Never in all our lives.

L. When a vein of rock which is going on smoothly, is interrupted by another troublesome little vein, which stops it, and puts it out, so that it has to begin again in another place—that is called a fault. *I* always think it ought to be called the fault of the vein that interrupts it ; but the miners always call it the fault of the vein that is interrupted.

DORA. So it is, if it does not begin again where it left off.

L. Well, that is certainly the gist of the business ; but, whatever good-natured old lecturers may do, the rocks have a bad habit, when they are once interrupted, of never asking ' Where was I ' ?

DORA. When the two halves of the dining table came separate, yesterday, was that a ' fault ' ?

L. Yes ; but not the table's. However, it is not a bad illustration, Dora. When beds of rock are only interrupted by a fissure, but remain at the same level, like the two halves of the table, it is not called a fault, but only a fissure ; but if one half of the table be either tilted higher than the other, or pushed to the side, so that the two parts will not fit, it is a fault. You had better read the chapter on faults in Jukes's *Geology ;* then you will know all about it. And this rent that I am telling you of in the Saléve, is one only of myriads, to which are owing the forms of the Alps, as, I believe, of all great mountain chains. Wherever you see a precipice on any scale of real magnificence, you will nearly always find it owing to some dislocation of this kind ; but the point of chief wonder to me, is the delicacy of the touch by which these gigantic rents have been apparently accomplished. Note, however, that we have no clear evidence, hitherto, of the time taken to produce any of them. We know that a change of temperature alters the position and the angles of the atoms of crystals, and also the entire bulk of rocks. We know that in all volcanic, and the greater part of all subterranean, action, temperatures are continually changing, and therefore masses of rock must be expanding or contracting, with infinite slowness, but with infinite force. This pressure must result in mechanical strain somewhere, both in their own substance, and in that of the rocks surrounding them ; and we can form no conception of the result of irresistible pressure, applied so as to rend and raise, with imperceptible slowness or gradation, masses thousands of feet in thickness. We want some experiments tried on masses of iron and stone ; and we can't get them tried, because Christian creatures never will seriously and sufficiently spend money, except to find out the shortest ways of killing each other. But, besides this slow kind of pressure, there is evidence of more or less sudden violence, on the same terrific scale ; and, through it all, the wonder, as I said, is always to me the delicacy of touch. I cut a block of the Saléve limestone from the edge of one of the principal faults which have formed the precipice ; it is a lovely compact limestone, and the fault itself is filled up with a red breccia, formed of the crushed fragments of the torn rock, cemented by a rich red crystalline paste. I have had the piece I cut from it smoothed, and polished across the junction ; here it is ; and you may now pass your soft little fingers over the surface, without so much as feeling the place where a rock which all the hills of England might have been sunk in the body of, and not a summit seen, was torn asunder through that whole thickness, as a thin dress is torn when you tread upon it.

(*The audience examine the stone, and touch it timidly ; but the matter remains inconceivable to them.*)

MARY (*struck by the beauty of the stone*). But this is almost marble ?

L. It is quite marble. And another singular point in the business, to my mind, is that these stones, which men have been cutting into slabs, for thousands of years, to ornament their principal buildings with—and which, under the general name of ' marble,' have been the delight of the eyes, and the wealth of architecture, among all civilised nations— are precisely those on which the signs and brands of these earth-agonies have been chiefly struck ; and there is not a purple vein nor flaming zone in them, which is not the record of their ancient torture. What a boundless capacity for sleep, and for serene stupidity, there is in the human mind ! Fancy reflective beings, who cut and polish stones for three thousand years, for the sake of the pretty stains upon them ; and educate themselves to an art at last (such as it is) of imitating these veins by dextrous painting ;— and never a curious soul of them, all that while, asks, ' What painted the rocks ? '

(*The audience look dejected, and ashamed of them-selves.*)

The fact is, we are all, and always, asleep, through our lives ; and it is only by pinching ourselves very hard that we ever come to see, or understand, anything. At least, it is not always we who pinch ourselves ; sometimes other people pinch us ; which I suppose is very good of them,— or other things, which I suppose is very proper of them. But it is a sad life ; made up chiefly of naps and pinches.

(*Some of the audience, on this, appearing to think that the others require pinching, the* LECTURER *changes the subject.*)

Now, however, for once, look at a piece of marble care-fully, and think about it. You see this is one side of the fault ; the other side is down or up, nobody knows where ; but, on this side, you can trace the evidence of the dragging and tearing action. All along the edge of this marble, the ends of the fibres of the rock are torn, here an inch, and there half an inch, away from each other; and you see the exact places where they fitted, before they were torn separate; and you see the rents are now all filled up with the sanguine paste, full of the broken pieces of the rock; the paste itself seems to have been half melted, and partly to have also melted the edge of the fragments it contains, and then to have crystallized with them, and round them. And the brecciated agate I first showed you contains exactly the same phenomena; a zoned crystallization going on amidst the cemented fragments, partly altering the structure of those fragments themselves, and subject to continual change, either in the intensity of its own power or in the nature of the materials submitted to it;—so that, at one time, gravity acts upon them and disposes them in horizontal layers, or causes them to droop in stalactites; and at another, gravity is entirely defied, and the substances in solution are crystallized in bands of equal thickness on every side of the cell. It would require a course of lectures longer than these (I have a great mind—you have behaved so saucily—to stay and give them) to describe to you the phenomena of this kind, in agates and chalcedonies only;—nay, there is a single sarcophagus in the British Museum, covered with grand sculpture of the 18th dynasty, which contains in the magnificent breccia (agates and jaspers imbedded in porphyry), out of which it is hewn, material for the thought of years; and record of the earthsorrow of ages in comparison with the duration of which, the Egyptian letters tell us but the history of the evening and morning of a day.

Agates, I think, of all stones, confess most of their past history; but all crystallization goes on under, and partly records, circumstances of this kind—circumstances of infinite variety, but always involving difficulty, interruption, and change of condition at different times. Observe, first, you have the whole mass of the rock in motion, either

contracting itself, and so gradually widening the cracks ;
or being compressed, and thereby closing them, and crush-
ing their edges ;—and, if one part of its substance be softer,
at the given temperature, than another, probably squeezing that softer substance out into the veins. Then the
veins themselves, when the rock leaves them open by its
contraction, act with various power of suction upon its
substance ;—by capillary attraction when they are fine—
by that of pure vacuity when they are larger, or by changes
in the constitution and condensation of the mixed gases
with which they have been originally filled. Those gases
themselves may be supplied in all variation of volume and
power from below ; or, slowly, by the decomposition of the
rocks themselves : and, at changing temperatures, must
exert relatively changing forces of decomposition and com-
bination on the walls of the veins they fill ; while water,
at every degree of heat and pressure (from beds of everlasting ice, alternate with cliffs of native rock, to volumes of
red hot, or white hot, steam), congeals, and drips, and throbs,
and thrills, from crag to crag ; and breathes from pulse to
pulse of foaming or fiery arteries, whose beating is felt
through chains of the great islands of the Indian seas, as
your own pulses lift your bracelets, and makes whole kingdoms of the world quiver in deadly earthquake, as if they
were light as aspen leaves. And, remember, the poor little
crystals have to live their lives, and mind their own affairs,
in the midst of all this, as best they may. They are wonderfully like human creatures,—forget all that is going on if
they don't see it, however dreadful ; and never think what
is to happen to-morrow. They are spiteful or loving,
and indolent or painstaking, and orderly or licentious, with
no thought whatever of the lava or the flood which may
break over them any day ; and evaporate them into air-
bubbles, or wash them into a solution of salts. And you
may look at them, once understanding the surrounding
conditions of their fate, with an endless interest. You

will see crowds of unfortunate little crystals, who have been forced to constitute themselves in a hurry, their dissolving element being fiercely scorched away ; you will see them doing their best, bright and numberless, but tiny.  Then you will find indulged crystals, who have had centuries to form themselves in, and have changed their mind and ways continually ; and have been tired, and taken heart again ; and have been sick, and got well again ; and thought they would try a different diet, and then thought better of it ; and made but a poor use of their advantages, after all.  And others you will see, who have begun life as wicked crystals ; and then have been impressed by alarming circumstances, and have become converted crystals, and behaved amazingly for a little while, and fallen away again, and ended, but discreditably, perhaps even in decomposition ; so that one doesn't know what will become of them.  And sometimes you will see deceitful crystals, that look as soft as velvet, and are deadly to all near them ; and sometimes you will see deceitful crystals, that seem flint-edged, like our little quartz-crystal of a housekeeper here (hush ! Dora), and are endlessly gentle and true wherever gentleness and truth are needed.  And sometimes you will see little child-crystals put to school like school-girls, and made to stand in rows ; and taken the greatest care of, and taught how to hold themselves up, and behave : and sometimes you will see unhappy little child-crystals left to lie about in the dirt, and pick up their living, and learn manners, where they can.  And sometimes you will see fat crystals eating up thin ones, like great capitalists and little labourers ; and politico-economic crystals teaching the stupid ones how to eat each other, and cheat each other ; and foolish crystals getting in the way of wise ones ; and impatient crystals spoiling the plans of patient ones, irreparably ; just as things go on in the world.  And sometimes you may see hypocritical crystals taking the shape of others, though they are nothing like in their minds ; and vampire crystals eating out the hearts of others ; and hermit-crab crystals living in the shells of others ; and parasite crystals living on the means of others ; and courtier crystals glittering in attendance upon others ; and all these, besides the two great companies of war and peace, who ally themselves, resolutely to attack, or resolutely to defend. And for the close, you see the broad shadow and deadly force of inevitable fate, above all this : you see the multitudes of crystals whose time has come ; not a set time, as with us, but yet a time, sooner or later, when they all must give up their crystal ghosts :— when the strength by which they grew, and the breath given them to breathe, pass away from them ; and they fail, and are consumed, and vanish away ; and another generation is brought to life, framed out of their ashes.

MARY. It is very terrible. Is it not the complete fulfilment, down into the very dust, of that verse : ' The whole creation groaneth and travaileth in pain ' ?

L. I do not know that it is in pain, Mary, at least, the evidence tends to show that there is much more pleasure than pain, as soon as sensation becomes possible.

LUCILLA. But then, surely, if we are told that it is pain, it must be pain ?

L. Yes ; if we are told ; and told in the way you mean, Lucilla ; but nothing is said of the proportion to pleasure. Unmitigated pain would kill any of us in a few hours ; pain equal to our pleasures would make us loathe life ; the word itself cannot be applied to the lower conditions of matter, in its ordinary sense. But wait till to-morrow to ask me about this. To-morrow is to be kept for questions and difficulties ; let us keep to the plain facts to-day. There is yet one group of facts connected with this rending of the rocks, which I especially want you to notice. You know, when you have mended a very old dress, quite meritoriously, till it won't mend any more——

EGYPT (*interrupting*). Could not you sometimes take gentlemen's work to illustrate by ?

L.   Gentlemen's work is rarely so useful as yours, Egypt ; and when it is useful, girls cannot easily understand it.

DORA.   I am sure we should understand it better than gentlemen understand about sewing.

L.   My dear, I hope I always speak modestly, and under correction, when I touch upon matters of the kind too high for me ; and besides, I never intend to speak otherwise than respectfully of sewing ;—though you always seem to think I am laughing at you.   In all seriousness, illustrations from sewing are those which Neith likes me best to use ; and which young ladies ought to like everybody to use. What do you think the beautiful word ' wife ' comes from ?

DORA (*tossing her head*).   I don't think it is a particularly beautiful word.

L.   Perhaps not.   At your ages you may think ' bride ' sounds better ; but wife's the word for wear, depend upon it.   It is the great word in which the English and Latin languages conquer the French and the Greek.   I hope the French will some day get a word for it, yet, instead of their dreadful ' femme.'   But what do you think it comes from ?

DORA.   I never *did* think about it ?

L.   Nor you, Sibyl ?

SIBYL.   No ; I thought it was Saxon, and stopped there.

L.   Yes ; but the great good of Saxon words is, that they usually do mean something.   Wife means ' weaver.'   You have all the right to call yourselves little ' housewives,' when you sew neatly.

DORA.   But I don't think we want to call ourselves ' little housewives.'

L.   You must either be house-Wives, or house-Moths ; remember that.   In the deep sense, you must either weave men's fortunes, and embroider them ; or feed upon, and

bring them to decay. You had better let me keep my
sewing illustration, and help me out with it.

DORA.  Well, we'll hear it, under protest.

L.  You have heard it before ; but with reference to
other matters.  When it is said, ' no man putteth a piece
of new cloth on an old garment, else it taketh from the old,'
does it not mean that the new piece tears the old one away
at the sewn edge ?

DORA.  Yes ;  certainly.

L.  And when you mend a decayed stuff with strong
thread, does not the whole edge come away sometimes,
when it tears again ?

DORA.  Yes ; and then it is of no use to mend it any more.

L.  Well, the rocks don't seem to think that : but the
same thing happens to them continually.  I told you they
were full of rents, or veins.  Large masses of mountain
are sometimes as full of veins as your hand is ;  and of veins
nearly as fine (only you know a rock vein does not mean
a tube, but a crack or cleft).  Now these clefts are mended,
usually, with the strongest material the rock can find ;
and often literally with threads ;  for the gradually opening
rent seems to draw the substance it is filled with into fibres,
which cross from one side of it to the other, and are partly
crystalline ;  so that, when the crystals become distinct, the
fissure has often exactly the look of a tear, brought together
with strong cross stitches.  Now when this is completely
done, and all has been fastened and made firm, perhaps some
new change of temperature may occur and the rock begin
to contract again.  Then the old vein must open wider ;  or
else another open elsewhere.  If the old vein widen, it
*may* do so at its centre ;  but it constantly happens, with
well filled veins, that the cross stitches are too strong to
break : the walls of the vein, instead, are torn away by
them ;  and another little supplementary vein—often three
or four successively—will be thus formed at the side of the
first.

105—J *

MARY. That is really very much like our work. But what do the mountains use to sew with?

L. Quartz, whenever they can get it : pure limestones are obliged to be content with carbonate of lime ; but most mixed rocks can find some quartz for themselves. Here is a piece of black slate from the Buet : it looks merely like dry dark mud ;—you could not think there was any quartz in it ; but, you see, its rents are all stitched together with beautiful white thread, which is the purest quartz, so close drawn that you can break it like flint, in the mass ; but, where it has been exposed to the weather, the fine fibrous structure is shown : and, more than that, you see the threads have been all twisted and pulled aside, this way and the other, by the warpings and shifting of the sides of the vein as it widened.

MARY. It is wonderful ! But is that going on still ? Are the mountains being torn and sewn together again at this moment ?

L. Yes, certainly, my dear : but I think, just as certainly (though geologists differ on this matter), not with the violence, or on the scale, of their ancient ruin and renewal. All things seem to be tending towards a condition of at least temporary rest ; and that groaning and travailing of the creation, as, assuredly, not wholly in pain, is not, in the full sense, ' until now.'

MARY. I want so much to ask you about that !

SIBYL. Yes ; and we all want to ask you about a great many other things besides.

L. It seems to me that you have got quite as many new ideas as are good for any of you at present : and I should not like to burden you with more ; but I must see that those you have are clear, if I can make them so ; so we will have one more talk, for answer of questions, mainly. Think over all the ground, and make your difficulties thoroughly presentable. Then we'll see what we can make of them.

DORA. They shall all be dressed in their very best ; and curtsey as they come in.

L. No, no, Dora ; no curtseys, if you please. I had enough of them the day you all took a fit of reverence, and curtsied me out of the room.

DORA. But, you know, we cured ourselves of the fault, at once, by that fit. We have never been the least respectful since. And the difficulties will only curtsey themselves out of the room, I hope ;—come in at one door—vanish at the other.

L. What a pleasant world it would be, if all its difficulties were taught to behave so ! However, one can generally make something, or (better still) nothing, or at least less, of them, if they thoroughly know their own minds ; and your difficulties—I must say that for you, children—generally do know their own minds, as you do yourselves.

DORA. That is very kindly said for us. Some people would not allow so much as that girls had any minds to know.

L. They will at least admit you have minds to change, Dora.

MARY. You might have left us the last speech, without a retouch. But we'll put our little minds, such as they are, in the best trim we can, for to-morrow.

# THE  CRYSTAL  REST

# LECTURE X

## THE CRYSTAL REST

*Evening.  The fireside.  L.'s arm-chair in the
comfortablest corner*

L. (*perceiving various arrangements being made of footstool, cushion, screen, and the like*).  Yes, yes, it's all very
fine I and I am to sit here to be asked questions till supper-
time, am I ?

Dora.  I don't think you can have any supper to-night :
—we've got so much to ask.

Lily.  Oh, Miss Dora I  We can fetch it him here, you
know, so nicely I

L.  Yes, Lily, that will be pleasant, with competitive
examination going on over one's plate ; the competition
being among the examiners.  Really, now that I know
what teasing things girls are, I don't so much wonder that
people used to put up patiently with the dragons who took
*them* for supper.  But I can't help myself, I suppose ;—
no thanks to St. George.  Ask away, children, and I'll
answer as civilly as may be.

Dora.  We don't so much care about being answered
civilly, as about not being asked things back again.

L.  'Ayez seulement la patience que je pare.'  There
shall be no requitals.

Dora.  Well, then, first of all—What shall we ask first,
Mary ?

Mary.  It does not matter.  I think all the questions
come into one, at least, nearly.

Dora.  You know, you always talk as if the crystals were

alive ; and we never understand how much you are in play, and how much in earnest. That's the first thing.

L. Neither do I understand, myself, my dear, how much I am in earnest. The stones puzzle me as much as I puzzle you. They look as if they were alive, and make me speak as if they were ; and I do not in the least know how much truth there is in the appearance. I'm not to ask things back again to-night, but all questions of this sort lead necessarily to the one main question, which we asked, before, in vain, ' What is it to be alive ? '

DORA. Yes ; but we want to come back to that : for we've been reading scientific books about the ' conservation of forces,' and it seems all so grand, and wonderful ; and the experiments are so pretty ; and I suppose it must be all right : but then the books never speak as if there were any such thing as ' life.'

L. They mostly omit that part of the subject, certainly, Dora : but they are beautifully right as far as they go ; and life is not a convenient element to deal with. They seem to have been getting some of it into and out of bottles, in their ' ozone ' and ' antizone ' lately : but they still know little of it ; and, certainly, I know less.

DORA. You promised not to be provoking, to-night.

L. Wait a minute. Though, quite truly, I know less of the secrets of life than the philosophers do ; I yet know one corner of ground on which we artists can stand, literally as ' Life Guards ' at bay, as steadily as the Guards at Inkermann ; however hard the philosophers push. And you may stand with us, if once you learn to draw nicely.

DORA. I'm sure we are all trying ! but tell us where we may stand.

L. You may always stand by Form, against Force. To a painter, the essential character of anything is the form of it ; and the philosophers cannot touch that. They come and tell you, for instance, that there is as much heat, or motion, or calorific energy (or whatever else they like to call it), in a tea-kettle as in a Gier-eagle. Very good ; that is so ; and it is very interesting. It requires just as much heat as will boil the kettle, to take the Gier-eagle up to his nest ; and as much more to bring him down again on a hare or a partridge. But we painters, acknowledging the equality and similarity of the kettle and the bird in all scientific respects, attach, for our part, our principal interest to the difference in their forms. For us, the primarily cognisable facts, in the two things, are, that the kettle has a spout, and the eagle a beak ; the one a lid on its back, the other a pair of wings ; —not to speak of the distinction also of volition, which the philosophers may properly call merely a form or mode of force ;—but then, to an artist, the form, or mode, is the gist of the business. The kettle chooses to sit still on the hob ; the eagle to recline on the air. It is the fact of the choice, not the equal degree of temperature in the fulfilment of it, which appears to us the more interesting circumstance ;—though the other is very interesting too. Exceedingly so ! Don't laugh, children ; the philosophers have been doing quite splendid work lately, in their own way : especially, the transforma-tion of force into light is a great piece of systematised discovery ; and this notion about the sun's being supplied with his flame by ceaseless meteoric hail is grand, and looks very likely to be true. Of course it is only the old gunlock—flint and steel—on a large scale : but the order and majesty of it are sublime. Still, we sculptors and painters care little about it. ' It is very fine, we say, and very useful, this knocking the light out of the sun, or into it, by an eternal cataract of planets. But you may hail away, so, for ever, and you will not knock out what we can. Here is a bit of silver, not the size of half-a-crown, on which, with a single hammer stroke, one of us, two thousand and odd years ago, hit out the head of the Apollo of Clazomenæ. It is merely a matter of form ; but if any of you philosophers, with your whole planetary system to hammer with, can hit out such another bit of silver as this,—we will take off our hats to you.  For the present, we keep them on.'

MARY.  Yes, I understand ; and that is nice : but I don't think we shall any of us like having only form to depend upon.

L.  It was not neglected in the making of Eve, my dear.

MARY.  It does not seem to separate us from the dust of the ground.  It is that breathing of the life which we want to understand.

L.  So you should : but hold fast to the form, and defend that first, as distinguished from the mere transition of forces.  Discern the moulding hand of the potter commanding the clay, from his merely beating foot, as it turns the wheel.  If you can find incense, in the vase, afterwards, well : but it is curious how far mere form will carry you ahead of the philosophers.  For instance, with regard to the most interesting of all their modes of force—light ;— they never consider how far the existence of it depends on the putting of certain vitreous and nervous substances into the formal arrangement which we call an eye.  The German philosophers began the attack, long ago, on the other side, by telling us there was no such thing as light at all, unless we chose to see it : now, German and English, both, have reversed their engines, and insist that light would be exactly the same light that it is, though nobody could ever see it.  The fact being that the force must be there, and the eyes there ; and ' light ' means the effect of the one on the other ;—and perhaps, also—(Plato saw farther into that mystery than any one has since, that I know of)—on something a little way within the eyes ; but we may stand quite safe, close behind the retina, and defy the philosophers.

SIBYL.  But I don't care so much about defying the philosophers, if only one could get a clear idea of life, or soul, for one's self.

L.  Well, Sibyl, you used to know more about it, in that cave of yours, than any of us.  I was just going to ask you about inspiration, and the golden bough, and the like ; only I remembered I was not to ask anything. But, will not you, at least, tell us whether the ideas of Life, as the power of putting things together, or 'making' them ; and of Death, as the power of pushing things separate, or 'unmaking' them, may not be very simply held in balance against each other ?

SIBYL. No, I am not in my cave to-night ; and cannot tell you anything.

L. I think they may. Modern Philosophy is a great separator ; it is little more than the expansion of Molière's great sentence, ' Il s'ensuit de là, que tout ce qu'il y a de beau est dans les dictionnaires ; il n'y a que les mots qui sont transposés.' But when you used to be in your cave, Sibyl, and to be inspired, there was (and there remains still in some small measure) beyond the merely formative and sustaining power, another, which we painters call ' passion ' —I don't know what the philosophers call it ; we know it makes people red, or white ; and therefore it must be something, itself : and perhaps it is the most truly ' poetic ' or ' making ' force of all, creating a world of its own out of a glance, or a sigh : and the want of passion is perhaps the truest death, or ' unmaking ' of everything ;—even of stones. By the way, you were all reading about that ascent of the Aiguille Verte, the other day ?

SIBYL. Because you had told us it was so difficult, you thought it could not be ascended.

L. Yes ; I believed the Aiguille Verte would have held its own. But do you recollect what one of the climbers exclaimed, when he first felt sure of reaching the summit ?

SIBYL. Yes, it was, ' Oh, Aiguille Verte, vous êtes morte, vous êtes morte ! '

L. That was true instinct. Real philosophic joy. Now can you at all fancy the difference between that feeling of triumph in a mountain's death ; and the exultation of your beloved poet, in its life—

' Quantus Athos, aut quantus Eryx, aut ipse coruscis
        Quum fremit ilicibus quantus, gaudetque nivali
        Vertice, se attollens pater Apenninus ad auras ' ?

DORA.   You must translate for us mere housekeepers,
please ;—whatever the cave-keepers may know about it.

MARY.   Will Dryden do ?

L.   No.   Dryden is a far way worse than nothing, and
nobody will ' do.'   You can't translate it.   But this is all
you need know, that the lines are full of a passionate
sense of the Apennines' fatherhood, or protecting power
over Italy ;  and of sympathy with their joy in their snowy
strength in heaven ;  and with the same joy, shuddering
through all the leaves of their forests.

MARY.   Yes, that is a difference indeed !  but then, you
know, one can't help feeling that it is fanciful.   It is very
delightful to imagine the mountains to be alive ;  but then
—are they alive ?

L.   It seems to me, on the whole, Mary, that the feelings
of the purest and most mightily passioned human souls are
likely to be the truest.   Not, indeed, if they do not desire
to know the truth, or blind themselves to it that they may
please themselves with passion ;  for then they are no longer
pure :  but if, continually seeking and accepting the truth
as far as it is discernible, they trust their Maker for the
integrity of the instincts He has gifted them with, and
rest in the sense of a higher truth which they cannot
demonstrate, I think they will be most in the right, so.

DORA and JESSIE (clapping their hands).   Then we really
may believe that the mountains are living ?

L.   You may at least earnestly believe that the presence
of the spirit which culminates in your own life, shows itself
in dawning, wherever the dust of the earth begins to assume
any orderly and lovely state.   You will find it impossible to
separate this idea of gradated manifestation from that
of the vital power.   Things are not either wholly alive, or
wholly dead.   They are less or more alive.   Take the

nearest, most easily examined instance—the life of a flower. Notice what a different degree and kind of life there is in the calyx and the corolla. The calyx is nothing but the swaddling clothes of the flower ; the child-blossom is bound up in it, hand and foot ; guarded in it, restrained by it, till the time of birth. The shell is hardly more subordinate to the germ in the egg, than the calyx to the blossom. It bursts at last; but it never lives as the corolla does. It may fall at the moment its task is fulfilled, as in the poppy ; or wither gradually, as in the buttercup ; or persist in a ligneous apathy, after the flower is dead, as in the rose ; or harmonise itself so as to share in the aspect of the real flower, as in the lily ; but it never shares in the corolla's bright passion of life. And the gradations which thus exist between the different members of organic creatures, exist no less between the different ranges of organism. We know no higher or more energetic life than our own ; but there seems to me this great good in the idea of gradation of life—it admits the idea of a life above us, in other creatures, as much nobler than ours, as ours is nobler than that of the dust.

MARY. I am glad you have said that ; for I know Violet and Lucilla and May want to ask you something ; indeed, we all do ; only you frightened Violet so, about the ant-hill, that she can't say a word ; and May is afraid of your teasing her, too ; but I know they are wondering why you are always telling them about heathen gods and goddesses, as if you half believed in them ; and you represent them as good ; and then we see there is really a kind of truth in the stories about them ; and we are all puzzled : and, in this, we cannot even make our difficulty quite clear to ourselves ;—it would be such a long confused question, if we could ask you all we should like to know.

L. Nor is it any wonder, Mary ; for this is indeed the longest, and the most wildly confused question that reason can deal with ; but I will try to give you, quickly, a few clear ideas about the heathen gods, which you may follow out afterwards, as your knowledge increases.

Every heathen conception of deity in which you are likely to be interested, has three distinct characters :—

I. It has a physical character. It represents some of the great powers or objects of nature—sun or moon or heaven, or the winds, or the sea. And the fables first related about each deity represent, figuratively, the action of the natural power which it represents ; such as the rising and setting of the sun, the tides of the sea, and so on.

II. It has an ethical character, and represents, in its history, the moral dealings of God with man. Thus Apollo is first, physically, the sun contending with darkness ; but morally, the power of divine life contending with corruption. Athena is, physically, the air ; morally, the breathing of the divine spirit of wisdom. Neptune is, physically, the sea ; morally, the supreme power of agitating passion ; and so on.

III. It has, at last, a personal character ; and is realised in the minds of its worshippers as a living spirit, with whom men may speak face to face, as a man speaks to his friend.

Now it is impossible to define exactly how far, at any period of a national religion, these three ideas are mingled ; or how far one prevails over the other. Each inquirer usually takes up one of these ideas, and pursues it, to the exclusion of the others : no impartial effort seems to have been made to discern the real state of the heathen imagination in its successive phases. For the question is not at all what a mythological figure meant in its origin ; but what it became in each subsequent mental development of the nation inheriting the thought. Exactly in proportion to the mental and moral insight of any race, its mythological figures mean more to it, and become more real. An early and savage race means nothing more (because it has nothing more to mean), by its Apollo, than the sun ; while a cultivated Greek means every operation of divine intellect and justice. The Neith, of Egypt, meant, physically, little more than the blue of the air ; but the Greek, in a climate of alternate storm and calm, represented the wild fringes of the storm-cloud by the serpents of her ægis ; and the lightning and cold of the highest thunder-clouds, by the Gorgon on her shield : while morally, the same types represented to him the mystery and changeful terror of knowledge, as her spear and helm its ruling and defensive power. And no study can be more interesting, or more useful to you, than that of the different meanings which have been created by great nations, and great poets, out of mythological figures given them, at first, in utter simplicity. But when we approach them in their third, or personal character (and, for its power over the whole national mind, this is far the leading one), we are met at once by questions which may well put all of you at pause. Were they idly imagined to be real beings ? and did they so usurp the place of the true God ? Or were they actually real beings—evil spirits —leading men away from the true God ? Or is it conceivable that they might have been real beings—good spirits— entrusted with some message from the true God ? These were the questions you wanted to ask ; were they not, Lucilla ?

LUCILLA. Yes, indeed.

L. Well, Lucilla, the answer will much depend upon the clearness of your faith in the personality of the spirits which are described in the book of your own religion ;— their personality, observe, as distinguished from merely symbolical visions. For instance, when Jeremiah has the vision of the seething pot with its mouth to the north, you know that this which he sees is not a real thing ; but merely a significant dream. Also, when Zechariah sees the speckled horses among the myrtle trees in the bottom, you still may suppose the vision symbolical ;—you do not think of them as real spirits, like Pegasus, seen in the form of horses. But when you are told of the four riders in the Apocalypse, a distinct sense of personality begins to force itself upon you. And though you might, in a dull temper, think that (for one instance of all) the fourth rider on the pale horse was merely a symbol of the power of death,—in your stronger and more earnest moods you will rather conceive of him as a real and living angel. And when you look back from the vision of the Apocalypse to the account of the destruction of the Egyptian first-born, and of the army of Sennacherib, and again to David's vision at the threshing floor of Araunah, the idea of personality in this death-angel becomes entirely defined, just as in the appearance of the angels to Abraham, Manoah, or Mary.

Now, when you have once consented to this idea of a personal spirit, must not the question instantly follow: ' Does this spirit exercise its functions towards one race of men only, or towards all men ?  Was it an angel of death to the Jew only, or the Gentile also ? '  You find a certain Divine agency made visible to a King of Israel, as an armed angel, executing vengeance, of which one special purpose was to lower his kingly pride.  You find another (or perhaps the same agency, made visible to a Christian prophet as an angel standing in the sun, calling to the birds that fly under heaven to come, that they may eat the flesh of kings.  Is there anything impious in the thought that the same agency might have been expressed to a Greek king, or Greek seer, by similar visions ?—that this figure, standing in the sun, and armed with the sword, or the bow (whose arrows were drunk with blood), and exercising especially its power in the humiliation of the proud, might, at first, have been called only ' Destroyer,' and afterwards, as the light, or sun, of justice, was recognised in the chastisement, called also ' Physician ' or ' Healer ' ?  If you feel hesitation in admitting the possibility of such a manifestation, I believe you will find it is caused, partly indeed by such trivial things as the difference to your ear between Greek and English terms ; but, far more, by uncertainty in your own mind respecting the nature and truth of the visions spoken of in the Bible. Have any of you intently examined the nature of your belief in them ? You, for instance, Lucilla, who think often, and seriously, of such things ?

LUCILLA. No ; I never could tell what to believe about them. I know they must be true in some way or other ; and I like reading about them.

L. Yes ; and I like reading about them too, Lucilla ; as I like reading other grand poetry. But, surely, we ought both to do more than like it ? Will God be satisfied with us, think you, if we read His words, merely for the sake of an entirely meaningless poetical sensation ?

LUCILLA. But do not the people who give themselves to seek out the meaning of these things, often get very strange, and extravagant ?

L. More than that, Lucilla. They often go mad. That abandonment of the mind to religious theory, or contemplation, is the very thing I have been pleading with you against. I never said you should set yourself to discover the meanings : but you should take careful pains to understand them, so far as they *are* clear ; and you should always accurately ascertain the state of your mind about them. I want you never to read merely for the pleasure of fancy ;—still less as a formal religious duty (else you might as well take to repeating Paters at once ; for it is surely wiser to repeat one thing we understand, than read a thousand which we cannot). Either, therefore, acknowledge the passages to be, for the present, unintelligible to you ; or else determine the sense in which you at present receive them ; or, at all events, the different senses between which you clearly see that you must choose. Make either your belief, or your difficulty, definite ; but do not go on, all through your life, believing nothing intelligently, and yet supposing that your having read the words of a divine book must give you the right to despise every religion but your own. I assure you, strange as it may seem, our scorn of Greek tradition depends, not on our belief, but our disbelief, of our own traditions. We have, as yet, no sufficient clue to the meaning of either ; but you will always find that, in proportion to the earnestness of our own faith, its tendency to accept a spiritual personality increases : and that the most vital and beautiful Christian temper rests joyfully in its conviction of the multitudinous ministry of living angels, infinitely varied in rank and power. You all know one expression of the purest and happiest form of such faith, as it exists in modern times, in Richter's lovely illustrations of the Lord's Prayer. The real and living death-angel, girt as a pilgrim for journey, and softly crowned with flowers, beckons at the dying mother's door ; child-angels sit talking face to face with mortal children, among the flowers ;—hold them by their little coats, lest they fall on the stairs ;—whisper dreams of heaven to them, leaning over their pillows ; carry the sound of the church bells for them far through the air ; and even descending lower in service, fill little cups with honey, to hold out to the weary bee. By the way, Lily, did you tell the other children that story about your little sister, and Alice, and the sea?

LILY. I told it to Alice, and to Miss Dora. I don't think I did to anybody else. I thought it wasn't worth.

L. We shall think it worth a great deal now, Lily, if you will tell it us. How old is Dotty, again ? I forget.

LILY. She is not quite three ; but she has such odd little old ways, sometimes.

L. And she was very fond of Alice ?

LILY. Yes; Alice was so good to her always !

L. And so when Alice went away ?

LILY. Oh, it was nothing, you know, to tell about; only it was strange at the time.

L. Well; but I want you to tell it.

LILY. The morning after Alice had gone, Dotty was very sad and restless when she got up; and went about, looking into all the corners, as if she could find Alice in them, and at last she came to me, and said, ' Is Alie gone over the great sea ? ' And I said, ' Yes, she is gone over the great deep sea, but she will come back again some day.' Then Dotty looked round the room; and I had just poured some water out into the basin; and Dotty ran to it, and got up on a chair, and dashed her hands through the water, again and again; and cried, ' Oh, deep, deep sea ! send little Alie back to me.'

L. Isn't that pretty, children ? There's a dear little heathen for you ! The whole heart of Greek mythology is in that; the idea of a personal being in the elemental power ;—of its being moved by prayer ;—and of its presence everywhere, making the broken diffusion of the element sacred.

Now, remember, the measure in which we may permit ourselves to think of this trusted and adored personality, in Greek, or in any other, mythology, as conceivably a shadow of truth, will depend on the degree in which we hold the Greeks, or other great nations, equal, or inferior, in privilege and character, to the Jews, or to ourselves. If we believe that the great Father would use the imagination of the Jew as an instrument by which to exalt and lead him; but the imagination of the Greek only to degrade and mislead him : if we can suppose that real angels were sent to minister to the Jews and to punish them ; but no angels, or only mocking spectra of angels, or even devils in the shapes of angels, to lead Lycurgus and Leonidas from desolate cradle to hopeless grave :— and if we can think that it was only the influence of spectres, or the teaching of demons, which issued in the making of mothers like Cornelia, and of sons like Cleobis and Bito, we may, of course, reject the heathen Mythology in our privileged scorn : but, at least, we are bound to examine strictly by what faults of our own it has come to pass, that the ministry of real angels among ourselves is occasionally so ineffectual, as to end in the production of Cornelias who entrust their child-jewels to Charlotte Winsors for the better keeping of them ; and of sons like that one who, the other day, in France, beat his mother to death with a stick ; and was brought in by the jury, ' guilty, with extenuating circumstances.'

MAY. Was that really possible ?

L. Yes, my dear. I am not sure that I can lay my hand on the reference to it (and I should not have said ' the other day '—it was a year or two ago), but you may depend on the fact ; and I could give you many like it, if I chose. There was a murder done in Russia, very lately, on a traveller. The murderess's little daughter was in the way, and found it out, somehow. Her mother killed her, too, and put her into the oven. There is a peculiar horror about the relations between parent and child, which are being now brought about by our variously degraded forms of European white slavery. Here *is* one reference, I see, in my notes on that story of Cleobis and Bito ; though I suppose I marked this chiefly for its quaintness, and the beautifully Christian names of the sons ; but it is a good instance of the power of the King of the Valley of Diamonds * among us.

In *Galignani* of July 21-22, 1862, is reported a trial of a farmer's son in the department of the Yonne. The father, two years ago, at Malay le Grand, gave up his property to his two sons, on condition of being maintained by them. Simon fulfilled his agreement, but Pierre would not. The tribunal of Sens condemns Pierre to pay eighty-four francs a year to his father. Pierre replies, ' he would rather die than pay it.' Actually, returning home, he throws himself into the river, and the body is not found till next day.

* See Note VI.

MARY. But—but—I can't tell what you would have us think. Do you seriously mean that the Greeks were better than we are; and that their gods were real angels?

L. No, my dear. I mean only that we know, in reality, less than nothing of the dealings of our Maker with our fellow-men; and can only reason or conjecture safely about them, when we have sincerely humble thoughts of ourselves and our creeds.

We owe to the Greeks every noble discipline in literature; every radical principle of art; and every form of convenient beauty in our household furniture and daily occupations of life. We are unable, ourselves, to make rational use of half that we have received from them; and, of our own, we have nothing but discoveries in science, and fine mechanical adaptations of the discovered physical powers. On the other hand, the vice existing among certain classes, both of the rich and poor, in London, Paris, and Vienna, could have been conceived by a Spartan or Roman of the heroic ages only as possible in a Tartarus, where fiends were employed to teach, but not to punish, crime. It little becomes us to speak contemptuously of the religion of races to whom we stand in such relations; nor do I think any man of modesty or thoughtfulness will ever speak so of any religion, in which God has allowed one good man to die, trusting.

The more readily we admit the possibility of our own cherished convictions being mixed with error, the more vital and helpful whatever is right in them will become: and no error is so conclusively fatal as the idea that God will not allow *us* to err, though He has allowed all other men to do so. There may be doubt of the meaning of other visions; but there is none respecting that of the dream of St. Peter; and you may trust the Rock of the Church's Foundation for true interpreting, when he learned from it that, ' in every nation, he that feareth God and worketh righteousness, is accepted with Him.' See that

you understand what that righteousness means ; and set
hand to it stoutly : you will always measure your neighbours' creed kindly, in proportion to the substantial fruits
of your own.  Do not think you will ever get harm by
striving to enter into the faith of others, and to sympathise,
in imagination, with the guiding principles of their lives.
So only can you justly love them, or pity them, or praise.
By the gracious effort you will double, treble—nay, inde-
finitely multiply, at once the pleasure, the reverence, and
the intelligence with which you read : and, believe me, it
is wiser and holier, by the fire of your own faith to kindle
the ashes of expired religions, than to let your soul shiver
and stumble among their graves, through the gathering
darkness, and communicable cold.

MARY (*after some pause*).  We shall all like reading
Greek history so much better after this !  but it has put
everything else out of our heads that we wanted to ask.

L.   I can tell you one of the things ; and I might take
credit for generosity in telling you ; but I have a personal
reason—Lucilla's verse about the creation.

DORA.  Oh, yes—yes ; and its ' pain together, until
now.'

L.   I call you back to that, because I must warn you
against an old error of my own.  Somewhere in the fourth
volume of *Modern Painters*, I said that the earth seemed to
have passed through its highest state : and that, after
ascending by a series of phases, culminating in its habitation
by man, it seems to be now gradually becoming less fit for
that habitation.

MARY.  Yes, I remember.

L.   I wrote those passages under a very bitter impression
of the gradual perishing of beauty from the loveliest scenes
which I knew in the physical world ;—not in any doubtful
way, such as I might have attributed to loss of sensation
in myself—but by violent and definite physical action ;
such as the filling up of the Lac de Chêde by landslips from

the Rochers des Fiz ;—the narrowing of the Lake Lucerne by the gaining delta of the stream of the Muotta-Thal, which, in the course of years, will cut the lake into two, as that of Brientz has been divided from that of Thun ;— the steady diminishing of the glaciers north of the Alps, and still more, of the sheets of snow on their southern slopes, which supply the refreshing streams of Lombardy ;— the equally steady increase of deadly maremma round Pisa and Venice ; and other such phenomena, quite measurably traceable within the limits even of short life, and unaccompanied, as it seemed, by redeeming or compensatory agencies. I am still under the same impression respecting the existing phenomena ; but I feel more strongly, every day, that no evidence to be collected within historical periods can be accepted as any clue to the great tendencies of geological change ; but that the great laws which never fail, and to which all change is subordinate, appear such as to accomplish a gradual advance to lovelier order, and more calmly, yet more deeply, animated Rest. Nor has this conviction ever fastened itself upon me more distinctly, than during my endeavour to trace the laws which govern the lowly framework of the dust. For, through all the phases of its transition and dissolution, there seems to be a continual effort to raise itself into a higher state ; and a measured gain, through the fierce revulsion and slow renewal of the earth's frame, in beauty, and order, and permanence. The soft white sediments of the sea draw themselves, in process of time, into smooth knots of sphered symmetry ; burdened and strained under increase of pressure, they pass into a nascent marble ; scorched by fervent heat, they brighten and blanch into the snowy rock of Paros and Carrara. The dark drift of the inland river, or stagnant slime of inland pool and lake, divides, or resolves itself as it dries, into layers of its several elements ; slowly purifying each by the patient withdrawal of it from the anarchy of the mass in which it was mingled.

Contracted by increasing drought, till it must shatter into fragments, it infuses continually a finer ichor into the opening veins, and finds in its weakness the first rudiments of a perfect strength. Rent at last, rock from rock, nay, atom from atom, and tormented in lambent fire, it knits, through the fusion, the fibres of a perennial endurance ; and, during countless subsequent centuries, declining, or, rather let me say, rising, to repose, finishes the infallible lustre of its crystalline beauty, under harmonies of law which are wholly beneficent, because wholly inexorable.

(*The children seem pleased, but more inclined to think over these matters than to talk.*)

L. (*after giving them a little time*). Mary, I seldom ask you to read anything out of books of mine ; but there is a passage about the Law of Help, which I want you to read to the children now, because it is of no use merely to put it in other words for them. You know the place I mean, do not you ?

MARY. Yes (*presently finding it*) ; where shall I begin ?

L. Here ; but the elder ones had better look afterwards at the piece which comes just before this.

MARY (*reads*) :

A pure or holy state of anything is that in which all its parts are helpful or consistent. The highest and first law of the universe, and the other name of life is, therefore, ' help.' The other name of death is ' separation.' Government and co-operation are in all things, and eternally, the laws of life. Anarchy and competition, eternally, and in all things, the laws of death.

Perhaps the best, though the most familiar, example we could take of the nature and power of consistence, will be that of the possible changes in the dust we tread on.

Exclusive of animal decay, we can hardly arrive at a more absolute type of impurity, than the mud or slime of a damp, over-trodden path, in the outskirts of a manufacturing town. I do not say mud of the road, because that is mixed with animal refuse ; but take merely an ounce or two of the blackest slime of a beaten footpath, on a rainy day, near a manufacturing town. That slime we shall find in most cases composed of clay (or brickdust, which is burnt clay), mixed with soot, a little sand, and water. All these elements are at helpless war with each other, and destroy reciprocally each

other's nature and power : competing and fighting for place at
every tread of your foot ; sand squeezing out clay, and clay
squeezing out water, and soot meddling everywhere, and defiling
the whole. Let us suppose that this ounce of mud is left in perfect
rest, and that its elements gather together, like to like, so that their
atoms may get into the closest relations possible.

Let the clay begin. Ridding itself of all foreign substance, it
gradually becomes a white earth, already very beautiful, and fit, with
help of congealing fire, to be made into finest porcelain, and painted
on, and be kept in kings' palaces. But such artificial consistence is
not its best. Leave it still quiet, to follow its own instinct of unity,
and it becomes, not only white, but clear ; not only clear, but hard ;
nor only clear and hard, but so set that it can deal with light in a
wonderful way, and gather out of it the loveliest blue rays only,
refusing the rest. We call it then a sapphire.

Such being the consummation of the clay, we give similar permission of quiet to the sand. It also becomes, first, a white earth ;
then proceeds to grow clear and hard, and at last arranges itself in
mysterious, infinitely fine parallel lines, which have the power of
reflecting, not merely the blue rays, but the blue, green, purple, and
red rays, in the greatest beauty in which they can be seen through any
hard material whatsoever. We call it then an opal.

In next order the soot sets to work. It cannot make itself white
at first ; but, instead of being discouraged, tries harder and harder ;
and comes out clear at last ; and the hardest thing in the world :
and for the blackness that it had, obtains in exchange the power of
reflecting all the rays of the sun at once, in the vividest blaze that
any solid thing can shoot. We call it then a diamond.

Last of all, the water purifies, or unites itself : contented enough
if it only reach the form of a dewdrop : but, if we insist on its proceeding to a more perfect consistence, it crystallizes into the shape
of a star. And, for the ounce of slime which we had by political
economy of competition, we have, by political economy of co-operation, a sapphire, an opal, and a diamond, set in the midst of a star of
snow.

L.  I have asked you to hear that, children, because,
from all that we have seen in the work and play of these
past days, I would have you gain at least one grave and
enduring thought. The seeming trouble—the unquestion-
able degradation—of the elements of the physical earth,
must passively wait the appointed time of their repose,
or their restoration. It can only be brought about for
them by the agency of external law. But if, indeed,
there be a nobler life in us than in these strangely moving

atoms ;—if, indeed, there is an eternal difference between the fire which inhabits them, and that which animates us—it must be shown, by each of us in his appointed place, not merely in the patience, but in the activity of our hope ; not merely by our desire, but our labour, for the time when the Dust of the generations of men shall be confirmed for foundations of the gates of the City of God. The human clay, now trampled and despised, will not be—cannot be—knit into strength and light by accidents or ordinances of unassisted fate. By human cruelty and iniquity it has been afflicted ;—by human mercy and justice it must be raised : and in all fear or questioning of what is or is not, the real message of creation, or of revelation, you may assuredly find perfect peace, if you are resolved to do that which your Lord has plainly required—and content that He should indeed require no more of you—than to do Justice, to love Mercy, and to walk humbly with Him.

# AUTHOR'S NOTES

# AUTHOR'S NOTES

Note I.—Page 148

*' That third pyramid of hers '*

THROUGHOUT the dialogues, it must be observed that ' Sibyl' is addressed (when in play) as having once been the Cumæan Sibyl; and ' Egypt ' as having been queen Nitocris,—the Cinderella, and ' the greatest heroine and beauty ' of Egyptian story. The Egyptians called ' Neith the Victorious ' (Nitocris), and the Greeks ' Face of the Rose ' (Rhodope). Chaucer's beautiful conception of Cleopatra in the *Legend of Good Women*, is much more founded on the traditions of her than on those of Cleopatra; and, especially in its close, modified by Herodotus's terrible story of the death of Nitocris, which, however, is mythologically nothing more than a part of the deep monotonous ancient dirge for the fulfilment of the earthly destiny of Beauty ; ' She cast herself into a chamber full of ashes.'

I believe this Queen is now sufficiently ascertained to have either built, or increased to double its former size, the third pyramid of Gizeh : and the passage following in the text refers to an imaginary endeavour, by the Old Lecturer and the children together, to make out the description of that pyramid in the 167th page of the second volume of Bunsen's *Egypt's Place in Universal History* —ideal endeavour—which ideally terminates as the Old Lecturer's real endeavours to the same end always have terminated. There are, however, valuable notes respecting Nitocris at page 210 of the same volume : but the *Early Egyptian History for the Young*, by the author of *Sidney Gray*, contains, in a pleasant form, as much information as young readers will usually need.

Note II.—Page 149

*' Pyramid of Asychis '*

THIS pyramid, in mythology, divides with the Tower of Babel the shame, or vain glory, of being presumptuously, and first among great edifices, built with ' brick for stone.' This was the inscription on it, according to Herodotus :

Despise me not, in comparing me with the pyramids of stone ; for I have the pre-eminence over them, as far as Jupiter has

301

pre-eminence over the gods.    For, striking with staves into
the pool, men gathered the clay which fastened itself to the
staff, and kneaded bricks out of it, and so made me.

The word I have translated 'kneaded' is literally 'drew;' in
the sense of drawing, for which the Latins use 'duco'; and thus
gave us our 'ductile' in speaking of dead clay, and Duke, Doge,
or leader, in speaking of living clay.    As the asserted pre-eminence
of the edifice is made, in this inscription, to rest merely on the
quantity of labour consumed in it, this pyramid is considered, in
the text, as the type, at once, of the base building, and of the lost
labour, of future ages ; so far at least as the spirits of measured
and mechanical effort deal with it : but Neith, exercising her
power upon it, makes it a type of the work of wise and inspired
builders.

NOTE III.—Page 149

*The Greater Pthah*

IT is impossible, as yet, to define with distinctness the personal
agencies of the Egyptian deities.    They are continually associated
in function, or hold derivative powers, or are related to each other
in mysterious triads; uniting always symbolism of physical
phenomena with real spiritual power.    I have endeavoured partly
to explain this in the text of the tenth Lecture ; here, it is only
necessary for the reader to know that the Greater Pthah more or
less represents the formative power of order and measurement :
he always stands on a four-square pedestal, 'the Egyptian cubit,
metaphorically used as the hieroglyphic for truth'; his limbs are
bound together, to signify fixed stability as of a pillar ; he has a
measuring-rod in his hand ; and at Philæ, is represented as holding
an egg on a potter's wheel ; but I do not know if this symbol occurs
in older sculptures.    His usual title is the 'Lord of Truth.'    Others,
very beautiful : 'King of the Two Worlds, of Gracious Countenance,'
'Superintendent of the Great Abode,' etc., are given by Mr. Birch
in Arundale's *Gallery of Antiquities*, which I suppose is the book
of best authority easily accessible.    For the full titles and utterances
of the gods, Rosellini is as yet the only—and I believe, still a very
questionable—authority ;    and Arundale's little book, excellent
in the text, has this great defect, that its drawings give the statues
invariably a ludicrous or ignoble character.    Readers who have
not access to the originals must be warned against this frequent
fault in modern illustration (especially existing also in some of
the painted casts of Gothic and Norman work at the Crystal Palace).
It is not owing to any wilful want of veracity : the plates in Arundale's
book are laboriously faithful : but the expressions of both face
and body in a figure depend merely on emphasis of touch ; and,

in barbaric art, most draughtsmen emphasise what they plainly
see—the barbarism ; and miss conditions of nobleness, which they
must approach the monument in a different temper before they
will discover, and draw with great subtlety before they can
express.

The character of the Lower Pthah, or perhaps I ought rather
to say, of Pthah in his lower office, is sufficiently explained in the
text of the third Lecture : only the reader must be warned that
the Egyptian symbolism of him by the beetle was not a scornful
one ; it expressed only the idea of his presence in the first elements
of life.    But it may not unjustly be used, in another sense, by us,
who have seen his power in new development ; and, even as it was,
I cannot conceive that the Egyptians should have regarded their
beetle-headed image of him (Champollion, *Pantheon*, pl. 12) without
some occult scorn.    It is the most painful of all their types of any
beneficent power ; and even among those of evil influences, none
can be compared with it, except its opposite, the tortoise-headed
demon of indolence.

Pasht (p. 149, line 8) is connected with the Greek Artemis,
especially in her offices of judgment and vengeance.  She is usually
lioness-headed ;  sometimes cat-headed ;  her attributes seeming
often trivial or ludicrous unless their full meaning is known ; but the
inquiry is much too wide to be followed here.  The cat was sacred
to her ;  or rather to the sun, and secondarily to her.    She is alluded
to in the text because she is always the companion of Pthah (called
' The beloved of Pthah,' it may be as Judgment, demanded and
longed for by Truth) ; and it may be well for young readers to have
this fixed in their minds, even by chance association.    There are
more statues of Pasht in the British Museum than of any other
Egyptian deity ;  several of them fine in workmanship ;  nearly
all in dark stone, which may be, presumably, to connect her, as
the moon, with the night ;  and, in her office of avenger, with
grief.

Thoth (p. 152, line 3) is the Recording Angel of Judgment ;  and
the Greek Hermes.  Phre (p. 152, line 6) is the Sun.

Neith is the Egyptian spirit of divine wisdom and the Athena
of the Greeks.  No sufficient statement of her many attributes,
still less of their meanings, can be shortly given ; but this should be
noted respecting the veiling of the Egyptian image of her by vulture
wings—that as she is, physically, the goddess of the air, this bird,
the most powerful creature of the air known to the Egyptians,
naturally became her symbol.    It had other significations ; but
certainly this, when in connection with Neith.    As representing her,
it was the most important sign, next to the winged sphere, in
Egyptian sculpture ; and, just as in Homer, Athena herself guides
her heroes into battle, this symbol of wisdom, giving victory, floats
over the heads of the Egyptian kings.    The Greeks, representing
the goddess herself in human form, yet would not lose the power

of the Egyptian symbol, and changed it into an angel of victory. First seen in loveliness on the early coins of Syracuse and Leontium, it gradually became the received sign of all conquest, and the so-called ' Victory ' of later times ; which, little by little, loses its truth, and is accepted by the moderns only as a personification of victory itself—not as an actual picture of the living Angel who led to victory.    There is a wide difference between these two conceptions—all the difference between insincere poetry and sincere religion. This I have also endeavoured farther to illustrate in the tenth Lecture ; there is, however, one part of Athena's character which it would have been irrelevant to dwell upon there ; yet which I must not wholly leave unnoticed.

As the goddess of the air, she physically represents both its benefi- cent calm, and necessary tempest : other storm-deities (as Chrysaor and Æolus) being invested with a subordinate and more or less malig- nant function, which is exclusively their own, and is related to that of Athena as the power of Mars is related to hers in war.   So also Virgil makes her able to wield the lightning herself, while Juno cannot, but must pray for the intervention of Æolus.    She has precisely the correspondent moral authority over calmness of mind, and just anger.   She soothes Achilles, as she incites Tydides ; her physical power over the air being always hinted correlatively. She grasps Achilles by his hair—as the wind would lift it—softly,

> ' It fanned his cheek, it raised his hair,
> Like a meadow gale in spring.'

She does not merely turn the lance of Mars from Diomed ; but seizes it in both her hands, and casts it aside, with a sense of making it vain, like chaff in the wind ;—to the shout of Achilles, she adds her own voice of storm in heaven—but in all cases the moral power is still the principal one—most beautifully in that seizing of Achilles by the hair, which was the talisman of his life (because he had vowed it to the Sperchius if he returned in safety), and which, in giving at Patroclus' tomb, he, knowingly, yields up the hope of return to his country, and signifies that he will die with his friend. Achilles and Tydides are, above all other heroes, aided by her in war, because their prevailing characters are the desire of justice, united in both, with deep affections ; and, in Achilles, with a passionate tenderness, which is the real root of his passionate anger.   Ulysses is her favourite chiefly in her office as the goddess of conduct and design.

### Note IV.—Page 187

#### ' Geometrical limitations '

It is difficult, without a tedious accuracy, or without full illustra- tion, to express the complete relations of crystalline structure, which dispose minerals to take, at different times, fibrous, massive, or foliated forms; and I am afraid this chapter will be generally skipped by the reader: yet the arrangement itself will be found useful, if kept broadly in mind; and the transitions of state are of the highest interest, if the subject is entered upon with any earnestness. It would have been vain to add to the scheme of this little volume any account of the geometrical forms of crystals: an available one, though still far too difficult and too copious, has been arranged by the Rev. Mr. Mitchell, for Orr's *Circle of the Sciences*; and, I believe, the 'nets' of crystals, which are therein given to be cut out with scissors, and put prettily together, will be found more conquerable by young ladies than by other students. There should also, when an opportunity occurs, be shown, at any public library, the diagram of the crystallization of quartz referred to poles, at p. 8 of Cloizaux's *Manuel de Minéralogie*: that they may know what work is; and what the subject is.

With a view to more careful examination of the nascent states of silica, I have made no allusion in this volume to the influence of mere segregation, as connected with the crystalline power. It has only been recently, during the study of the breccias alluded to in page 263, that I have fully seen the extent to which this singular force often modifies rocks in which at first its influence might hardly have been suspected; many apparent conglomerates being in reality formed chiefly by segregation, combined with mysterious brokenly-zoned structures, like those of some malachites. I hope some day to know more of these and several other mineral phenomena (especially of those connected with the relative sizes of crystals, which otherwise I should have endeavoured to describe in this volume.

### Note V.—Page 249

#### ' St. Barbara '

I WOULD have given the legends of St. Barbara and St. Thomas if I had thought it always well for young readers to have everything at once told them which they may wish to know. They will remember the stories better after taking some trouble to find them! and the text is intelligible enough as it stands. The idea of St. Barbara as there given, is founded partly on her legend in *Peter de Natalibus*, partly on the beautiful photograph of Van Eyck's picture of her at Antwerp; which was some time since published at Lille.

### Note VI.—Page 292

#### ' King of the Valley of Diamonds '

ISABEL interrupted the Lecturer here, and was briefly bid to hold her tongue; which gave rise to some talk, apart, afterwards, between L. and Sibyl, of which a word or two may be perhaps advisably set down.

SIBYL.  We shall spoil Isabel, certainly, if we don't mind : I was glad you stopped her, and yet sorry ; for she wanted so much to ask about the Valley of Diamonds again, and she has worked so hard at it, and made it nearly all out by herself.  She recollected Elisha's throwing in the meal, which nobody else did.

L.  But what did she want to ask ?

SIBYL.  About the mulberry trees and the serpents ; we are all stopped by that.  Won't you tell us what it means ?

L.  Now, Sibyl, I am sure you, who never explained yourself, should be the last to expect others to do so.  I hate explaining myself.

SIBYL.  And yet how often you complain of other people for not saying what they meant.  How I have heard you growl over the three stone steps to purgatory ; for instance !

L.  Yes ; because Dante's meaning is worth getting at ; but mine matters nothing ; at least, if ever I think it is of any consequence, I speak it as clearly as may be.  But you may make anything you like of the serpent forests.  I could have helped you to find out what they were, by giving a little more detail, but it would have been tiresome.

SIBYL.  It is much more tiresome not to find out.  Tell us, please, as Isabel says, because we feel so stupid.

L.  There is no stupidity ; you could not possibly do more than guess at anything so vague.  But I think you, Sibyl, at least, might have recollected what first dyed the mulberry ?

SIBYL.  So I did ; but that helped little ; I thought of Dante's forest of suicides, too, but you would not simply have borrowed that ?

L.  No.  If I had had strength to use it I should have stolen it, to beat it into another shape ; not borrowed it.  But the idea of souls in trees is as old as the world ; or at least, as the world of man.  And I *did* mean that there were souls in those dark branches ; —the souls of all who had perished in misery through the pursuit of riches ; and that the river was of their blood, gathering gradually, and flowing out of the valley.  Then I meant the serpents for the souls of those who had lived carelessly and wantonly in their riches ; and who have all their sins forgiven by the world, because they are rich : and therefore they have seven crimson-crested heads, for the seven mortal sins ; of which they are proud : and these, and the memory and report of them, are the chief causes of temptation to others, as showing the pleasantness and absolving power of riches ; so that thus they are singing serpents.  And the worms are the souls of the common money-getters and traffickers, who do nothing but eat and spin : and who gain habitually by the distress or foolishness of others (as you see the butchers have been gaining out of the panic at the cattle plague, among the poor)—

so they are made to eat the dark leaves, and spin, and perish.

SIBYL. And the souls of the great, cruel, rich people who oppress the poor, and lend money to governments to make unjust war, where are they ?

L. They change into the ice, I believe, and are knit with the gold ; and make the grave-dust of the valley. I believe so, at least, for no one ever sees those souls anywhere.

(SIBYL *ceases questioning.*)

ISABEL (*who has crept up to her side without any one's seeing*). Oh, Sibyl, please ask him about the fireflies !

L. What, you there, mousie ! No ; I won't tell either Sibyl or you about the fireflies ; not a word more about anything else. You ought to be little fireflies yourselves, and find your way in twilight by your own wits.

ISABEL. But you said they burned, you know ?

L. Yes ; and you may be fireflies that way too, some of you, before long, though I did not mean that. Away with you, children. You have thought enough for to-day.

# INDEX

Oxide of Copper, red, 187

PASHT, 149; connection with Artemis, 303
Passion, from the painter's standpoint, 283
Patience, best part of fortitude, 176
Pearlspar, 215
Philosophy, modern, 283
Phre (=the sun), reference to, 152
Pisa, leaning tower of, 255
Plato, referred to, 282
Poetry, on understanding it, 204
Political economy of competition and co-operation, 296
Prophets, visions of the, 287
Pthah, the Greater, dream concerning, 149; meaning of, 302
Pthah, the Lower, or Little, 153; his meaning, 167; 171, 257, 303
Pyramid, dream of building a, 149–154

QUARTZ, 192, 213; its caprices, 246; ill-disposed, 249; 257, 262, 274

RELIGIONS, early, 285; Christianity and heathen, 285–294
Repentance, not a virtue, 195
Riches, uselessness of, 139
Rocks, fibrous, 186; tearing and mending of, 262–274; veins in, 273; fissures in, 273; limestone, 274
Rock-crystal, 211; of Dauphiné and St Gothard, 246
Rosellini, an authority on Egyptology, 302
Ruby, 135, 186

SALEVE, Mont, 264
Saints, their characteristics, 250, 251
St. Gothard, rock-crystals of, 246
Sand, turns to opal, 297
Sapphire, 186; from clay, 297

Sarcophagus, ancient Egyptian, 268
Self-sacrifice, not lovely, 215; foolish when sought, 218
Serpents, the seven-headed, 135; their significance, 306
Sewing, 272
Silver, branched, 214
Slate, 274
Soot, turns to diamond, 297
Sophia, same as Neith, 155
Soul-sickness, 203
Strata, movements of, 262
Suffering, no virtue in, 218
Sulphide of antimony, 187; of bismuth, 187
Sulphur, crystallization of, 161
Sun, his supply of flame, 281 (see also Phre)

TAKING up one's cross, its meaning, 233
Thomas, St., not the true patron of architects, 250
Thoth, reference to, 152; meaning of, 303
Thun, Lake of, 295
Titian, referred to, 219
Tourmaline, 261
Turner's St. Catherine's Hill, 168

UNCRYSTALLIZATION, 160
Uran-Mica, 185

VEINS in rocks, 273
Victory, Goddess of, 301, 304
Virgil quoted, 284; referred to, 304
Virtues, of crystals, 188, 191–206; the two essential, 192; the three, in girls, 226; meaning of the word, 219, 234
Visions of the Prophets, 287
"Vita," meaning of, 220

WEARDALE, fluor of, 246
"Wife," its meaning, 272
Will of God respecting us, the, 218
Wrong, the two sorts, 196
Wrong-doing unnecessary, 195, 198

RICHARD CLAY & SONS, LIMITED,
BREAD STREET HILL, E.C., AND
BUNGAY, SUFFOLK.